Africa in the Twenty-First Century

African Governance and Development

African Governance and Development identifies and elaborates on the strategic place of governance and development within the African studies. Reflecting the fact that life in Africa continues to change; particularly in political, development, and socio-economic arenas; this series explores issues focusing on the ongoing mobilization for good governance and the search for sustainable and economic development. The *African Governance and Development* series address gaps and larger needs in the developing scholarship on Africa and the African Diaspora. This series provides scholarly monographs and edited collections in the humanities, social science, and social scientific traditions. Contributors are encouraged to submit book length manuscripts that encompass, besides the above named topics, those focusing on: Africa's political economy and economic development, Africa's place in world trade development, democratization of African countries, the inclusion and representation of ethnic minorities, and the role of gender in Africa's development. Works can be focused on a single African country, a region of African countries, or the African continent's place as a global player.

Recent Titles

Pan-Africanism in Modern Times: Challenges, Concerns, and Constraints, edited by Olayiwola Abegunrin and Sabelle Ogbobode Abidde

Nigeria, Africa, and the United States: Challenges of Governance, Development, and Security, by Olayiwola Abegunrin

Human Rights in Nigeria's External Relations: Building the Record of a Moral Superpower, by Philip C. Aka

Nigeria's Niger Delta: Militancy, Amnesty, and the Post-Amnesty Environment, by Sabella Ogbobode Abidde

Trade Unions and the Age of Information and Communication Technologies in Kenya, by Eric E. Otenyo

Africans and the Exiled Life: Migration, Culture, and Globalization edited by Sabella Ogbobode Abidde and Brenda I. Gill

The Illusion of the Post-Colonial State: Governance and Security Challenges in Africa by W. Alade Fawole

Nigeria-United States Relations 1960–2016 by Olayiwola Abegunrin

Africa in the Twenty-First Century: The Promise of Development and Democratization edited by Gashawbeza W. Bekele and Adebayo Oyebade

Africa in the Twenty-First Century

The Promise of Development and Democratization

Edited by
Gashawbeza W. Bekele
and Adebayo Oyebade

LEXINGTON BOOKS
Lanham • Boulder • New York • London

Published by Lexington Books
An imprint of The Rowman & Littlefield Publishing Group, Inc.
4501 Forbes Boulevard, Suite 200, Lanham, Maryland 20706
www.rowman.com

6 Tinworth Street, London SE11 5AL, United Kingdom

British Library Cataloguing in Publication Information Available

Library of Congress Cataloging-in-Publication Data Available

ISBN 978-1-4985-6451-9 (cloth: alk. paper)
ISBN 978-1-4985-6452-6 (electronic)

∞™ The paper used in this publication meets the minimum requirements of American National Standard for Information Sciences—Permanence of Paper for Printed Library Materials, ANSI/NISO Z39.48-1992.

Printed in the United States of America

Contents

Preface vii

Acknowledgments ix

Introduction xi
Gashawbeza W. Bekele and Adebayo Oyebade

PART I: GOVERNANCE, DEMOCRACY, AND DEVELOPMENT **1**

1 African Development and Democratization Trajectories 3
Gashawbeza W. Bekele and Adebayo Oyebade

2 The Political Ecology of Sustainable Development in Africa 19
Tadesse Kidane-Mariam

3 Revisiting the Promise of Democracy and Development in Africa 35
Phillip E. Agbebaku, William E. Odion, and Mohammed Itakpe

4 Beyond the Millennium Development Goals: Localizing the Development Agenda in Nigeria 49
Funmi Adewumi

5 Fallacy of Development in Africa 63
Sunday Layi Oladipupo

6 Political Economy of Postcolonial Rail Transportation Management in Africa 77
Tokunbo A. Ayoola

PART II: DEMOCRATIZATION, DEMOCRATIC INSTITUTIONS, AND UNEVEN REGIONAL DEVELOPMENT **99**

7 The Legislature and Tenure Elongation in African Presidential Democracies 101
Joseph Yinka Fashagba and Rotimi Ajayi

8 The African Diaspora and the Quest for Democracy in Africa: Revisiting the June 12, 1993 Presidential Election in Nigeria 115
Udida A. Undiyaundeye

9 Bill of Rights for Africa: Uneven Regional Development and Indigenous Peoples Protests 127
Rufus T. Akinyele

PART III: GENDER RELATIONS, HEALTH CARE, AND DEVELOPMENT **147**

10 Vanishing or Emerging Voices? Nigerian Women and Political Participation 149
Ngozi U. Emeka-Nwobia

11 Women, Conflict, and Nigeria's Sustainable Development Agenda 165
Adaora Osondu-Oti

12 Gabon's Giant Step in Health Care 179
Biale Zua

Bibliography 199

Index 211

About the Contributors 217

Preface

In the last decades of the twentieth century, Africa witnessed a wave of political liberalization and democratization. In the twenty-first century, the continent has made significant strides in both economic growth and democratization, as apparent in states such as Mauritius, Cape Verde, Botswana, South Africa, Tunisia, Gabon, Ghana, and Nigeria. The international media and organizations such as the World Bank and the International Monetary Fund have noted that several African states are among the fastest growing economies in the world with rapidly rising middle class. Significant achievements have been made in many areas such as health care, education, access to technology, and poverty alleviation. While there are many bright spots and the continent's economic and democratic prospects are promising, it is still a truism that large numbers of Africans presently languish in poverty.

It is equally valid to say that Africa's democracy, for the most part, is limited to formal elections without the necessary independent institutions to support the rule of law such as an independent judiciary to safeguard human and civil rights, and freedom of the press, speech, and assembly. Institutionalized political corruption, detrimental to good governance, is also still very rampant. Hence, although it is often assumed that democracy is a path that must, out of necessity, lead to development, almost two decades into the twenty-first century, the dividends of democracy in terms of development and good governance are yet to be realized in most African countries.

This book examines within a multidisciplinary location milestones and challenges in development and democratization in contemporary Africa, which undoubtedly are two pillars that are critical to the future of the continent. The collection of essays in this volume, written by African scholars on both sides of the Atlantic, interrogate contemporary debates, controversies, achievements, challenges, and future prospects of African development and democratization from multidisciplinary and diverse theoretical perspectives. The diverse issues and subthemes addressed in this volume include tenets of governance such as democracy, democratization, democratic institutions, presidential term limits, and dynamics of development such as uneven regional development, sustainable development, transportation development, gender relations, and health.

Acknowledgments

Original versions of papers in this book were first presented at the Fourth Annual Africa Conference held at Tennessee State University in Nashville, Tennessee, organized by the Department of History, Political Science, Geography, and Africana Studies. As conveners of the Annual Africa Conference, we would like to acknowledge the contributions of several individuals whose support is critical to the success of the conference. We would like to extend our appreciation to Dr. Gloria Johnson, dean of the College of Liberal Arts, Tennessee State University, and Dr. Joel Dark, associate dean of the College for their continued, unwavering support for the conference. We are especially grateful to our colleagues, Dr. Michael Bertrand, Ms. Pamela Bobo, Dr. Rebecca Dixon, Dr. K. T. Ewing, Dr. Kyle Murray, Dr. Erik Schmeller, Dr. Learotha Williams, and Dr. Wosene Yefru for their scholarly encouragement and support. Our heart-felt thanks and gratitude go to Dr. Olayiwola Abegunrin, professor of International Relations and African Studies, Howard University, Washington, DC and Dr. Mayowa Ogedengbe, adjunct professor of Africology at Temple University, Philadelphia and director of research and development, Oodua Foundation, Wilmington, DE who delivered the plenary and banquet keynote addresses, respectively. Finally, this book would not have been in its final form without all our contributors from both sides of the Atlantic, who made their research work available for this volume.

Gashawbeza W. Bekele and Adebayo Oyebade,
Tennessee State University,
Nashville,
Summer 2018

Introduction

Gashawbeza W. Bekele and Adebayo Oyebade

The twin concepts of development and democracy have certainly consumed academic energies over the years, especially in the context of Africa. Great expectations for rapid economic and political development attended the arrival of African states into the community of independent states in the post–Second World War period. By the end of the twentieth century, however, it became clear that Africa had wholly failed to meet the expectations that greeted the end of colonial authoritarianism and the advent of self-rule.

It is true that in the last decades of the twentieth century, a wave of political and economic liberalization swept across Africa. As many countries transitioned from one-party and military regimes toward multiparty systems in the 1990s, some have argued that a "third wave" of democratization has been taking place in Africa.[1] Similarly, with improved governance and strong economic performance across the continent in the twenty-first century, some employed the "Africa rising" narrative to describe rapid economic growth, rising income, and an emerging middle class. Even though these narratives shed a positive light on Africa and its people by focusing on the success stories than the stereotypical images of the past such as "the dark continent" and "the hopeless continent," the dividends of democracy in terms of development are yet to be realized in most countries almost two decades into the twenty-first century. Hence, a more nuanced, balanced, and cautionary approach is needed to examine the dynamics of African development and democratization. This volume is a modest attempt to fill this gap: the collection of chapters in this volume, written by African scholars on both sides of the Atlantic, interrogate contemporary debates, controversies, achievements, and challenges in African development and democratization from multidisciplinary and diverse theoretical perspectives.

ORGANIZATION OF THE BOOK

The twelve chapters of this book are organized into three parts, each of which contains chapters that address substantive and interrelated themes within the framework of democracy and development issues in Africa. Part I, titled, "Governance, Democracy, and Development," begins with chapter 1 of the book where Gashawbeza W. Bekele and Adebayo Oyebade revisit the trajectories of African development and democratization. The authors provide a synopsis of governance systems and development models adopted in Africa since colonial times, and an overall assessment of progress made in Africa in democratization and development in the last three decades. Drawing examples from several African states and assessing overall progress and trends in democratization using both the minimalist and expansive measures of democracy, they note that there is genuine ground for optimism regarding Africa's transition toward democracy, as many African countries have pervasively embraced some form of multiparty democracy since the 1990s. Bekele and Oyebade argue that while formal or procedural democracy has been instituted in many parts of Africa where regular elections are held and citizens enjoy some political rights, many countries have experienced major setbacks and challenges in their efforts to transition toward a more substantive liberal form of democracy based upon the principles of liberty and equality. The authors point out the absence of strong democratic institutions, an independent judiciary, and adequate checks and balances or separation of powers between different branches of government in many countries as notable problems compounding the adoption, implementation, consolidation, and sustenance of democracy. In addition, they show the notable successes that many African countries have made in economic growth and other indicators of social progress such as education and health in the new millennium. However, they argue that the pro-rich growth that is associated with the neoliberal economic policies in Africa is characterized by rising inequalities, uneven development, and did not bring significant gains in income to the average citizen, substantial reductions in poverty, and meaningful improvements in standard of living or development.

In chapter 2, Tadesse Kidane-Mariam examines Africa's sustainable development achievements, opportunities, and challenges employing a political ecology perspective, essentially integrating both the biophysical factors and the political economy structures of African societies that affect sustainability. Kidane-Mariam discusses in details critical opportunities and challenges of sustainable development to reduce poverty, accelerate economic growth, and protect Africa's highly diversified and vulnerable environment. Major areas of action to bring sustainable development in Africa include improving the following areas: poor governance and political instability, external economic dependence and extreme poverty, lack of economic integration, agricultural stagnation, rapid population growth that contributes to youth unemployment and underemployment, inadequate energy access, deterioration in the quality of education, and degradation of natural resources and the natural environment. The author noted that African leaders and the international economic and political institutions continue to dictate Africa's development in a top-down approach without the meaningful participation of citizens as stakeholders. However, he argues that sustainable development cannot be promoted and realized without democratic governance and citizen's full participation in the decision making process. He calls for broad-based, bottom-up, and participatory development approaches and strong government/public partnerships that hold the key for ensuring adequate safeguards and management tools for sound environmental management at different geographic scales.

In chapter 3, Phillip E. Agbebaku, William E. Odion, and Mohammed Itakpe situate their discourse on development within the context of the centrality of democracy. They argue that the vitality of democracy in a given society defines the level at which the society develops. They begin their theoretical discourse by pointing out the obvious, that the African democratic experiment, which in itself is challenging in many states, has failed woefully to produce development in virtually all areas of human endeavor. However, the authors are quick to point out that democracy does not necessarily mean good governance, as the African context has clearly demonstrated. For development to take place, the authors argue, democracy must guarantee good governance, which is measurable in terms of equal opportunities for all in the civil society and respect for the rule of law by the governing elite. The chapter further analyzes the concepts of democracy and development, and the interrelationship between the two components, while also engaging critical discussions on the crisis of African development in historical perspective and developmental strategies adopted by African states.

In chapter 4, Funmi Adewumi tackles the issue of development agenda in Nigeria by looking at the Millennium Development Goals (MDGs). An audacious initiative of the United Nations, the MDGs was instituted at the beginning of this century to address the developmental needs of developing states such as Nigeria by proposing eight developmental goals expected to be met by the year 2015. Adewumi provides a comprehensive discourse on the history of the development agenda in Nigeria with a focus on the various development plans instituted by the states. The chapter assesses the reality of contemporary Nigeria, evident in increasing rampant poverty among the civil population despite enormous human and material resources, and concludes that the country has failed to live up to the expectations of the MDGs. He categorically rejects the modernization argument as a viable developmental model, and suggests that African states must define and develop their own strategies for development in the light of resources at their disposal. He argues that external interventions have not always augured well for Africa, such that development, particularly in economics terms, has remained sporadic, rather than sustained.

Sunday Layi Oladipupo further pursues the dilemma of development models for Africa in chapter 5. Adopting a philosophical approach, he attempts to discredit both the modernization and dependency theories. For him, any prescription of Western developmental modalities for Africa as a *sine qua non* is wrong-headed. In the same vein, he is of the opinion that Africa's underdevelopment could not be adequately explained by Western imperial intervention in African history. Oladipupo proposes a development trajectory that takes into cognizance African cultural values and systems. While admitting the impracticality of absolute return to precolonial dispensation, Oladipupo concludes that Africa must, at least, endeavor to incorporate elements of its culture in any developmental model.

Transportation development is a vital component of economic development in any nation. In chapter 6, Tokunbo A. Ayoola explores the development and management of rail transportation in postcolonial Africa from a historical perspective. He documents railway development in Africa from colonial times to the present and links how the development and management of rail transport has been affected by the various economic policies pursued by African countries. While transportation networks were constructed to serve the narrow economic interests of the colonial powers in the past, postcolonial governments in many parts of Africa often neglected railroad infrastructure after independence because their focus was mainly on industrialization as part of the import-substitution industrialization strategy. In addition, as the railway systems were government-run, many became inefficient and unprofitable due to mismanagement. Hence, because of pressure from World Bank and the International Monetary Fund, African governments have embarked upon a program of privatization under the auspices of neoliberal policies. However, Ayoola argues that the neoliberal policies and strategies adopted in the late 1980s and early 1990s designed to resolve the inherent contradictions and mismanagement of Africa's railways through privatization in fact compounded the problem. The railroad privatization programs to foreign contingents, rather than helping the continent's railroads to become profitable, effective, and efficient, have rather become avenues through which African governments are subsidizing foreign railroad concessionaires in Africa in what can be considered as "neocolonialism."

Part II on "Democratization, Democratic Institutions, and Uneven Regional Development," consists of three chapters. While noting the growth of constitutional democracies in Africa since the 1990s, in chapter 7, Joseph Fashagba and Rotimi Ajayi examine the ever-growing voracious appetite of African incumbent presidents to change the constitutional provisions to elongate their power, which undermines democratization efforts in many parts of Africa. The chapter interrogates the variations in legislative capacity of African countries to resist the executive branch's attempt in amending the national constitutions to elongate their tenure by using four African states as a case study, namely Nigeria, Malawi, Burundi, and Rwanda. Their study finds that while legislatures in Nigeria and Malawi were able to resist executive pressure to continue in office after the constitutionally permitted two terms successfully, the legislature in Rwanda caved in to presidential pressure to amend the constitution to elongate the tenure of the president. In the case of Burundi, although the legislature resisted the attempt to elongate the tenure of the president, the president still had his way by using the court. Fashagba and Ajayi conclude that a viable and uncompromising opposition in the form of the media, civil society, and the general public in tandem play a large role in taming this problem by spurring the legislature into serving as a bulwark for the constitution.

In chapter 8, Udida A. Undiyaundeye uses the annulled June 12, 1993, presidential election to interrogate the dilemma of the quest for democracy in Nigeria. The General Ibrahim Babangida ruling military junta abruptly annulled the election, the first to be free and fair in the history of Nigeria's electoral politics. Widely considered unwarranted, the annulment epitomized the crisis of democratization in Nigeria, which accounts for why scholars have extensively written on it.[2] However, Undiyaundeye takes a different approach to the failed transition regime; his consideration is on the role of the African Diaspora on the democratization project, particularly its involvement in the election saga. Undiyaundeye uses the botched Nigerian democratic transition attempt and the crisis that attended its failure to examine the investment of the African American leadership in the promotion of democracy and good governance in Africa.

The need for a bill of rights in a democracy cannot be overemphasized, as the bill of rights protects the inalienable and natural rights and freedoms of individuals, including freedom of speech, religion, privacy, due process of law, and equality before the law. In chapter 9, Rufus T. Akinyele proposes the need for a bill of rights in Africa to protect the rights of minorities, as they are often trampled on by majority rule even in democratic societies. He situates the need for protecting ethnic minority rights within the context of uneven regional development, which is an indication of exploitative relationship between the dominant and minority groups. Akinyele argues that in addition to a constitutional provision prohibiting discrimination, there is a need for a bill of rights to safeguard group rights since political power often follows population size. By using four ethnic groups as case studies, namely, the Tonga of Zimbabwe, the Ogiek of Kenya, and the Ogoni and Igbo of Nigeria, Akinyele examined the struggle of indigenous minorities to maintain their identities, particularly through the control of their ancestral land and the practice of their culture and tradition. He observed that in almost all cases, minority groups have been denied their rights to their ancestral homelands and resources in the name of modernization and development. This subsequently led to their marginalization, destruction of their economic livelihood and identity, lack of representation in government, and segregation into areas with a greater amount of environmental degradation and contamination. Hence, Akinyele concludes that uneven regional development is the root cause of the minority agitations and suggests the need for bill of rights to protect the social, economic, and cultural rights of indigenous minorities in an era of globalization and modernization.

The last section of this book, Part III, on the subtheme of "Gender Relations, Health Care, and Development," consists of three chapters that probe Africa's health care system, women's evolving role in Africa's political environment, and the intersection of the two dynamics to the question of development. In chapter 10, Ngozi U. Emeka-Nwobia takes on the important issue of women's political empowerment in Africa, a subject that has rightly attracted scholarly attention in political discourse in recent times. It is true that in the last thirty years, there has been a progressive increase in the number of African women actively participating in politics, from votes casting, to electoral offices candidacy. The often-cited example is Rwanda, which boasts of the highest number of women parliamentarians in the world. Other countries have made significant strides as well in women's political participation. However, in general, gender disparity in Africa, to the detriment of women, still very much permeates virtually all sectors of the society. In the chapter, Emeka-Nwobia examines women's struggle from the perspective of political participation in Nigeria. Focusing on the Fourth Republic, particularly the 2015 general elections, the author argues that since Nigeria's independence in 1960, women had been consistently underrepresented in elective positions and denied unfettered political participation despite constituting half of the Nigerian electorate. The chapter gauges women's political involvement through their participation in political campaigns and rallies, their record in contesting for electoral positions, and their role in governance and decision-making. In addressing these issues, Emeka-Nwobia contends that a combination of political, social, economic, and cultural factors has consistently posed a threat to women political participation in Nigeria. In her view, the full dividends of democracy would remain unattainable a long as Nigerian women continue to lack real political empowerment and are underrepresented in the democratic process and in governance and decision-making.

In chapter 11, Adaora Osondu-Oti underscores the need for actionable commitments to address the challenges that women face in times of conflict, as women disproportionately suffer more harm (both short term and long term) than other segments of society in conflict zones. By employing as examples, the Niger Delta conflict and the Boko Haram insurgency in Nigeria, where kidnapping and abduction of young girls were used as a strategy, Osondu-Oti documented the ways in which women are subjected to gender-based violence, which has a devastating impact on the lives and dignity of women both in war and peace times. Furthermore, Osondu-Oti examined the commitments of the Nigerian government to gender dimension of sustainable development. Her findings indicate that despite the country being party to several international agreements concerning women, in practice, women are often marginalized in many spheres of life, and adequate strategies have not been proposed or implemented for the protection of women during conflict. By using Nigeria as reference point, Osondu-Oti advances the need for the social dimension of sustainable development goals to have adequate provisions that address challenges faced by women who are adversely affected during and after conflict. Osondu-Oti recommends a more proactive strategy and inclusive sustainable development agenda that focuses on the protection of women's rights while building gender equity and a socially sustainable society.

The subject of health care in Africa is the concern of the last chapter by Biale Zua. Indeed, health care is a critical component of social development and largely a measure of national advancement. Few African states have working health care systems adequate for the heath demand of the twenty-first century. The crisis of public health in Africa is evident, characterized by a combination of factors ranging from outdated or inadequate facilities and infrastructure, lack of adequate and qualified health care professionals, to lackluster government funding of health institutions. The result is poor standards of clinical care which falls short of the needs of the populace.

Nothing demonstrates the general mistrust for health care in Africa by the people more than the practice of seeking medical care in Western and Asian countries by those who can afford it. In 2017, for instance, the Nigerian president Muhammadu Buhari shunned his country's health care system, apparently out of mistrust, to spend more than three months in London, undergoing medical treatment.[3] Although, many African countries rank in the rear in the global health care index, some have made appreciable strides toward improvement in recent years. One of such countries is Gabon, noted for one of the most advanced health care systems in West Africa, which provides for almost the entire populace irrespective of gender and socioeconomic status. In her chapter, Biale Zua takes up the theme of health care in Africa as a development dynamic, using Gabon as an example of the possibility of an African success story in health care delivery. Zua examines the remarkable strides Gabon had made in its health care system by focusing on its bold program of infrastructural development, universal and comprehensive health insurance coverage, and other elements that have significantly enhanced its preventive care capability and capacity to address a myriad of health problems, including the HIV/AIDS pandemic. The chapter provides an optimistic viewpoint of the otherwise underdeveloped health care industry in Africa.

NOTES

1. Gabrielle Lynch and Gordon Crawford, "Democratization in Africa 1990-2010: An Assessment," *Democratization* 18, no. 2 (2011): 275–310.

2. See, for instance, Larry Diamond, Anthony Kirk-Greene, and Oyeleye Oyediran, eds., *Transition Without End: Nigerian Politics and Civil Society Under Babangida* (Boulder, CO, Lynne Rienner, 1997).

3. Stephanie Busari and Nicole Chavez, "Nigerian President Returns to Nigeria after Medical Treatment," *CNN*, Aug. 19, 2017, accessed May 15, 2018, https://www.cnn.com/2017/08/19/africa/nigeria-president-buhari/index.html.

Part I

GOVERNANCE, DEMOCRACY, AND DEVELOPMENT

Chapter 1

African Development and Democratization Trajectories

Gashawbeza W. Bekele and Adebayo Oyebade

INTRODUCTION

Democracy and development represent two pillars that are critical to the future of Africa, and African countries have made notable progress in both areas in recent years. Pragmatic evidence shows that democratic states are generally more developed than those that are not. While other dynamics are involved in development, the link between development and democracy cannot be underestimated. Indeed, democracy, to the extent that it more easily provides the political and economic space for sustainable growth, is fundamentally interwoven with development. In addition to widespread economic progress, elimination of extreme poverty, implementation of community-building policies, and environmental protection, the world-renowned American economist Jeffrey Sachs added the essentiality of "good governance" as important component of sustainable development.[1]

Given the aforementioned linkages between democracy, development, and good governance, and as a result of internal and external pressure, many African countries have widely embraced some form of multiparty democracy since the 1990s. There is indeed genuine ground for optimism regarding Africa's transition toward democracy, as democracy is slowly but surely taking root in the continent. Formal or procedural democracy has been instituted in many parts of Africa where regular elections are held and citizens enjoy some political rights. Despite the important strides that have been made by a number of African states toward democracy, however, many countries have experienced major setbacks and challenges in their efforts to transition toward a more substantive, liberal form of democracy. In general, nascent democracy in contemporary Africa often has been devoid of the fundamental principles of democracy such as rule of law and independent judiciary;

political pluralism; respect for civil and human rights; free, fair, and competitive elections; and freedom of the press and individual expression.

In addition, Africa has made significant strides in the areas of economic, health, and social development in recent years. Economic growth has expanded sharply since the turn of the millennium, and in fact, half of the fastest growing economies in the world since 2000 have been in Africa.[2] Also, tremendous progress has been recorded in reducing maternal mortality, infant and child mortality, and improving life expectancy. Despite the economic and social progress, however, economic growth has hardly translated into broad-based, sustainable development, which is needed to improve the welfare of the people, as gains in per capita income, improvements in standard of living, and poverty reduction are negligible. Concomitantly, one can argue that Africa has demonstrated quite glaringly all the elements of stunted development. This chapter provides a synopsis of governance systems and development models adopted in Africa since colonial times, and an overall assessment of progress in democratization and development in the last three decades by drawing examples from several African states and employing appropriate indices of democracy and economic and social development.

A HISTORICAL OVERVIEW OF GOVERNANCE SYSTEMS IN AFRICA

African states have not been formed based on their indigenous systems of socioeconomic and political institutions and heritage, as precolonial African administrative structures and norms have been replaced by colonially inspired political and economic institutions, administrative structures, and practices. The colonial administrative framework rested on the centralization of power and resources by the state, creating an authoritarian system of governance, employing both direct and indirect rule.[3] The colonial system not only undermined indigenous systems of administration and sociopolitical organization but also created authoritarian leadership and stiff competition for state power and economic resources in African states.

A number of nationalist leaders who led the struggle against colonial rule assumed power following independence and inaugurated personal rule in their countries. These leaders, such as Kwame Nkrumah of Ghana and Jomo Kenyatta of Kenya, developed a personality cult during the nationalist struggle; however, they maintained the authoritarian system of governance that was inherited from colonial rule. Hence, independence did not bring a quality break from the colonial past, as colonial political and economic systems were still intact. Following independence, many African countries opted for a single national party, ostensibly to safeguard national unity in the face of diversity. Chinua Achebe, one of the foremost Nigerian novelists, qualified this sentiment toward a one-party state in his novel as "all argument should cease and the whole people speak with one voice and that any more dissent and argument outside the door of the shelter would subvert and bring down the whole house."[4]

A one-party system, however, became the instrument of perpetuating personal rule as it offered political elites the desired power to exercise a tight control over all segments of state affairs. It was common in these states such as Ghana, Guinea, Ivory Coast (now Côte d'Ivoire), Kenya, Zambia, Tanzania, Algeria for the leader to proscribe or deliberately render democratic political institutions weak, ignore the rule of law with impunity, and employ state's security apparatus to suppress dissent. Invariably, personal rule constitutes a dictatorship as the ruler wields control over practically all aspects of the machinery of governance.

Hence, the postcolonial African state, for the most part, has been characterized by predatory leadership, the construction of personality cult, autocratic rule, consequent repression of civil society, and unbridled corruption. Furthermore, as Pierre Englebert and Kevin Dunn rightly pointed out, many postcolonial African states became patrimonial states, where political leaders exercised absolute authority over state resources and appropriated power and resources based on loyalty and political patronage, involving a complex network of patron-client relationships.[5]

Several African states introduced multiparty democratic systems in the 1990s as a result of internal and external pressure. Consequently, patrimonial states gave way to "patronage democracies."[6] In patronage democracies, political leaders take office via elections but still control and distribute state resources and government positions at their discretion to buy the loyalty of supporters and voters, often along ethnic lines. Hence, although many African countries transitioned toward multiparty democracy and formal elections become the norm in the last three decades, there has been an increased realization that instituting liberal democracy and transforming patrimonial and authoritarian systems of governance to responsible democratic governance is a challenging, slow, and complex political process.

DEMOCRATIC CONSOLIDATION IN AFRICA'S FLEDGLING DEMOCRACIES

Democracy, defined by Abraham Lincoln as "government of the people, by the people, and for the people," is arguably considered the best form of government in many parts of the world, including Africa, as it ensures transparency and fairness, promotes an egalitarian society, and prevents tyranny.

In addition, democracy is often accompanied by economic growth, progress, and the all-around development of a society. A number of African countries have made a successful transition to a multiparty democratic system and many are at various stages of transition, partly to realize the aforementioned benefits of democratic governance and partly due to internal and external pressure. Since democracy entails citizen participation and competition of groups in a polity via multiparty elections, Africa has made remarkable gains in electoral democracy over the last three decades. As a result of pressure from civil society organizations, churches, trade unions, students, and international organizations, many African countries hold elections on a regular basis and allow certain forms of multiparty democratic participation. Indeed, formal (procedural) democracy has been instituted in many parts of Africa where regular elections are held and citizens enjoy some political rights. Available statistics shows that forty-two African countries held multiparty elections between 1990 and 2004.[7] However, as elections are not entirely free or fair in some countries, and citizens are deprived of basic rights and freedoms, some of the African countries might be considered at best "illiberal" democracies. Thus, only very few countries could be considered liberal democracies, where there is not only free and fair elections but also citizens have civil rights and freedoms that are protected by rule of law.

We employ the two most widely used indices of democracy in academia, Polity IV and Freedom House, to assess democratic progress in Africa.[8] Polity scores from the Political IV project, compiled by political scientists at the University of Maryland, are considered minimalist measures of democracy that assess competitiveness and openness of elections, the nature of political participation, and the extent of checks on executive authority by parliament. Based on the polity scores from this project, we tabulated the number of African regimes that fall into the three categories of governance: democracies, anocracies, and autocracies between 1979 and 2011. As it is shown in figure 1.1, while the number of democracies in Africa stayed almost the same (below five) until 1991, the number of democracies rose from six to seventeen between 1991 and 2011. The increase in the number of democracies was accompanied by an associated decrease in autocracies, as the number of autocracies, which were dominant before the 1990s, fell down from thirty-nine in 1990 to five in 2011, indicating a radical shift in governance. However, in 2011, Africa still had few democracies (seventeen), as the majority of African governments are considered anocracies (twenty-eight), or "hybrid regimes" that are partly democratic but with autocratic features. Thus, based on a "minimalist" measure of democracy, it would seem that democracy has spread rapidly in Africa mainly due to increases in the procedural democratic practices across the continent,[9] but largely without substantive gains in democracy.

Figure 1.1 Africa Governance Trends, 1979–2011. *Source*: Authors' computations based on Polity IV Project. The Polity IV Project is a quantitative research project that contains annual information on regime and authority characteristics for all independent states with a total population of 500,000 or more. The Polity dataset can be used for time-series analyses of political behavior and for studying the effects of regime authority. Monty G. Marshall, Societal-Systems Research Inc. is the Principal Investigator and Ted Robert Gurr, Emeritus and Distinguished Professor of Government and Politics, University of Maryland is the founder of the project. The dataset can be accessed via http://www.systemicpeace.org/polity/polity4.htm.

It is clearly evident that many African countries are more open and democratic than they were in the 1980s, with citizens enjoying greater set of political rights and civil liberties. While a growing number of African countries meet the limited set of criteria for procedural or electoral democracy, very few countries are considered as liberal democracies, with a fuller set of civil liberties and freedoms.[10] Freedom House's index of democracy focuses on individual rights and freedoms. Based on the latest *Freedom in the World Report*, there are only ten countries in Africa that can be considered as fully liberal democracies (see figure 1.2). As is shown in figure 1.2, in 2016, more than 60 percent of African people are living in countries that are classified as free (19 percent) or partly free (41 percent). In the year 1989, only 43 percent of African countries were considered free (8 percent) and partly free (35 percent). Despite the progress in the state of freedom through the early 2000s, the state of freedom remained almost the same ever since with instances of democratic backsliding in recent years.

Overall, the aforementioned figures clearly indicate that democratic consolidation is gradually taking place in Africa. Recent political changes in the

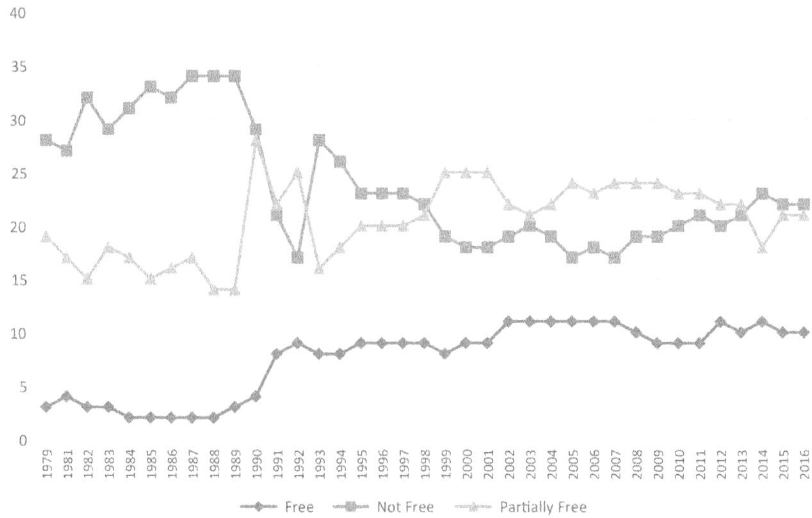

Figure 1.2 Democratic Trends in Africa, 1979–2016. *Source*: Authors' computations based on data from Freedom House titled "Freedom in the World Comparative and Historical Data: Country and Territory Ratings and Statuses." https://freedomhouse.org/content/freedom-world-data-and-resources.

continent also attest to the fact that democracy is slowly but surely taking root in the continent and that the political landscape is changing. For instance, the year 2017 has been an eventful year in African politics. One of the longest serving authoritarian leaders in Africa, Robert Mugabe, who ruled Zimbabwe for thirty-seven years, was forced to resign by his own military and political allies. In Angola, long-serving leader, José Eduardo dos Santos, stepped aside after thirty-eight years in power. In Gambia, Yahya Jammeh, who ruled the country for twenty-two years, grudgingly relinquished power after losing an election. The exodus of these long-serving authoritarian leaders may signal the beginning of a new wave of leadership change and the waning of autocratic and personal rule in Africa.

However, with the exception of Gambia, changes of leadership in Zimbabwe and Angola did not usher in a new wave of democratic governance because the statuesque has been maintained and the ruling parties in these countries still remain in power. Mugabe was replaced by his vice president Emmerson Mnangagwa, who in turn appointed military leaders and party loyalists from the Zimbabwe African National Union Patriotic Front (ZANU-PF), the ruling party in Zimbabwe since 1980. Despite dos Santos's exit, the Popular Movement for the Liberation of Angola (MPLA) has maintained a monopoly in Angolan politics since independence in 1975.

Similar examples can be found in many parts of Africa. The ruling party, Chama Cha Mapinduzi (CCM), or Party of the Revolution, has also dominated Tanzanian politics since independence. Furthermore, although Hosni Mubarak who held power in Egypt for nearly thirty years was ousted from power with a brief interlude of Muslim Brotherhood's Mohamed Morsi, Egypt's political structure has not changed in the last sixty years. The ascendance to power of Egypt's current president Abdel Fattah el-Sisi, via the "Arab Spring," has been viewed as a continuation of military rule in Egypt and Egypt's failed revolution toward democracy.

There are, however, many bright spots. African countries that have made democratic transitions in the late 1990s and early 2000 remain stable and democratic. In Liberia, President Ellen Sirleaf-Johnson left power peacefully after serving two terms to be succeeded by George Oppong Weah, who defeated her preferred successor, Vice President Joseph Boakai, at the ballot box. In Sierra Leone, Julius Maada Bio of the Sierra Leone People's Party (SLPP) became the country's new president, defeating the previously ruling All People's Congress (APC) candidate Samura Kamara. In the Gambia, Yahya Jammeh's eviction after losing the election to Adama Borrow is also a sign of recent democratic gains in Africa. The democratic transfer of power in this small African country has resulted in its monumental rise to become one of the most democratic countries in Africa in 2017 based on the U.K.-based Economist Intelligence Unit's Democracy Index.

The election of Nana Akufo-Addo in Ghana after winning Ghana's seventh democratic election shows that democracy in fact is taking root in African countries that adopted multiparty democracy in the 1990s. The recent election in 2017 was the fourth peaceful transition of power in Ghana between two dominant political parties that alternated power, the National Democratic Congress and the New Patriotic Party. Former president Barack Obama acknowledged the democratic consolidation in Ghana in his speech to Ghana's Parliament on July 11, 2009 as follows:

> The people of Ghana have worked hard to put democracy on a firmer footing, with peaceful transfers of power even in the wake of closely contested elections. And with improved governance and an emerging civil society, Ghana's economy has shown impressive rates of growth. To realize that promise, we must first recognize a fundamental truth that you have given life to in Ghana: development depends upon good governance. That is the ingredient which has been missing in far too many places, for far too long. That is the change that can unlock Africa's potential. And that is a responsibility that can only be met by Africans.[11]

Moreover, in an apparent but small victory for the rule of law and independent judiciary, the Kenyan Supreme Court nullified the August 2017 presidential election in which Uhuru Kenyatta was declared the winner, citing election irregularities. However, the country's Supreme Court rejected two subsequent petitions to nullify the election results of the repeated election in October 2017, which was boycotted by the main opposition leader Raila Odinga and his supporters. This case provides genuine grounds for optimism and underscores the need for independent judiciary to protect civil and human rights and serve as a check and balance to the excesses of the executive branch of government.

THE CHALLENGES OF DEMOCRATIZATION

The aforementioned cases involving the consolidation of democracy in countries that have already made democratic transitions, the institutionalization of electoral democracy, occasional peaceful transfer of power without bloodshed, and adoption of multiparty systems in general are areas of progress that should be regarded as important milestones in Africa's transition toward democracy. However, what we have learned in the last three decades is also the fact that building a strong and enduring democratic system is a very slow and arduous process, as the nascent democracies in Africa have experienced major setbacks, rollbacks, or challenges enumerated below.

Multiparty democracy in Africa was introduced with no guarantees for civil rights and liberties. Even though many African countries included a bill of rights in their constitutions, individual rights and liberties are often violated on a regular basis in many countries. Absence of political and academic freedom, freedom of speech and assembly, human right violations, extra-judicial killings, stifling of dissent, arbitrary arrest of opposition party officials, and intimidation are still common place in many counties. This is clearly evident in Freedom House's categorization of many African countries as partly free and not free (see figure 1.2).

African leaders who were hailed as "the new breed" of African leaders by President Clinton in the mid-1990s, including Uganda's Yoweri Museveni, Rwanda's Paul Kagame, Eritrea's Isaias Afwerki, and Ethiopia's Meles Zenawi (deceased) were once thought to espouse democratic governance in Africa. However, they have not transferred political power via electoral democracy. Even though there are variations in leadership style and extent of oppression, these leaders have remained in power by silencing opposition leaders, the media, free press, journalists, and stifling dissent in general.

The other challenge to democracy in Africa is nonadherence to constitutional term limits and omnipresent attempts to extend or remove term limits of incumbents through constitutional amendments. Several African leaders who promised to institute democratic systems of governance have pressured legislatures to repeal term limits enshrined in their constitutions to stay in power. The most often outcome is repealing the term limit of the sitting president that leads toward authoritarian stability, even though some legislatures successfully resisted constitutional change. In a similar vein, some leaders were hell-bent on scrapping age limits to run for life. For instance, Museveni successfully pressured the Ugandan Parliament to remove the age limit of seventy-five from the country's constitution, which effectively allows the seventy-three-year-old (who has been in power for thirty-one years) to extend his rule and essentially become a ruler for life in Uganda. As a result of these manipulations, Africa, the youngest continent with a median age of 19.5 years, continues to be ruled by oldest men.[12]

Other obstacles to democratization in Africa include rigged elections or electoral fraud, politicization of ethnic identity and ethnic voting, underrepresentation of women in politics, unbridled corruption, absence of independent judiciary and strong civil institutions, and sporadic military intervention in African politics.[13] Hence, one can argue that given the weak institutions of civil society and the continued "big man rule" in Africa using legal tactics, multi-party system of democracy in Africa is at its infancy at best, making the transition to liberal democracy a daunting challenge.

CONCEPTUALIZING DEVELOPMENT

The concept of development is quite complex and somewhat problematic in terms of grasping its whole essence. In effect, it has been articulated in a number of different ways in development studies. In a rather simplistic format, and perhaps from the perspective of the average person, development translates to the existence of opportunities in which economic, political, and social advancement can be attained. An environment is thus created that ensures reduction in rampant poverty, reasonably decent quality of life in which basic necessities are met, transparent governance and a political and ruling elite that is not corrupt, equal opportunities and respect for rights of people irrespective of ethnicity and social and economic class, and other things that make life better for all. If this provides a succinct definition of development, certainly, Africa could be said to still belong to the underdeveloped segment of the world. This assessment is aptly put in the report of the UN Plan of Action that came out of the World Summit on Sustainable Development in Johannesburg, in 2002. The report states:

> Since the United Nations Conference on Environment and Development, sustainable development has remained elusive for many African countries. Poverty remains a major challenge and most countries on the continent have not benefited fully from the opportunities of globalization, further exacerbating the continent's marginalization. Africa's efforts to achieve sustainable development

> have been hindered by conflicts, insufficient investment, limited market access opportunities and supply side constraints, unsustainable debt burdens, historically declining levels of official development assistance and the impact of HIV/AIDS.[14]

Some studies have emphasized the element of sustainability in the concept of development. They note that the idea of development entails more than the ability to cater for present human essential needs and that development, to be real value, must be sustainable. This position is, perhaps, best underscored by the UN commissioned Brundtland Report published in 1987. According to the report, sustainable development is defined as "development that meets the needs of the present without compromising the ability of future generations to meet their own needs."[15]

However, the debate on African development hardly factors in the sustainability element, as it is focused largely on overall economic growth as measured by Gross National Product (GDP) or Gross National Income (GNI). It is an understatement to state that developmental plans are often haphazardly planned and shortsighted, lacking clear vision for the future; plans are often underfunded or ill executed to the extent that they fail to produce any sustainable transformations that would help the majority of the people lay claim to decent, quality living.

MODELS FOR AFRICAN DEVELOPMENT

The question of what developmental path Africa should pursue has never ceased to be a subject of intense debate, particularly in the academy. In the array of developmental theories, two main strands stand out: the Modernization School and Political Economy perspectives. The Modernization Theory of development economics, popular in Western scholarly discourses in the 1960s, proposed a particular development chart for the less-developed and the underdeveloped world, or the Global South, including Africa. Proponents of modernization theory draw what they consider a necessary distinction between two types of societies, the traditional of the underdeveloped Global South, and the modern of the developed Global North. Modernizers contend, in absolute terms, that traditional societies fundamentally lack necessary internal forces required to bring about progress and development. Modernization theory thus concludes that development in the underdeveloped world is feasible provided that it adopts Western style development models.

By the mid-1970s, an alternative development paradigm championed by political economists began to mount a challenge to the modernization constructs. Many of the scholars from this school of thought emerged from the Global South, mainly from Latin America, the Caribbean, and Africa. They included noted leftist intellectuals like the Guyanese historian and revolutionary Walter Rodney; the West Indian psychoanalyst and social philosopher Franz Fanon; the Egyptian-French Marxian economist Samir Amin; and the Nigerian political scientist Claude Ake. However, the most enterprising scholar of this genre was, perhaps, the German-born American economic historian Andre Gunder Frank, who published extensively in the 1970s and 1980s on issues of development, underdevelopment, and the political economy of the Global South.[16]

Generally, political economists adopt a neo-Marxist approach to problematize the trajectory of underdevelopment in the Global South. Essentially, Africa's underdevelopment was construed as a function of the historical, brutal Western capitalist exploitation of the continent, through slavery, colonialism, and subsequently neocolonialism, unequal terms of trade, and the entrenchment of African economies into the Western-dominated and exploitative global capitalist system. The proposed solution was to reduce links with the Western capitalist system, eradicate excessive external dependence, and bring about autocentric economic growth and self-sufficiency. In line with this call for a new international economic order, African leaders, through the works of the Economic Commission for Africa (ECA), prepared development plans to restructure African economies and extricate the continent from its peripheral position in the world economy. The ECA played a major role not only in preparing two seminal documents but also in initiating a series of actions in the 1970s. This activity in turn led to the adoption of the Monrovia Strategy in 1979 and the Lagos Plan of Action for Economic Development in 1980 by African Heads of States and Governments, which called for national and collective self-reliance and self-sustainment.[17] The main purpose of such plans was to offer an alternative economic policy or strategy that would lead to the economic decolonization of the continent, as inherited colonial and neocolonial policies failed to bring economic progress in Africa. In addition, to curb Africa's external dependence on imports of skills, technology, capital goods, and services, the plan called for due consideration to be given to transform domestic markets, cultivate local entrepreneurship, and develop skilled labor force and technology. As a result, many African countries adopted state-led Import Substitution Industrialization (ISI) as an economic strategy to produce industrialized goods locally and thereby reduce dependence on imported goods.

In the 1980s, however, there was a realization that ISI and state intervention in the economy failed to produce results, as the majority of African countries were saddled with huge debt and other macroeconomic crisis. Hence, the World Bank and the International Monetary Fund (IMF) pushed for economic reforms to replace inward-looking, import substitution strategies with outward-oriented, liberalization strategies aimed at reducing government intervention in the economy, privatizing the public-sector, cutting government spending and subsidies, and opening up local markets to worldwide competition and investment. The World Bank and IMF led efforts toward the implementation of such market liberalization strategies, often called Structural Adjustment Programs (SAPs), in Africa in the 1980s and 1990s. While liberalization of trade and capital markets and privatization of national industries led to increases in exports and productivity for some countries, the draconian austerity measures in the policy reform package, however, had disastrous consequences, especially on the poor and other vulnerable groups of society. For instance, the reductions in expenditure on health and education and the introduction of user fees exacerbated social hardships.[18]

TRENDS IN ECONOMIC GROWTH AND SOCIAL DEVELOPMENT

Economic growth in Africa has expanded sharply since the turn of the millennium. As clearly shown in figure 1.3, there has been steady increase in per capita income since the early 2000s. However, growth has slowed in majority of the countries in recent years, reaching its lowest level in 2016 while some countries still continue to expand strongly. According to the IMF, a third of the countries in Africa south of the Sahara continue to grow at 5 percent or more, twelve countries comprising over 40 percent of the region's population, but economic growth barely surpass population growth in the majority of the countries.[19]

However, we should consider the reality of contradictory trends, as a number of African countries are considered some of the fastest growing economies in the world, boosting average GDP growth above 6 percent. According to World Bank, in 2018, five of the world's ten fastest growing economies are from Africa (see figure 1.4). These include Ethiopia (9.6 percent), Côte d'Ivoire (7.4 percent), Ghana (6.9 percent), Senegal (6.8 percent), and Rwanda (6.8 percent).

Nevertheless, given the slow rate of economic growth in many countries, averaging 1.4 percent in 2016, 2.6 percent in 2017, 3.4 percent (expected) in 2018 and rapid population growth in the continent, gains in per capita income, or improvements in standard of living are negligible.[20] The pro-rich growth in the continent has not been accompanied by rising income to average citizens, and the progress that was made in poverty reduction is insignificant. Hence, as Lynch and Crawford rightly argue, Africa's economic performance when cast in terms of development rather than economic growth is inconsequential.[21]

Furthermore, the rapid growth in population outstripping economic growth exacerbates development challenges in the continent, as the imbalance between population and economic growth often results in youth unemployment, underemployment, and poverty. Hence, given rapid growth in population and urbanization, there are fears that the rapid population growth may trample economic growth and depress standard of living.

Africa has made significant strides in the areas of health and social development in recent years. For instance, in the areas of health, tremendous progress has been recorded in reducing maternal mortality, infant and child mortality, and improving life expectancy (see figure 1.5). In the areas of education, the

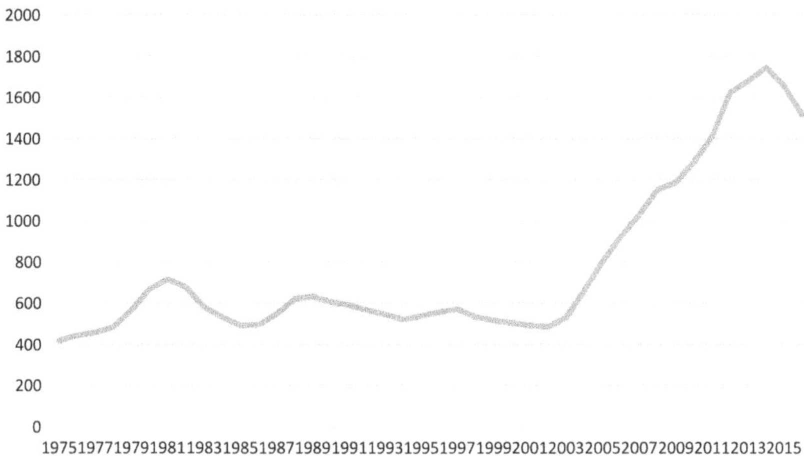

Figure 1.3 Africa South of the Sahara: GNI per Papita, Atlas Method in Current U.S.$. *Source*: World Bank national accounts data, and Organisation for Economic Co-operation and Development (OECD) National Accounts data files.

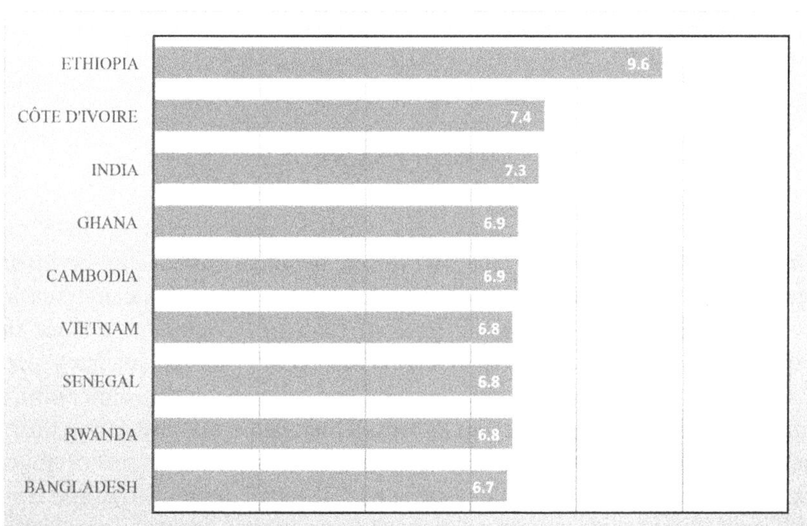

Figure 1.4 The Top Ten Fastest Growing Economies in the World in 2018 Based on Real Gross Domestic Product (GDP) Growth at Market Prices. *Source*: World Bank, Global Economic Prospects, 2018.

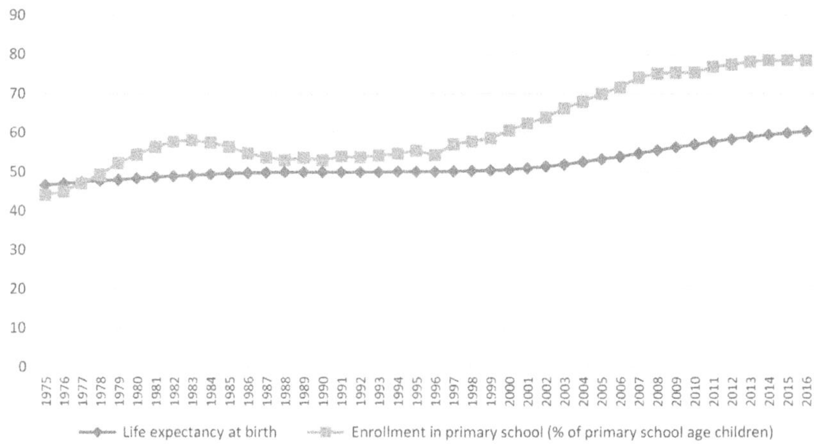

Figure 1.5 Trends in Primary Education Enrollment and Life Expectancy in Africa South of the Sahara, 1975–2016. *Source*: UNESCO Institute for Statistics and World Bank. Data for life expectancy at birth compiled by the World Bank from the following sources: United Nations Population Division. World Population Prospects: 2017 Revision, or derived from male and female life expectancy at birth from sources such as: Census reports and other statistical publications from national statistical offices, Eurostat: Demographic Statistics, United Nations Statistical Division Population and Vital Statistics Report (various years), U.S. Census Bureau: International Database, and Secretariat of the Pacific Community: Statistics and Demography Programme.

pace of progress toward universal primary education has been remarkable, with the average primary education enrollment for both sexes increasing from 44 percent in 1975 to 79 percent in 2016 (see figure 1.5).

CONCLUSION

An overall assessment of progress and trends in democratization in Africa in recent years shows that there is indeed genuine ground for optimism regarding Africa's transition toward democracy, as many African countries have pervasively embraced some form of multiparty democracy since the 1990s. Formal or procedural democracy has been instituted in many parts of Africa where regular elections are held and citizens enjoy some political rights. However, there has been an increased realization that instituting liberal democracy and transforming patrimonial and authoritarian systems of governance to responsible democratic governance is a challenging, slow, and complex political process, as many countries have experienced major setbacks and challenges in their efforts to transition toward a more substantive, liberal form of democracy based upon the principles of liberty and equality. This is largely due to absence of strong democratic institutions, an independent judiciary, and adequate checks and balances or separation of powers between different branches of government in many countries.

In addition, many African countries have made significant strides in economic growth and other indicators of social progress such as education and health in the new millennium. However, the pro-rich growth that is associated with the neoliberal economic policies in Africa is characterized by rising inequalities, uneven development, and did not bring significant gains in income of the average citizen, substantial reductions in poverty, and improvements in standard of living. Despite faster economic growth, in many parts of Africa, there is concern about rising debt, a problem exacerbated by poor governance in the form of corruption, lack of transparency, and accountability. That is why development, good governance, and democracy have to be linked, as they are largely inseparable. It is also imperative to note that the sustenance of rapid economic growth and improvements in social development and health require democratic and responsible governance. Without economic growth and improvement in citizens' well-being, political leaders loose the support of voters, which, in turn, finds expression in civil violence and mass protests, making budding democracies fragile. This thus necessitates a strong nexus between democratization, development, and improved governance in Africa.

NOTES

1. Jeffery D. Sachs, *The Age of Sustainable Development* (New York: Columbia University Press, 2015), 3.

2. Landry Signe, "Capturing Africa's High Returns," Project Syndicate, March 13, 2018, accessed May 10, 2018, https://www.project-syndicate.org/commentary/africa-investment-high-returns-by-landry-signe-2018-03?barrier=accesspaylog.

3. For an authoritative work on this subject, see Obaro Ikime, "Reconsidering Indirect Rule: The Nigerian Example," *Journal of the Historical Society of Nigeria* 4, no. 3 (1968): 421–438.

4. Chinua Achebe, *A Man of the People* (New York: Penguin Books, 1996), 37.

5. Pierre Englebert and Kevin C. Dunn, *Inside African Politics* (Boulder, CO: Lynne Rienner Publishers, 2013), 132–133.

6. Kanchan Chandra, "Caste in our social imagination," conference paper, the Republic of Ideas: A Symposium on Some Concerns and Concepts Engaging our Society, 2009, accessed May 25, 2018, http://www.india-seminar.com/2009/601/601_kanchan_chandra.htm. See also Kanchan Chandra, *Why Ethnic Parties Succeed Patronage and Ethnic Head Counts in India* (New York: NY, Cambridge University Press, 2004), 6.

7. Lise Rakner and Lars Svåsand, "Stuck in Transition: Electoral Processes in Zambia, 1991–2001," *Democratization* 12, no.1 (2005): 85.

8. These measures are developed based on Western conceptions of democracy, and some critiques suggest that a non-Western or an African-centered conceptualization of democracy and indices is needed to assess democratic progress.

9. Stephenie Burchard, "Democratic Trends in Sub-Saharan Africa, 1990–2014," Institute for Defense Analyses Document NS D-5393, Alexandria: Virginia, 2014.

10. Gabrielle Lynch and Gordon Crawford, "Democratization in Africa 1990–2010: An Assessment," *Democratization* 18, no. 2 (2011): 293.

11. For full text of the speech, see "Obama Ghana Speech: FULL TEXT," *Huffington Post*, August 11, 2009, https://www.huffingtonpost.com/2009/07/11/obama-ghana-speech-full-t_n_230009.html.

12. David Kiwuwa, "Africa Is Young. Why Are Its Leaders so Old?" *CNN*, October 15, 2009, accessed May 25, 2018, https://www.cnn.com/2015/10/15/africa/africas-old-mens-club-op-ed-david-e-kiwuwa/index.html.

13. For a more detailed list and analysis of shortcomings in Africa's democratization effort, see Lynch and Crawford, "Democratization in Africa," 277–296.

14. United Nations, "Plan of Implementation of the World Summit on Sustainable Development, VIII. Sustainable development for Africa," September 4, 2002, accessed May 28, 2018, http://www.un-documents.net/jburgpln.htm#VIII.

15. United Nations, "Brundtland Report: Report of the World Commission on Environment and Development, Chapter 2. Towards Sustainable Development," General Assembly Resolution 42/187, December 11, 1987, accessed May 28, 2018, https://en.wikisource.org/wiki/Brundtland_Report/Chapter_2._Towards_Sustainable_Development.

16. On this subject, see the following works, for instance: Andre Gunder Frank, *Underdevelopment of development* (Stockholm, Sweden: Bethany Books, 1991); Claude Ake, *A Political Economy of Africa* (Harlow, Essex: Longman Group Ltd., 1981); and Samir Amin, *Accumulation on a World Scale: A Critique of the Theory of Underdevelopment, Vol. 2* (New York: Monthly Review Press, 1974).

17. Adebayo Adedeji, "The Monrovia Strategy and the Lagos Plan of Action for African Development—Five Years After," United Nations Economic Commission for Africa, 1984–11. A paper presented at the ECA/Dalhousie University Conference on the Lagos Plan of Action and Africa's Future International Relations: Projections and Implications for Policy-Makers in Nova Scotia, Canada, November 2–4, 1984.

18. Aderanti Adepoju, *The Impact of Structural Adjustment on the Population of Africa: The Implications for Education, Health, & Employment* (London: James Curry, 1993).

19. International Monetary Fund, "Regional Economic Outlook: Sub-Saharan Africa: Fiscal Adjustment and Economic Diversification," Washington, DC, October 2017.

20. International Monetary Fund, "Regional Economic Outlook: Sub-Saharan Africa: Restarting the Growth Engine," Washington, DC, April 2017; International Monetary Fund, "Regional Economic Outlook: Sub-Saharan Africa: Fiscal Adjustment and Economic Diversification," Washington, DC, October 2017.

21. Lynch and Crawford, "Democratization in Africa," 293.

Chapter 2

The Political Ecology of Sustainable Development in Africa

Tadesse Kidane-Mariam

INTRODUCTION

This chapter revolves around the political ecology of sustainable development in the African region. Political ecology approaches to the study of the dynamics of population, resources, environment, and development establish a systemic link between resource endowments and the policy, institutional, and organizational arrangements for their sustainable exploitation, use, and management. The contributions of many researchers to the understanding of the nature and dynamics of the complex interaction between these critical factors of national development are varied in their approaches and perspectives. Some have privileged biophysical forces to explain the serious problems facing the region's population, environment, and development management while others have focused their analysis on political economy structures and institutional arrangements. This chapter is a modest attempt at understanding the multifaceted problems facing Africa's sustainable development from a political ecology perspective, essentially integrating both the biophysical factors and the political economy structures of African societies. Natural resources are fundamentally technological and social appraisals in the dynamics of any society's development and transformation. As such, both technological and political organizations of society play decisive roles in meeting basic needs, promoting sustainable development, protecting the environment, and facilitating the growth of a harmonious relationship between nature and society.

The capacity of successive African societies to understand, exploit, conserve, and manage their diverse human and natural resources has increased both qualitatively and quantitatively with the introduction of modernity over the last 100 years. Unfortunately, the nature of the relationship between humans and the physical environment has been unfavorably inclining in the direction of unsustainable use and management of the natural resources of the environment. Hence, the researcher is faced with the daunting task of explaining or making sense of why one of the world's best resource-endowed continents has remained one of the weakest, environmentally challenged and most underdeveloped part of the modern world system. Why did successive generations of Africans fail to deal with structural political, economic, environmental and population problems in an effective, socially just and sustainable manner? Why have successive postindependence governments failed to institute a system of governance based on accountable and transparent public administrations that could manage the resources of the environment more soundly and meet the basic needs of their fast growing and highly expectant populations? Why have African societies failed to disengage themselves from crippling dependency on external forces to drive their own dynamics of development management? These are daunting questions that defy simplistic and overarching answers, as they require systematic analysis and objective answers. In this chapter, I want to raise what I consider to be critical challenges and opportunities in promoting sustainable development in Africa without losing sight of the complex global, continental, country and local environments that affect the region's development dynamics. Following the brief introduction, I offer a synoptic overview of Africa's sustainable development experiences since the late 1980s. The third part highlights the critical opportunities and challenges facing the region in realizing the objectives and goals of sustainable development. The last part provides a brief conclusion.

I would like to highlight some geographical facts of the African continent before I present my reflections on its sustainable development achievements, opportunities, and challenges. Africa has an area of 11.8 million sq. miles (30 million sq. kilometers) and is the second largest continent after Asia. It covers about 20 percent of the earth's surface. It is three times larger than the United States. Its estimated population of 1.2 billion makes it the second most populous world region. It is a region of tremendous physical and demographic diversity. More than 75 percent of Africa lies within the tropics and hence is the hottest and driest of all continents. It is also the only continent where major biomes repeat north and south of the equator thus giving it a unique endowment of resources and climatic opportunities and challenges. Its wildlife resources are known for their legendary variety and abundance. Culturally, it is the most diverse world region with six major language families and more than 1,000 languages and many ethnic and universalistic religions including Christianity, Islam, Judaism, and Indigenous African religions.[1]

AFRICA'S SUSTAINABLE DEVELOPMENT EXPERIENCE: A SYNOPTIC OVERVIEW

Africa's development has been strongly impacted by major global historical events and trends including slavery, colonialism, neocolonialism and globalization. Frederick Cooper in his recent book noted that "Africa's progress has been impeded by its international relations."[2] The postindependence experience of Africa is variegated and complex. Adebayo Adedeji, the former executive secretary of the UN Economic Commission for Africa, summed up the three decades of the postindependence African experience in a rather unflattering manner. He noted that the failure of postindependence African governments to make fundamental changes alienated the energetic independence generation. As he put it, "colonialism became neocolonialism; old colonial masters became donors, African countries became recipients."[3] These structures and forces continue to define and shape the current dynamics and configuration of the region's development and social transformation. The recent role of The International Monetary Fund (IMF), World Bank (WB), and African Development Bank (ADB) to cast a new macroeconomic model for Africa's renaissance following the meeting in Germany is viewed as a continuation of the last fifty years of dominance of these institutions in formulating and forcing the implementation of economic and social policies in the region. In his 2017 critique, Fekadu Bekele noted that there was ample evidence that the macroeconomic, business, and financial frameworks that the three institutions developed and applied in the region in the postindependence period failed to deal with the structural problems facing Africa today.[4] The renewed attempt to apply these macroeconomic models to the economic and social conditions of Africa is not likely to lead to needed structural changes. The scattered economic and social activities that operate in most African countries function independently without clear-cut division of labor, market structures that are of a subsistence and nontransparent nature. Bekele alleges that the fast rate of growth registered in the last decade has not succeeded in creating true natural wealth and multiplier effects due to the lack of coherent, integrated, dynamic economic, and social structures. Africa's position as a dependent partner makes its global participation quite difficult, complex, and based on unequal exchange.[5]

Despite complex challenges, the last fifty years of Africa's development have registered significant improvements and achievements in different sectors of socioeconomic endeavors. The emergence of fifty-three countries from colonialism and the establishment of independent states with their own governments, sovereignty, development, and national economies is a historic achievement. The phenomenal expansion of education, healthcare, transportation, manufacturing, modern agricultural development, mining, energy, and information have all contributed to the improvement of the standard of living of millions of Africans. At the same time, Africa's dependence on foreign trade and international aid continues to arrest, distort, and stunt the dynamics of national development and social transformation. Coupled with bad governance, distorted priorities and management practices, exploding populations, and rising social expectations, Africa today finds itself as the least developed and politically unstable part of the world region.

It is against such a broad brush of the postindependence history of development that the current opportunities and challenges of sustainable development should be critically analyzed and properly understood.

It should be remembered that in 1987, the UN Commission on Environment and Development (Bruntland Commission) came out with an important document, "Our Common Future," highlighting the significance of sustainable development for the world community. It defined sustainable development as one that "meets the needs of the current generations without compromising the ability of future generations to meet their needs."[6] The idea of sustainability stood on the three interrelated legs of promoting economic growth to generate the wealth that is required to meet societal need: a more equitable distribution of the wealth among peoples, regions, and the protection of the natural environment that provides the very resources for our survival. Since the 1980s, the concept of sustainable development incorporating these critical dimensions has thrust itself into both academic and public discourse as well as development practice.

African countries used sustainable development as the main theme in the preparation of National Environmental Action Plans for the 1991 Rio Conference on Environment and Development. The expanded definition of sustainable development given by a Nigerian Environmental Action Team encapsulates the views of African countries as follows:

> Sustainable development is a notion, a movement, and an approach which has developed into a global wave of concerns, study, political mobilization, and organization around the twin issues of environmental protection and economic development. The approach embodies the notion and ideal of a development process that is equitable and socially responsive, recognizing the excessive nature of poverty, deprivation, and inequality between and within nations, classes, and communities. It also advocates that the world be seen as one ecosystem and that the economic development process should include ecological and environmental issues as an essential component.[7]

Academic and development research has anchored the discourse of economic development reflecting, according to Lakshman Yapa,

> the three paradigms of neoclassical economic theories of underdevelopment concerning overpopulation, transfer of technology and the diffusion of development; neo-Marxist theories of uneven development concerned with imperialism, dependency and world systems, and the environmentalist conception of sustainable development.[8]

Yapa argues that despite their profound differences in their world views, the three paradigms essentially reflect the central belief that "poverty arises from lack of development or underdevelopment, a condition which can be eradicated with more development."[9] He countered with the argument that "poverty is not about failed development, poor technology, lack of resources, mismanagement or poor planning . . . rather poverty represents a routine, everyday, normal manifestation of the very process of economic development, indeed development has created modern poverty."[10]

Notwithstanding differences in the paradigms of discourses on economic development, Africa's population, natural resources, and development dynamics pose both challenges and opportunities for any kind of scholarly work. The paucity of timely and reliable information on these critical areas forces the researcher to seek all kinds of sources to make sense of the complex and fast changing social and physical reality. The continuously evolving nature of the structures of the state and governance systems often poses insurmountable challenges in understanding the changes and continuities that accompany such transformations. The legislative, institutional, and policy changes accompanying such transformations make it difficult for anyone to distinguish between the remnants of the old and the novelties of the present. Likewise, the dramatic changes in the physical environment due to both natural processes and human pressure are immense and complex.

Geographical analysis of places and peoples essentially revolves around understanding interrelated themes of location (absolute and relative); physical and human attributes of places; the interaction between humans and the physical environment; movement or spatial interaction; and regional structures that evolve over time.[11] A systematic understanding of these basic geographic themes unfolds the underlying reasons as to why certain patterns of development persist at different places, times, and societies. Since geography and public policy are intimately related, studies should ask the bigger questions about the organization of society, and how political, economic, social, and environmental factors affect the overall dynamics of change over space and time. Hence, a systematic analysis of the political ecology of population, resources, development, environment, and technology in Africa should of necessity address such critical issues as the biophysical characteristics of places, the historical evolution of states, the role of population distribution and dynamics in development and resource management, and the impact of institutions, policies, and strategies on ameliorating and/or aggravating the contradictions that are inevitably manifested in human-environment relationships.

Africa's development, environment, and population challenges have often been described in tones of despair and exasperation. In a 1983 report entitled, "ECA and Africa's Development, 1983-2008: A Preliminary Perspective Studies," the UN Economic Commission for Africa projected a grim scenario in which Africa's socioeconomic conditions in a quarter of a century would be "a degradation of the very essence of human dignity."[12] Probably the best example of such characterization was Basil Davidson's caricature of Africa in his 1992 book *The Black Man's Burden*:

> The actual and present condition of Africa is one of deep trouble, sometimes a deeper trouble than the worst imposed during the colonial years. For some time now, deserts have widened year by year, broad savannas and their communities have lost all means of existence, or else are sorely threatened. Tropical forests such as the world will never see again have fed the export maw. Cities that barely deserve the name have spawned plagues of poverty on a scale never known before in earlier times, or even dreamed of. Harsh governments or dictatorships rule over peoples who distrust them to the point of hatred, and usually for good and sufficient reasons; and all too often one dismal tyranny gives way to a worse one. Despair rots civil society, the state becomes an enemy, and bandits flourish. Meanwhile, the developed world, the industrial world, has continued to take its cut of Africa's dwindling wealth. Transfers of this wealth to the developed countries of Europe and North America have annually expanded in value. And multitudes starved.[13]

A quarter of a century later, his highly illustrative caricature could be considered rather tame given the significant deterioration in Africa's nature-society relationship since the late 1980s.

African countries adopted the sustainability paradigm in their development policies and registered significant achievements in reducing population growth, accelerating economic growth, opening-up employment opportunities, and putting in place policy, legislative, and institutional mechanisms for protecting the environment. Yet, the region remains the poorest and most unstable part of the world community with tremendous challenges in the spheres of governance and political instability, population, economic growth and integration, agricultural change, poverty reduction, energy access, education, information, technology, and environmental management.

The regional effort to implement sustainable development policies, strategies, and action programs has taken many forms and dimensions. All countries of Africa adopted the 2000 UN Millennium Development Goals (MDG) and promoted the objectives and goals of sustainable development.

One of the fundamental objectives of the MDGs was to ensure environmental sustainability through the integration of the principles of sustainable development into national development policies and programs and reverse the loss of environmental resources. The quest for sustainable development and resource management has been grounded in the complex interaction between the changing size and distribution of its population and the demands that modern development is putting on the production, distribution, consumption of goods and services, and growing need for the judicious use and management of its diversified human and natural resources.

It is against such a broad brush of Africa's sustainable development experience that I would like to highlight the following critical sustainable development-related challenges and opportunities facing the region.

CRITICAL OPPORTUNITIES AND CHALLENGES OF SUSTAINABLE DEVELOPMENT

Africa's sustainable development efforts have taken place under complex domestic and international settings. The continued articulation of its political, economic, and cultural development to essentially colonial and neocolonial institutions and the lack of progress in the democratization of governance have thwarted the full realization of the objectives and goals of sustainable development. I believe that the region should deal with critical opportunities and challenges of sustainable development, discussed in the following sections, to reduce poverty, accelerate economic growth, and protect its highly diversified and vulnerable environment.

Political Instability and Poor Governance

The most significant challenge to sustainable development in African countries does not emanate from ecological concerns or deficiencies, but from political instability and poor governance. Political instability and poor governance have defined the postindependence history of African development. Genocidal civil wars, countless coup d'états, vicious dictatorships, Apartheid, ethnic conflict, serious violation of human and civil rights, and a wide range of "unfreedoms" have closed or truncated the possibility of enduring political stability and the evolution of genuine democratic governance. To a large extent, democracy in Africa has mainly been related to meaningless voting that is not connected to the true preparation of the population in critical decision making on matters that concern its overall welfare and development. As a result, the populace has lost faith in bringing change through democratic means and instead has resorted to all kinds of dangerous actions such as massive migration to foreign lands seeking economic opportunities and peace. Africa hosts the largest number of refugees and displaced persons in the world today; it is no wonder that the 2014 Mo Ibrahim index on governance, economic development, human rights, safety, and the rule of law top-rated only tiny Mauritius and Botswana. More than 50 percent of the 50 countries evaluated were found to be regressing in safety and the rule of law. Sustainable economic opportunity show signs of having stalled, and poverty, oppression, and political violence continue to define the fate of many African countries and societies.[14] The World Bank uses aggregate factors in six areas in its world governance indicator, including government effectiveness, voice and accountability, political stability and absence of violence, regulatory quality, rule of law, and control of corruption. The average rank for Sub-Saharan Africa (SSA) was 30.1, the lowest figure among world regions. Only Botswana and Mauritius scored above 70 points.[15] Governments and leaders have sanctioned systematic human rights abuses and violations, often invoking internal state sovereignty principles and practices. In many instances, governments and parties have fanned ethnic, regional, and class conflicts to stay in power indefinitely.

The increased flow of military hardware into the continent has been destabilizing many countries and wasting tremendous resources that could have been used to promote sustainable development and reduce poverty in the region. Hence, Africa today faces the structural challenge of establishing and maintaining political stability and instituting fundamental changes in the way Africans are governed. The fight for dignity, democracy, accountable, and transparent governments is not only a moral imperative but also an existential prerogative for African societies to achieve sustainable development and growth and improve the quality of life of a fast-increasing population.

Economic Dependence and Persistent Poverty

Africa's postindependence economic development and social change have been defined by its external economic dependence and the persistence of unacceptable levels of poverty. Despite the crippling dependence, the last decade has witnessed significant strides in economic growth and social transformation in many parts of Africa. Yet, the region remains stifled by a condition of economic dependence, the prevalence of widespread poverty, and a rather marginal role in international trade. About 70 percent of Sub-Sahara's exports come from oils, metals, and agricultural commodities for which it has no control over quantities, qualities, and prices. This debilitating dependence on a few natural resources and external markets is making growth both limited and unsustainable. Economic diversification through improvements in agriculture, manufacturing, commerce, tourism, education services, banking, information technology, and so on remains a structural policy and development challenge. Africa's vast natural resources provide tremendous opportunities for producing goods and services for meeting the needs of its fast-growing population. The failure of African countries to tap into their vast and diverse natural resources has led to the persistence of pervasive poverty at all levels. Concrete poverty reduction strategies and programs are needed on a sustained basis to deal with the growing problems of unemployment, underemployment, and abject poverty. The flow of African youth to Europe, the Middle East, and other parts of the world through illegal migration and human trafficking is a symptom of the inability of African countries to generate employment opportunities for a youthful population with rising expectations. The tragic death of thousands of young people trying to cross the Mediterranean Sea into Europe in search of economic opportunities is indicative of the failure of African societies to put their houses in order. The November 2017 CNN TV report on the sale of West Africans as slaves in Libya's lawless state is an egregious portrayal of the dire state of affairs in Africa's development.

Market Integration

The globalization of the world economy has necessitated the integration of markets. Africa's participation in the global market place as a buyer and seller of goods and services determines its capacity to promote sustainable development at national, subregional, and regional levels. On average, only 10–12 percent of Africa's trade goes to other African countries.[16] This is quite pitiful when we compare it with Europe's 60 percent, North America's 40 percent, and Asia's 30 percent. This situation is taking place despite the existence of such regional integration organizations such as Southern Africa Development Commission (SADC), Economic Community of West African States (ECOWAS), East African Community (EAC), Commission on Eastern and Southern Africa (COMESA), and Intergovernmental Authority on Drought and Development (IGAD). Regional integration is often seen as a rational response in Africa because the continent is faced with many small national economies and fifteen land-locked countries.[17] The ECA in 2010 raised doubts about the appropriateness of the strategy. The lack of political will and adequate resources to promote cross-border infrastructures and reduce tariffs and red-tape is not only arresting Africa's interregional trade and sustainable development but also contributing to the hemorrhaging of its hard-earned foreign exchange, thus perpetuating and increasing the region's dependence on traditional sources of products and services.

Part of the problem may lie in the paradigm of linear market integration, marked by stepwise integration of goods, labor and capital markets, and eventually monetary and fiscal integration. This tends to focus on border measures such as the import tariff. However, supply-side constraints may be more important. A deeper integration agenda that includes services, investment, competition policy, and other behind-the-border issues can address the national-level supply-side constraints

The World Trade Organization (WTO) study sees regional integration problems in Africa from "the paradigm of linear market integration, marked by stepwise integration of goods, labor, capital markets, and eventually, monetary and financial integration. This tends to focus on border measures such as the import tariff."[18] However, it proposed the adoption of a "deeper integration agenda that includes services, investment, competition policy, and other behind the border issues which can address the national level supply side constraints far more effectively than an agenda which focuses almost exclusively on border measures."[19] In addition, the WTO noted that need for changes in trade composition, industrialization, improvement in infrastructure and structural transformation as key processes in Sub-Saharan Africa's sustainable development efforts.[20]

The fact that fifteen countries are landlocked and most SSA economies are small and poor leads to high trade transaction costs. In 2000, twelve SSA states had populations of less than 2 million, while nineteen had a Gross Domestic Product (GDP) of less than $U.S. 5 billion. Africa's contribution to total world exports decreased from 8 percent in 1948 to 6 percent in 1980 and 2.3 percent in 2000.[21] The March 21, 2018, signing of the African Free Trade Area Agreement in Kigali, Rwanda, was hailed as a major step toward boosting African trade by the signatory countries.[22] On the other hand, a South African weekly newspaper referred to it as Africa's "free trade fairy tale," citing the reluctance of Nigeria to join the club.[23] The chair of the African Union Commission sounded a note of caution about the implementation of the grand vision, fully aware of the great disconnect between noble ideas and declarations and its no-can-do record.[24]

Agricultural Stagnation

Africa's sustainable development challenge comes from a largely stagnating agricultural economy. It is estimated that Africa has 50 percent of the world's available land for new farming, yet, forty of the forty-eight Sub-Saharan countries are net importers of food, and 30 percent of agricultural production is lost due to rotting and insects. Agriculture not only provides employment to 70 percent of the population but also most of the raw materials for manufacturing and commerce. Most countries in Sub-Saharan Africa practice subsistence agriculture involving mixed agriculture, horticulture, shifting cultivation, and agroforestry. These activities are largely engaged in the production of food and fiber for the farmer's family. The modernization of agriculture through the introduction of cash crops has brought both advantages and disadvantages in terms of productivity, price fluctuation, and environmental degradation. In 1991, Robert McNamara, the then president of the World Bank, underlined the three major trends and crises in African development, namely agricultural stagnation, explosive population growth, and degradation of the natural resource base.[25] Hence, investment in technology, storage, transportation, marketing, research, and environmental protection is an urgent priority. The balance between food and cash crop production should be carefully analyzed and managed if the region is to meet its goals of ending hunger and reducing poverty on a meaningful level. Ensuring food security is a political, socioeconomic, environmental, and moral imperative for African countries. The regression of the continent from a net exporter of agricultural products to one of a net importer is a catastrophic trend that needs to be reversed. Africa has the human and physical resources to bring about this reversal if the right policies, strategies, and programs of action are put in place and are genuinely supported by those in control of the financial and technological tools of African society.

Population Dynamics

The dynamics of Africa's population presents a tremendous challenge and opportunity for the promotion and achievement of the objectives and goals of sustainable development. Africa's population has grown from 289 million in 1960 to 1 billion in 2014, which is almost a 350 percent rate of growth in half a century. The urban population has grown even faster, from an estimated 65 million in 1960 to 460 million in 2014, or from 20 percent to 46 percent of the population as a whole.[26] Africa's current estimated population of 1.2 billion is growing at 2.5 percent/year, which is almost twice the global average. If this trend continues, and it most likely will, the region will have 2 billion people by 2050. Given the fact that 70 percent of the population is below the age of thirty and 45 percent below the age of fifteen, the food, energy, service, environment, and security ramifications of the current dynamics of population growth are huge and scary to contemplate. Some estimates put the current unemployment rates of Sub-Saharan countries as falling between 40 and 50 percent at any given time.[27] Given such a reality, it is imperative that African decision makers, the public, and the broader global community fully realize the challenge and chart out sustainable and implementable strategies of population management. The current "burying the head in the sand" and business as usual strategy is creating a time bomb that is ticking with every passing day. Hence, education, training, improving the reproductive health of girls and mothers, and the gainful deployment of the exploding young population are critical challenges facing sustainable development in the region. While the downward trend in fertility and the annual rates of population growth are welcome signs, stronger and committed local, national, and regional actions are called for to realize the objectives and goals of sustainable development. The judicious deployment of Africa's huge population in productive activity presents a great opportunity for the region to realize its huge resource potential. Resources are basically technological and organizational appraisals and the education and proper deployment of Africa's huge human resources to productive labor is a foundational prerequisite for sustained growth and improvement of the quality of life for its people.

Energy Access

Africa's access to modern sources of energy is the lowest among developing regions of the world. In 2014, more than 620 million people, or two-thirds of the total population in SSA, had no access to electricity, and 730 million people used solid biomass for cooking. Energy demand grew by 45 percent between 2000 and 2012 but accounted for only 4 percent of the world total despite having 13 percent of the world's population. Twenty-five of the fifty-four countries had an energy crisis. Only 10 percent of Africans are believed to have access to the electrical grid.[28] It can be safely concluded that electricity has reached the wealthy, the middle class, and urban areas. Most Africans living in the rural areas have essentially been bypassed. The generating capacity of African countries grew by only 1.2 percent/year over the 2001–2005 period. The region has used only between 5 and 7 percent of its hydroelectric potential. Given the sector's strong link with economic growth, income, and improvement in the standard of living of the people, African leaders and the international community should give high priority to the development, wide distribution, and use of modern energy. No meaningful economic transformation and improvement in the standard of living of Africa's population is possible without a radical departure from the current low level of energy consumption. Energy development is a capital-intensive sector, but the multiplier effect of easy energy access more than compensates for the high cost and lumpiness of energy investments.

Education, Information, and Technology

Africa's significant strides in the expansion of modern education, information, and technology have contributed to the improvement of the quality of life for a wide segment of the region's population. A recent report on the education sector noted that "education is critical to the development of knowledge-societies as it is the source of basic skills, a foundation for knowledge acquisition and innovation and an engine for socio-economic development."[29]

It indicated that Africa's educational objective of "Education for All" (EFA) had resulted in dramatic enrollment increases at all levels of education. Primary school enrollment increased from 23 million in 1970 to 87 million in 1980 and 129 million in 2009, while secondary enrollment increased from 4 million to 22 million and 36 million during the same years. Likewise, tertiary education enrollment increased from 200,000 to 2.5 million and 4.5 million. The investment in teacher education and expenditure on education grew phenomenally; SSA spent an average of 18.2 percent of government budgets on education—a figure considered at the highest threshold level.[30]

The quantitative achievements in the expansion of modern education have been increasingly compromised by worrisome qualitative weaknesses. Both World Bank reports and Mo Ibrahim's index of governance point out that young people are coming out of twelve to sixteen years of education with few skills and little hope for gainful employment. A recent education sector study report prepared for the African Development Bank, the World Bank, and African Union noted the need for a strategic application of information and communication technologies in the education system integrated with a range of twenty-first-century skills, including the capacity "to think creatively, solve problems, communicate effectively, identify and analyze existing information, and create knowledge."[31]

Africa's colonially structured education system has largely failed to build a meaningful regional capacity to generate, utilize, and manage information and technology to accelerate and promote sustainable development. Adedeji summed up Africa's predicament perceptively when he noted that:

> the failure of African leaders to rediscover, acknowledge and act upon their continent's wealth of collective wisdom—whether social, economic and political organization—of knowledge or ways of thinking—largely accounts for the endemic crisis that has confronted the region since independence.[32]

Environmental Protection and Management

The other critical challenge to sustainable development in Africa is the degradation of its complex biophysical resources of its complex environment. The massive degradation of land and soil, deforestation of vast tracts of land for agriculture, construction and energy, the relentless advance of the Sahara and other marginal zones into the savannah zones, the loss of wildlife habitats, the dramatic growth of urban populations, the proliferation of slums, the stubborn persistence of crushing poverty in both rural and urban areas, the lack of access to clean water and sanitation, poor access to health services and affordable modern energy, etc. all pose serious challenges to Africa's very survival as a viable and competitive partner in world development.

Africa's environmental degradation has manifested itself in critical ecosystemic and economic crises. Loss of arable land, decline in crop yields, decreasing livestock carrying capacity, water scarcity, severe firewood deficiency, and the loss of wildlife and plant life habitat are important challenges across the region. The World Resources Institute estimated that 64 percent of original wildlife habitat was lost by the 1990s.[33] Hence, there is an urgent need for African countries and societies to use their tremendous and varied natural resources and ecosystems to promote sustainable development, reduce poverty, and protect the integrity of the environment. Sustained programs of public awareness and active participation in policy, legal, and institutional measures should be undertaken at various levels of societal organization. Broad-based and participatory development and strong government/public partnership hold the key for ensuring adequate safeguards and management tools for sound environmental management at continental, subregional, national, and local levels.

CONCLUSION

I would like to conclude my chapter by citing Joseph Ki-Zerbo's excellent summation of the major sources of Africa's sustainable development crisis. He noted that it emanated from the synergistic burden imposed by the state (signifying power), the market (signifying poverty) and science and technology (signifying lack of knowledge).[34] Africa today finds itself as a dependent and weak economy with high level of indebtedness, weak institutional and human resources, a narrow technological base, and a highly vulnerable relationship with powerful global institutions such as the World Bank, IMF, and the World Trade Organization. The objectives, strategies, and targets of sustainable development cannot be promoted and realized meaningfully unless these and other critical challenges and opportunities find resolution through a genuinely democratic order that allows the people to exercise their inalienable rights as free and independent thinking citizens, secure from arbitrary and extra-judicial administrative actions by mostly illegitimate and unrepresentative governments and ruling parties. Dictatorships can neither deliver the goods and services nor create a conducive environment for the emergence of a vibrant, productive, and enterprising civil society. Sustainable development is a long-term strategic task; African societies have the requisite tenacity and perseverance to achieve its objectives and goals if they are given the opportunity by their leaders and the international system that continues to dictate Africa's development without their meaningful participation as stakeholders and decision-makers.

NOTES

1. Robert Stock, *Africa South of the Sahara: A Geographical Interpretation* (New York: the Guilford Press, 2013).
2. Frederick Cooper, *Africa in the World: Capitalism, Empire, Nation-State* (Cambridge: Harvard University Press, 2014).
3. Adebayo Adedeji, "Marginalization and Marginality: Context, Issues and Viewpoints," in *Africa within the World: Beyond Dispossession and Dependence,* ed. Adebayo Adedeji (London: Zed Books, 1993).
4. Fekadu Bekele, "Compact with Africa or Dismantling Africa and Making it Helpless," *Ethiomedia* (October 5, 2017), http://www.ethiomedia.com/1000bits/compact-with-africa-or-dismantling-africa.html.
5. Ibid.
6. Word Commission on Environment and Development, *Our Common Future* (London: Oxford University Press, 1987).
7. Tade Akin Aina, "Environmental Management and Social Equity," in *Sustaining the Future: Economic, Social, and Environmental Change in Sub-Saharan Africa,* eds. George Benneh, Juha I. Uitto, and William B. Morgan (Tokyo: United Nations University Press, 1996).
8. Lakshman Yapa, "What Are Improved Seeds? An Epistemology of the Green Revolution," *Economic Geography* 69, no. 3 (1993): 254–255.
9. Ibid., 259.
10. Ibid.
11. Sallie Marston, Paul Knox, and Diana Liverman, *World Regions in Global Contexts: People, Places and Environments* (Upper Saddle River, NJ: Prentice Hall: 2002).
12. United Nations Economic Commission for Africa, *Africa's Development, 1983-2008: A Preliminary Perspective Study* (Addis Ababa, Ethiopia: UNECA, 1983), 93–94.
13. Basil Davidson, *The Black Man's Burden: Africa and the Curse of the Nation-State* (London: James Currey, 1992), 9.
14. See Rachel Hamada, "Government Accountability Takes a Nosedive," *Opinion*, September 29, 2014, https://thisisafrica.me/mo-ibrahim-index-2014-government-accountability-takes-nosedive.
15. World Bank, "Africa's Pulse: An analysis of Issues Shaping Africa's Future," *Africa's Pulse*, 3 (2011).
16. Trudi Hartzenberg, "Regional Integration in Africa," World Trade Organization, Economic Research and Statistics Division, Staff Working Paper, ERSD 2011–14 (2011), 9.
17. World Trade Organization, *World Trade Report 2011: The WTO and Preferential Trade Agreements: From Coexistence to Coherence.* https://www.wto.org/english/res_e/booksp_e/anrep_e/world_trade_report11_e.pdf.
18. Hartzenberg, "Regional Integration," 1.
19. Ibid.
20. World Trade Organization, *World Trade Report 2011*, 4.

21. Hartzenberg, "Regional Integration," 3, 9.

22. Eskinder Kifle, "Signing of African Continental Free Trade Agreement Expected to Boost African Trade by 52%," *Capital,* Year 20, no. 1007, Addis Ababa, March 25, 2018, 14.

23. Simion Allison, "Africa's Free Trade Fairy Tale," *Mail and Guardian*, March 22, 2018.

24. Ibid.

25. Robert McNamara, "*Africa's Development Crisis. Agricultural Stagnation, Population Explosion and Environmental Degradation*" (Washington, DC: World Bank, 1991). This paper was a presidential address by Robert McNamara, presented to the Africa Leadership Forum on June 21, 1990, in Ota, Nigeria, at the invitation of General Olusegun Obasanjo, the former President of Nigeria.

26. Akinyinka Akinyoade, Jos Damen, Ton Dietz, BlandinaKilama, and Gerrit van Omme, "Africa Population Dynamics," ASC themakaart research paper, no. 9 (Leiden University, Netherlands: African Studies Centre, 2014).

27. McNamara, *Africa's Development Crisis.*

28. International Energy Agency, *Africa Energy Outlook: A Focus on Energy Prospects in Sub-Saharan Africa, World Energy Outlook Special Report* (Paris: International Energy Agency, 2014), 21–33.

29. Lishan Adam, Neil Butcher, F. Tusubira, and Claire Sibthorpe, "Transformation-Ready: The Strategic Application of Information and Communication Technologies in Africa," Education Sector Study Prepared for the African Development Bank, the World Bank, and the African Union, ICT Development Associates Ltd. December 2011, 16.

30. Ibid., 13–16.

31. Ibid., 16; Hamada, "Government Accountability," 2014.

32. Adedeji, *Africa within the World*, 1993.

33. McNamara, *Africa's Development Crisis*, 1991.

34. Joseph Ki-Zerbo, "Which Way Africa? Reflections on Basil Davidson's The Black Man's Burden," *Development Dialogue* 2 (1995): 103–108.

Chapter 3

Revisiting the Promise of Democracy and Development in Africa

Phillip E. Agbebaku, William E. Odion, and Mohammed Itakpe

INTRODUCTION

African countries have made several attempts at developing the continent. Through policies, programs, and partnership with the international community and donor agencies, Africa has initiated plans to lift itself up from its undeveloped state. The irony is that the continent is blessed with abundant natural resources. More importantly, the promises of democracy and development have become unfulfilled dreams owing to several challenges. Efforts may have been made in Africa to advance the course of democracy and development beyond the superficial level, but unfortunately, said efforts have not yielded the desired result.

A lot has been discussed and written about Africa's development. What appears to be lacking in these discussions is a critical assessment of the nexus between democracy and development in the African context. The issue of democracy and development is central in the discussions on the implementation and attainment of development goals in Africa; many African countries have embraced democracy or a semblance of it with the belief that it can usher into the continent the much-awaited development. This has also raised questions of the feasibility of democratic consolidation in Africa.[1]

This chapter argues that democracy, as practiced in Africa, has not been able to affect development in the continent. It is further argued that the issues of development represent the basic concern of everyday governance in most states in Africa. In this chapter, too, the promise of democracy and development in Africa is examined, bearing in mind that there exists a nexus between them. Drawing from secondary sources, it posits that democracy and development have eluded Africa due to factors such as corruption, leadership failure, insecurity, and political instability.

Conceptual Discourse

Democracy is a concept that lacks universally accepted definitional consensus. Diverse experiences of countries and the different stories flowing from the experiences have been revealed through the massive works of scholars and the lack of consensus. Democracy appeared first in ancient Greek political and philosophical thought in the city-state of Athens. In a simple conception, the democratic system can be defined in procedural terms as that institutional arrangement for arriving at political decisions in which individuals acquire the power to decide by means of a competitive struggle for the people's vote.[2] This definition is further expanded to identify seven key criteria that are essential for democracy, or what is referred to as "polyarchy." These include the following:

- Control over governmental decisions about policy constitutionally vested in elected officials
- Relatively frequent, fair, and free elections
- Universal adult suffrage
- The right to run for public office
- Freedom of expression
- Access to alternative sources of information that are not monopolized by either the government or any other single group
- Freedom of association (i.e., the right to form and join autonomous associations such as political parties, interest group, etc.)[3]

On the other hand, besides procedural features of democracy such as the existence of civil and political rights, democracy requires substantive values or features such as economic, social, and cultural rights.[4] This is particularly so since the practice of democracy, even in the African context, has revealed that political elites that drive representative democracies undermine substantive values of democracy.

Modern or full democracies have also been described as those systems in which there are universal suffrage, regular elections, an independent judiciary, relatively equal access to power for all groups, and extensive civil liberties that are combined with protection for minorities and disadvantaged groups.[5] There is, however, a broad consensus that democracy involves participation and accountability and includes members of a society in choosing their leaders. Democracy as conceived in this case refers to:

> Meaningful competition for political power amongst individuals and organized groups, inclusive participation in the selection of leaders and policies, at least through free and fair elections and a level of civil and political liberties sufficient to ensure the integrity of political competition and participation.[6]

Democracy in itself does not guarantee good governance, but at least it gives the people the opportunity to make choices. It is a means to good governance.[7] It therefore has a link with equality, consent, and legitimacy. Equality in this sense holds that everyone should enjoy equal opportunity to be involved in the affairs that affect them, particularly in the exercise of choice. The issue of consent is recognized as the authority to rule in a democracy, which must necessarily emanate from the people—while legitimacy is the element by which power and authority may be evaluated.

Political parties are useful indexes of democracy and the level of political development.[8] The structure and operation of party politics, as have been argued, tend to serve as a measuring rod for determining the fragility or otherwise of democratic systems.[9] However, where political parties are poorly structured to perform articulative, aggregative, communicative, and educative functions, such a political system is likely going to be associated with poor political culture that tends to make the democratic process very fragile. Conversely, where political parties are well structured to perform the above functions, such a political system is often associated with participant culture, which tends to ensure a stable democratic process.[10]

Development, like democracy, is another complex issue, often difficult to define and measure, as it is characterized by many different and contentious definitions; there is no consensus on the best measure for development. Until recently, the main indexes for measuring development have been the Gross Domestic Product (GDP), Gross National Product (GNP), and Per Capita Income. Yet, as the African experience in particular has shown, increases in national income do not necessarily translate to solutions for social, economic, and political problems.[11]

The UN Development Program (UNDP) developed the Human Development Index (HDI) as an alternative variant/approach to understanding development, focusing on measures of health, life expectancy, education, and access to resources. It defines human development as:

> The process of enlarging the range of people's choices—increasing their opportunities for education, health care, income and employment, and covering the full range of human choices from a social physical environment to economic and political freedoms. Human development is concerned both with developing human capabilities and with using them productively. The former requires investments in people, the latter that people contribute to GNP growth and employment.[12]

The Physical Quality of Life Index (PQLI), developed by the UN Research Institute for Social and Economic Development (UNRISD) is another good measure of human development. It combines three component indicators of infant mortality, life expectancy at age one, and basic literacy at age fifteen to measure performance in meeting the most basic needs of the people.[13]

Other perspectives of development are political development and sustainable development. Political development is the ability of a state to successfully resolve the problems that include participation, penetration, distribution, legitimacy, identity, and integration. On the other hand, sustainable development is defined as "meeting the needs of the present generation without compromising the needs of future generation."[14] Sustainable development, therefore, puts emphasis on accelerating economic development in order to conserve and enhance the stock of environmental, human, and physical capital without endangering future generations.

Furthermore, development connotes a multidimensional process involving major changes in social structures, political attitudes, and national institutions as well as the acceleration of economic growth, the reduction of inequality, and the eradication of absolute poverty.[15] It is also perceived as coterminous with capacity expansion and freedom. As capacity expansion, it requires adequate empowerment of the state and society that they can adequately distill their complimentary responsibilities. It also requires an enhanced state capacity as well as institutional and governmental stability. As freedom, it demands greater latitude of autonomy for the political community as its constituent parts as well as the individual members of such communities. In all, development has assumed various meaning to include economic growth, modernization, socioeconomic transformation, and distributive justice.[16]

Though there is the debate concerning the relationship between democracy and development, three conclusions have been reached. One is supportive of a negative relationship between democracy and development, the other is of a positive relationship, and the third is agnostic (not knowing whether democracy fosters or hinders economic development).[17] However, what has been generally agreed upon is that democracy is related to the state of economic development, hence democracy and development share common attributes such as popular empowerment, participation, and freedom.[18]

THE CRISIS OF AFRICAN DEVELOPMENT IN HISTORICAL PERSPECTIVE

It is imperative to note that as a continent, Africa possesses certain features such as richness in culture, religion, social dynamism, energy, natural resources, population, etc. Africa is home to abundant natural, mineral, and human resources evenly spread across the continent, making it a region with tremendous investment opportunities. These resources include crude oil, minerals (iron ore, steel, copper, gold, diamond, coal, and magnesium), timber, and agricultural products that can be harnessed and transformed to greatness and development. Ninety percent of cobalt and the bulk of the world's diamonds are found in Africa. Sixty-four percent of the world's manganese, 50 percent of world's phosphate and gold, 40 percent of platinum, 35 percent of the world's uranium, and more than 20 percent of oil reserves are found in Africa.[19] Ironically, the same continent is home to diseases, poverty, homelessness, conflict, instability, terrorism, etc. Twenty-eight of the fifty independent African countries constitute 65 percent of the world's forty-three poorest countries. Over half of the fifty African countries have adopted the Structural Adjustment Program (SAP) sanctioned by International Monetary Fund (IMF) and World Bank since 1988. The countries remain unindustrialized, with eighteen out of the world's forty primary exporting countries being in Africa. African countries also represent the heaviest official borrowers of the World Bank.[20] The implication of the above analysis is that the African record of development has been dismal and one of a deep sense of frustration and hopelessness, but the position has always been to blame the colonial masters for African woes.[21]

African leaders admit that the West packaged Africa's development strategies and goals in the postcolonial period without taking cognizance of African peculiarities, including its historical experience. Also held is the view that these strategies and goals were designed to further strengthen Africa's malintegration into the world economy, packaged by Westerners to address their own problems, but implemented for Africa by Africans. The result has thus been continued generalized poverty, misery, political instability, mounting debt crisis, socioeconomic tension, and widening gap that have rendered Africa incapable of solving its own development problem.[22]

It is obvious that the African continent has gone through a series of crisis of development. African countries have been characterized by persistent crisis, including civil wars and communal crisis, which usually devastate entire communities of able-bodied men and women who are highly prized developmental tools.[23] The low level of development in the continent finds explanation in the above. Examples are found in Liberia, Sierra Leone, Rwanda, the Gambia, Sudan, Ethiopia, Nigeria, Mali, Tanzania, and Eritrea. It is on record that these countries have experienced civil war, military dictatorship, authoritarian one-party rule, and corrupt sit-tight leaders since they gained independence than they have practiced democracy.[24] The latest is The Gambia where Yahya Jammeh almost refused to relinquish power.

The attainment of independence in most African countries has not brought any significant improvement in the material condition of Africans even though very few have been massively empowered. The authoritarian and undemocratic practices of most of the postcolonial regimes in Africa are evidenced in the gagging of the press, manipulation of the legislature and the judiciary, rigging of elections, harassment, intimidation, victimization, detention, and elimination of political opponents and repression of mass-based democratic and professional organizations.[25]

A nexus exists between the quality of governance and the fortune of states. Many African countries are bedeviled by poor governance and service delivery of political goods. This has reflected in the decline in the quality of governance. This decline has manifested in profound institutional failure and lack of national development; in poor social and physical infrastructure exemplified in deplorable communication network, poor health care, and educational facilities. States may either be weak or strong depending on their capabilities to carry out their responsibilities.

STRATEGIES AND MEASURES ADOPTED BY AFRICAN COUNTRIES

A number of strategies have been adopted by African countries. They include *increase and diversification of export commodities*, which sought not only to expand the production of agricultural export commodities for increased foreign earning but also to escape the consequence of unfavorable terms of trade for primary products while opening up other production areas such as manufacturing. *Import substitution* emphasized curtailment of foreign imports and production of local substitutes. *Export promotion* encouraged industrial development, diversification, economic self-reliance, and better terms of trade. *Integrated rural development* was intended to redress existing disparities between rural and urban areas. The aim was to transform rural areas where more than 70 percent of the population in Africa lives. In addition to those strategies, *regional cooperation, integration, and collective self-reliance* were also adopted. The main idea behind the formation of regional unions was to foster collective self-reliance through regional cooperation and integrative socioeconomic relations. Other measures are indigenization, the unified approach, and a call for a New International Economic Order.[26]

Worthy of mention here are African initiatives such as the adoption of Africa's Priority Program for Economic Recovery (APPER) by the Organization of African Unity (OAU) Heads of State and Government in Addis Ababa in July 1985, the African Peer Review Mechanism (APRM), and the New Economic Partnership for African Development (NEPAD). The APRM serves as a self-monitoring mechanism for African political leaders to improve good governance, development, and eliminate arbitrary rule by peer reviewing each country's democratic, socioeconomic, and corporate governance structures. It is a voluntary process by which (in theory at least) participating countries submit themselves for examination and then undertake identifying and remedying governance problems. NEPAD represents the African initiative to partner with each other with the hope to develop the continent and integrate it with the global economy. African countries also keyed into international collaboration for development such as the Millennium Development Goals (MDGs) and the African-Caribbean and Pacific Economic Partnership Agreement (ACP-EPA). The MDGs pursued eight goals, among which were reducing the number of people who lived on less than a dollar by the year 2015, eradication of poverty and hunger, achieving universal primary education, and reducing child mortality. This has since been changed to Sustainable Development Goals (SDGs) since the end of 2015. The ACP is currently made up of seventy-nine members—forty-eight African, sixteen Caribbean, and fifteen Pacific. It was created by the Georgetown Agreement in 1975. The objective included the pursuit of sustainable development and poverty reduction within its member states as well as their greater integration in the world economy.

THE NEXUS BETWEEN DEMOCRACY AND DEVELOPMENT IN THE AFRICAN CONTEXT

There are three perspectives concerning the relationship between democracy and development. They are the compatibility perspective, the conflict perspective, and the skeptical/neutral perspective.[27] The compatibility perspective argues that democracy does no harm to economic and political development, but rather it is an indispensable element for development. The conflict perspective argues that democracy impedes development, while the skeptical/neutral perspective advises caution in projecting the relationship between regime type and development.

Be that as it may, it has been argued that democracy could be an instrument for the development of society if it guarantees popular participation in the affairs of the state, social justice, and good governance. A number of ways exist in which democracy can be linked with development. They are:

1. The possibility that it provides a resolution for participation crisis, which is one of the major problems faced by most states in the process of development. This means that the stress and strains on the political system, which may arise as new issues and demands emerge from the configuration of interests and groups in the society, are more easily resolved within the context of popular politics that democracy provides.

2. By ensuring that governance is made relevant to society, and it is people oriented. This essentially refers to the values of political responsibility and accountability, stressed in democracy, which serves as political guarantee against irrationality and arbitrariness in governance and a strategy for development of the society.
3. The rational use of power in democracy offers greater prospects for the resolution of fundamental crisis associated with the process of development such as those of identity, distribution, penetration, legitimacy, and integration. Deduced from the above is that a rational use of power requires that power is not self-appropriated, privatized, and not used to advance private, parochial, sectional, and selfish ends at the expense of public interest.
4. Democracy is also linked with development in relation to the fundamental ends and goals which states expressly seek.[28] Deduced from this is that since happiness of the citizens and fulfillment of their personality are attainable only within the context of the state, the democratic character of the state is to an extent an important factor in ensuring development for both citizens and society.[29]

Critically speaking, the above arguments have not been true as the African democratic and development experience show. This position is sustained by the fact that successive governments in Africa have not been able to drive development with democracy and semblance of it. The expectation that democracy should serve as a springboard for development as well as good governance in Africa is a mirage. Leaders and past governments have only paid lip service to the fundamentals and imperatives that can drive development in African societies. Examples of the above are reflected in annual budget speeches, independence anniversary speeches, and special national broadcasts by top government functionaries and statesmen, national constitutions, and outlines of development plans. Elite dominance has not worked in tandem with advancing the course of political participation, hence successive democratic regimes or semblance of it have not been people oriented and relevant to African society.

The process of political recruitment and succession is often marred by irregularities, manipulations, conflict, violence, uncertainty, and instability. The fundamentals of credible elections, which include competition and popular participation, have been breached without any sense of wrongdoing. Democratic principles such as responsiveness, responsibility, accountability, and transparency, which are all stressed in democracy, have been lacking. The main instrument of control and political survival, sovereignty, is eroded while the capacity to mobilize the people for development has been significantly reduced. Since there exists a disconnection between the citizens in Africa and the political systems, problem of legitimacy often occurs. Yet Africa is replete with "sit tight" political leaders, such as Paul Biya of Cameroon, Idris Deby of Chad, Julius Nyerere of Tanzania, and Paul Kagame of Rwanda. Others are Yoweri Museveni of Uganda, and recently ousted leaders such as Jammeh of Gambia and Robert Mugabe of Zimbabwe, who were all in power for decades. Uhuru Kenyatta of Kenya was on trial for election violence at the International Criminal Court, even though the case was withdrawn for insufficient evidence.

Elections in Africa are very contentious with heated pre- and postelection contestations. Recent examples are found in Nigeria, Rwanda, Gambia, and Kenya. Oftentimes, the electorates were left in the dark while it was obvious that the parties and candidates generally lacked clear political programs as the main focus was on personal qualities, personality bashing, and party criticism rather than issues and political party ideology during campaigns. With political parties that could not be differentiated markedly by ideology, it confirmed that elections in Africa were not won or lost on the basis of how hard a candidate campaigned on an ideological basis but more on the interlocking issues of electoral manager's manipulations, electoral malpractice, power of incumbency, and influence of money captured in the "stomach infrastructure" analogy.[30]

In the African context, democracy has not brought development because of the irrational use of power. The use of power has been significantly abused, hence the philosophy and apparatus of government as the African experience has shown are deployed toward the satisfaction and development of a few. Accordingly, for the rulers (elites), the struggle for power, political survival, relevance, and the reproduction of their domination is intense and absorbing, and it is perhaps the major preoccupation. Political power is absolutized, self-appropriated, privatized, and used to advance private, parochial, sectional, and selfish ends instead of public interest. Politics for the political leadership and the entire political class has become the means for appropriation and accumulation of wealth as evidenced in the mouthwatering corruption revelations in Nigeria and other African countries. African history is replete with political leaders who are mired in excessive corruption. Access to and means of state power has become the principal means of appropriation and accumulation. Therefore, what is at stake in politics is no longer just power but more importantly, the possibility of wealth accumulation, thus making the quest for power to be increasingly absorbing.

Political parties have not presented a robust ideological leaning except that they continue to mirror elite features that advertise accumulation, expropriation, and outright pillage of the national purse. The number of high profile cases being investigated by the Economic and Financial Crimes Commission (EFCC) and Independent Corrupt Practices and Related Offences

Commission (ICPC) in Nigeria attest to the fact that political leaders have not rationally used the power gained in democracy to attract development. A situation of underdevelopment as manifested/reflected in conflicts, high unemployment rate, hunger, squalor, increased corruption, decayed infrastructure, socioeconomic anxiety, and insecurity (which are common features of the African States) have clearly indicated that the polity has not experienced increased rational use of democratically acquired power to drive development in the society. Also, the confidence and trust between the rulers and the ruled, required for development of the society, have not been sufficiently established due to years of failed promises and disappointments. This has led to mutual alienation between the rulers and the ruled, as was the case during tenure elongations.

Rational use of power in this context is used for maintaining order, resolving disputes, selecting authoritative leaders, and thus promoting community among two or more social forces. As a society becomes more complex and heterogeneous, it becomes more dependent upon the workings of political institutions.[31] The capacity to fulfill essential functions requires the possession of certain structural requisites, all of which provide every polity the basis for effectiveness and legitimacy. Thus the variation in the degree of effectiveness and legitimacy in different political systems may be explained or accounted for on the basis of existing requisite structures and institutions. Various dimensions of contradictions and contending forces exist within the socioeconomic and political formations, which needed to be identified and resolved to attain development.

In the African situation, the problem of identity, distribution, penetration, participation, legitimacy, and integration remain prevalent. For example, the processes of political recruitment are almost continuously fraught with massive irregularities, manipulations, conflict, violence, uncertainty, and instability. The fundamentals of credible elections, which include competition and popular participation, are observed more in their breaches. Citizens therefore have lost faith in the political process and in the ruling elite/leadership; therefore, such regimes have suffered a legitimacy problem. In the polities, mass participation has essentially become a new form of response to elite manipulations rather than credible electoral process. Though elections are held in African states with relative success, democratic culture has continued to elude the nations as political office holders turned their offices into instruments for impunity, personal enrichment, and abuse of human rights of African citizens. Ethnic rivalries, religious bigotry, and acts of terrorism are common features of the African State that struggles to surmount such problems as it marches to modernity. These problems represent the ventilation of bottled up anger against failed institutions of the State.

Finally, it is impossible for democracy to be linked with development when and where citizens are not happy and free from restrictions, hindrances, fear, and want. Social justice in the light of the purpose of the State is lacking in this context. Citizens in Africa absolutely live in fear and in an atmosphere of insecurity. Religious crises, electoral violence, kidnapping and armed robbery, militancy, and insurgency by groups such as Boko Haram in Nigeria, the Tuareg in Mali, al-Shabaab in Somalia, Ansar al-Sharia in Libya, and Islamic State in Northern Africa are issues that citizens daily contend with. Unemployment and hunger force citizens to resort to alternative avenues for survival, having lost faith in the ability of the state to provide solution to same.

Other manifestations are the adoption of the IMF/World Bank imposed policies such as the Austerity Measures and SAP. The consequence of this has been worsening conditions of underdevelopment than the promotion of growth and development. For example, instability occasioned by government policies such as removal of subsidy from petroleum products and the consequent increase in petrol pump price; the withdrawal of government subsidy on education, health, and other social services; as well as retrenchment/downsizing of workers through deliberate government implementation of foreign-induced policies in recent times/years has further compounded the crisis of development in Africa despite attempts at democratizing. The inability and nonimplementation of promised programs have generated consequences such as political upheavals, deindustrialization, and poverty, which made Africa fall back on the EU, China, and other donor agencies for support and assistance, and thus sustaining the apron string and dependency syndrome. Under this atmosphere, characterized by lack of mutual trust among its members, creating stable and effective political institutions via democracy required for development is difficult.

Stability, when it merely produces stagnation, and order, when it is arbitrary support of the status quo, clearly do not produce development except when the alternative is manifestly a worst state of affairs. It has been argued that order itself is a crucial objective in developing countries. The primary argument is that violence and instability were in large part the products of rapid social change and the rapid mobilization of new groups into politics coupled with the slow development of political institutions. The responses of African States to such conflicts have been increasing repressive use of power of the state, which includes police violence, detention without trial, and torture. The rampant use of repression, duplicity, deceit, faulty assumptions, and purposeful blindness in effecting reforms further alienates citizens. With incidences such as corruption, looting, repression, human rights abuses, and lack of accountability, and transparency in governance in Africa coupled with

African government's inability to withstand or mediate pressures, contradictions, and conflict, social forces confront each other with little restraint, thus destroying the very foundation of democracy and development.

The rentier states in Africa are built on corruption. The boom and bust mode of economic management, encouraged by a dominance of mono resource, has led to increased income and a corresponding increased public-sector spending. The consequence of this is fiscal indiscipline and spiraling debt that stunted Africa development. Consequently, corruption, lack of transparency, and accountability in governance are the bane of development in Africa.

The resources that abound in Africa, which could provide the basis for diversification and sustainable development, are mismanaged and wasted. Unfortunately, widespread leakages, mismanagement, and corrupt use of economic and other resources represent the hallmark of bad governance in Africa. In turn, there is an inability to use economic resources as a sustainable basis for development. As a result, many African countries suffer underdevelopment, which manifests itself in the form of endemic poverty, proliferation of urban slums, soaring unemployment, lack of industrialization, energy crisis, incidences of debt, high mortality rate, disempowerment, minimal participation in politics and economy, spiraling inflation, infrastructural and general institutional failure, large-scale suffering, and social dislocation.

CONCLUSION

From the foregoing argument, it is difficult to conclude that there is a strong nexus between development and democracy based on the experiences of African countries. The dismal record and failure of democracy and development in Africa made scholars apprehensive, who in turn predicted in 2007 that Africa was not meeting the colossal MDG goals.[32] It is clear that democracy has not been able to drive development. The effect of unfulfilled promises of local and global development strategies has been more sharply felt in Africa than in other continents of the world.[33] Therefore, emphasis on the management of African economies must necessarily shift from liberal to social democracy. This not only emphasizes the role of the state in development but also seeks to cultivate the ideals of popular participation in the process of development. Furthermore, in line with the "New World Order," what Africa needs is a responsive and responsible democratic government that is capable of steering the continent to the desired goals of development. This means adherence to world's best practices in good governance, democracy, and rule of law.

NOTES

1. James Apam, "Democracy, Good Governance and the Realization of Millennium Development Goals (MDGs) in Africa," in *Millennium Development Goals and Challenges: Issues on Education and Poverty*, eds. Christian Ewhrudjakpor and Atare A. Otite (Abraka: Faculty of the Social Sciences, Delta State University, 2009), 49–60.
2. Joseph Schumpeter, *Capitalism, Socialism and Democracy* (London: Allen and Unwin, 1976).
3. Robert A. Dahl, *Polyachy: Participation and Opposition* (New Haven: Yale University Press, 1971).
4. Julia Leininger, "Bringing the Outside in Illustration from Haiti and Mali for the Reconceptualization of Democracy Promotion," *Contemporary Politics* 16, no. 11 (2010): 63–80.
5. Tom Lansford, "Democracy, Future Of," in *International Encyclopedia of Political Science*, ed. George Thomas Kurian (Washington, DC: CQ Press, 2010): 391–392.
6. Apam, "Democracy," 53.
7. Adebayo Adedeji, "Popular Participation, Democracy and Development: Is There a Dialectical Linkage?" in *Nigeria: Renewal from the Roots? The Struggle for Democratic Development*, eds. Adebayo Adedeji et al. (London: Zed, 1995): 23–31.
8. Joseph Lapalombara and Myron Weiner, "The Origin and Development of Political Parties," in *Political Parties and Development*, eds. Joseph Lapalombara and Weiner Myron (Princeton: Princeton University, 1966), 7.
9. S.M. Omodia, "Political Parties in Nigeria Fourth Republic," *Trakia Journal of Science*, 8, no. 3 (2010): 65–69.
10. Akindiyo Oladiran, Imoukhuede Benedict Kayode, and Siyaka Mohammed, "Democracy and Development Paradigm Relationship: Emulation Possibility for Nigeria?" *America International Journal of Social Sciences*, 4, no. 2 (April 2015): 166, accessed May 21, 2018, http://www.aijssnet.com/journals/Vol_4_No_2_April_2015/15.pdf.
11. Ibid., 167.
12. United Nations Development Programme (UNDP), *Human Development Report* (New York: Palgrave, 1992), 2.
13. M. L. Jhingan, *The Economics of Development and Planning* (Delhi: Vrinda Publications, Ltd., 2007), 14–16.
14. Ibid., 22.
15. Jan-Erik Lane and Svante Ersson, *Comparative Political Economy: A Development Approach* (London: Pinters, 1997), 54.
16. A. L. Mabogunje, *The Development Process: A Spatial Perspective* (Englewood: Prentice Hall, 1980), cited in Stephen K. Omorogbe, *Main Currents in Sociology of Development* (Benin City: Lucosem Publishing House, 2000), 2–3.
17. Oladiran, et al., "Democracy and Development Paradigm," 167.
18. Shola J. Omotola, "Democratization, Good Governance and Development in Africa: The Nigerian Experience, 1999-2003," paper presented at the International

Conference on Rethinking Governance and Development in the 21st Century, Ambrose Alli University, Ekpoma, June 2003, 25–27.

19. Odilim Enwegbara, "US-Africa Leaders Summit: In Whose Interest?" Accessed May 29, 2018 https://www.inigerian.com/us-africa-leaders-summit-in-whose-interest.

20. Emmanuel Nwafor Mordi, "The Millennium Development Goals and the Challenges of Sustainable Development in Africa: A Historical Discourse," in *Millennium Development Goals and Challenges: Issues on Education and Poverty*, eds. Christian Ewhrudjakpor and Atare A. Otite (Abraka: Delta State University, 2009), 123–136.

21. Walter Rodney, *How Europe Underdeveloped Africa* (Abuja: Panaf Publishing Inc., 2005), 108–361.

22. Mordi, "The Millennium Development Goals," 125.

23. M. Shima, "The NEPAD and Africa's Development: A Critical Analysis," in *NEPAD and the Challenges of Development in Nigeria*, eds. Dennis Ityavyar and Zacharys Gundu (Jos: Inter-GENDER Monograph Series, 2006): 26–38.

24. Ibid., 26–38.

25. Apam, "Democracy," 51.

26. Claude Ake, *Democracy and Development in Africa* (Ibadan: Spectrum Books Limited, 2001), 66–78.

27. Shola J. Omotola, "No Democracy, No Development or Vice Versa?" in *Democracy and Development in Nigeria: Conceptual Issues and Democratic Practice. Vol. 1,* eds. Hassan A. Saliu, et al. (Ilorin: Mushin Lagos, Nigeria: Concept Publications, 2006), 25–45.

28. S.O.J. Ojo, "Democracy and Political Development: Towards an Alternative Paradigm," *Ekpoma Political Review – IJPA:* 4, (1997): 115–130.

29. W. E. Odion, *Studies in Political Economy* (Akure: Sylva Publishing Inc, 2014), 123.

30. F. A. Surajudeen, "2007 General Election Campaign Strategy and Democratic Consolidation in Nigeria," *The Constitution* 8, no. 2 (2008): 15–32.

31. Samuel Huntington, *Political Order in Changing Societies* (New Haven, CT: Yale University Press, 1968), 9.

32. E. Sampson, "MDGs: Is Africa Meeting These Colossal Goals?" *Zenith Economic Quarterly* 2, no 12 (2007): 62–73.

33. Ake, "Democracy and Development in Africa," 22.

Chapter 4

Beyond the Millennium Development Goals

Localizing the Development Agenda in Nigeria

Funmi Adewumi

INTRODUCTION

In contemporary Nigeria, most people are on the wrong side of the social divide, suffering from impoverishment and pauperization, and denied access to the basic necessities of life including shelter, food, clothing, health care, education, and potable water. Yet, there are constitutional provisions that practically create a social contract between the government and the governed, and the least that is expected in a democratic polity is a faithful adherence to the terms of contract. This is particularly so given the fact that "governance is about people and how they organize themselves to achieve their common objectives. In a democracy people are the ultimate source of constitutional and political legitimacy."[1]

After sixteen years of democratic rule, the unemployment rate in Nigeria remains high at 23.9 percent; 62.6 percent of the people live in extreme poverty, that is below $1.25 per day, while 76.6 percent of the people can be categorized as poor, living on $1.90 a day. Life expectancy at birth is put at 52.8 years, 42 percent of the population has no access to clean water supply, 68 percent has no access to improved sanitation facilities, and the electrification rate is 55.6 percent. In the education sector, the adult literacy rate is 51.1 percent, with only 10.1 percent of those qualified enrolled in tertiary institutions. For the secondary level, only 43.8 percent are enrolled. Additionally, just 66.1 percent of primary school teachers are qualified to teach. Public health expenditure currently stands at 3.9 percent of GDP, while there are 4.1

physicians per 10,000 patients. Infant mortality is 41 per 1,000 live births. Overall, Nigeria is ranked 152 on the Human Development Index (HDI) for 2015.[2]

This reality contrasts sharply with the expectations that propelled the involvement of a broad coalition of groups in the struggles that led to the termination of military rule in the late 1990s. After fifteen years of the Millennium Development Goals (MDGs) and decades of development planning, the vast majority of Nigerians' lives have not improved significantly. This brings about the need to question the development planning that has led to a situation in which there is a rich country but very poor people. Of course, this untoward situation could not have been different given the class character of the Nigerian society, the dependent nature of its economy, the comprador status of its ruling class, and the failure of the citizenry to contest the development agenda with the thieving political elite. It is largely because the dependent ruling elite have surrendered the country's sovereignty to the operators of the international capitalist system that makes it easy for the development agenda to be dictated by outside interests.

Deriving from the foregoing, the major submission of this chapter is that if Nigerians are to benefit from the development process, its planning must be localized and factor in the basic needs of the people. The major task for those genuinely concerned in bettering the lot of the people is the need to enthrone a truly democratic welfare state guided by the principles of accountability, transparency, and popular participation. In this context, all disadvantaged social groups and classes, including peasants, workers, artisans, market women, and youths, would need to join forces to assure for themselves a better tomorrow, which has already been mortgaged by the predatory ruling class for their own today.

DEVELOPMENT PLANNING IN NIGERIA: AN OVERVIEW

The concept of national development connotes a qualitatively higher level or stage of evolution of a given country. It involves a transformation from a lower level of life that harnesses available resources, both human and material, for the benefit of all, thereby securing for the people an improvement in their standard of living. Ojetunji Aboyade's conceptualization is quite insightful:

> Development is essentially a continuous process of generating and more efficiently allocating resources for achieving greater socially satisfying ends. It is thus made up of two basic and interrelated parts: (a) increasing the availability

of resources and (b) improving the utilization of available resources. The first component can be further sub-divided into three broad groups: natural, human and financial. The second component is a complex function of social organization, level of technology, efficiency of management and the content of public policy.[3]

Planning, which is a subtheme of this section, is a process that involves defining goals, instituting strategy, and developing plans designed to harmonize actions. It entails developing goals and objectives and also the actions required to achieve them, thus necessitating decision making. It can therefore be said that plans constitute a consciously thought out approach in achieving objectives that have been preselected. Development planning can therefore, be taken as a conscious effort by nation states to define the parameters and framework for a qualitative transformation of the society.

Arising from the above is that apart from the availability or nonavailability of human and material resources, the vision (or lack of it) of the national leadership as enunciated in various policy documents(plans) and measures will be instrumental in determining the direction in which society moves. This point was also underscored by the World Bank, which argued that history and recent experience have also taught us that development is not just about getting the right economic and technical inputs. It is also about the underlying institutional environment: the rules and customs that determine how these inputs are used.[4]

The development process, it should be stressed, must also address substantial improvements in social services such as education, health, and reduction in social inequality. The possibilities in these areas are a function of the resources available and their judicious allocation. Within the Nigerian experience, the totality of the development process has been officially acknowledged. This much is reflected in the philosophical underpinning of the Second National Development Plan, 1970–1974, which was meant to achieve the following:

a. A united, strong, and self-reliant nation
b. A great and dynamic economy
c. A just and egalitarian society
d. A land of bright and full opportunities for all citizens.
e. A free and democratic society[5]

Another important factor that determines the direction of national development is the reality of interdependence of the different countries of the world. This means that developments outside national boundaries have effects on what obtains locally. Nation states engage in international activities such as trade while also entering into bilateral and multilateral agreements with their concomitant effects on the development process. To be sure, there is nothing wrong about this as long as a country enters into such international transactions from a position of strength.

From the foregoing, it goes without saying that a combination of factors, both internal and external, impacts the development process. For instance, the subordination of Nigeria to international finance capital (the dependency syndrome) is an external factor, while the gross mismanagement of national resource, lack of visionary, and selfless leadership are critical internal factors in Nigeria's development equation.

Development aspirations of nation states are usually reflected and encapsulated in national development plans (NDPs). The history of development planning in Nigeria dates to the colonial period when the government put together a ten-year development plan (1945–1956). Although this plan was criticized for lack of coordination and coherence,[6] at least it laid the foundation for subsequent development plans that were instituted by postcolonial governments.

The First National Development Plan, 1962–1968, was the one initiated by an indigenous government in Nigeria. The objectives of this NDP were the following:

1. to bring about equal distribution of national income;
2. to speed up the rate of economic growth;
3. to generate savings for investments so as to reduce its dependence on external capital for the development of the nation;
4. to get enough manpower for the development of the country; and
5. to increase the standard of living of the masses particularly in respect of food, housing, health, and clothing and to develop infrastructure of the nation.[7]

The political upheaval and the civil war that ensued during the period of the first NDP are considered obstacles to the attainment of the objectives of the plan. However, landmark projects such as the Nigerian Security, Printing and Minting Company, the Jebba Paper Mill, the Bacita Sugar Plant, the Kainji Dam, the Niger Bridge, Onitsha, and the Port Harcourt Refinery, were, among others, delivered under the plan.

The second NDP covered the period of 1970 to 1974. The exigencies thrown up by the thirty-month civil war informed the concern of the NDP with national reconstruction and rehabilitation. The objectives of this NDP have already been highlighted above. Of course, not unexpectedly, there was a shortfall between set targets and actual accomplishments. Perhaps, in order to demonstrate its seriousness as a means of ensuring genuine national development, the objectives of the second NDP were incorporated into the 1979

Constitution of the Federal Republic of Nigeria, reflected in Chapter II as "Fundamental Objectives and Directive Principles of State Policy."[8] Unfortunately, these objectives remain nonjusticiable.

The third NDP covered the period of 1975 to 1980, and had the following objectives:

1. increase in per capita income;
2. more even distribution of income;
3. reduction in the level of unemployment;
4. increase in the supply of higher level manpower;
5. diversification of the economy; and
6. balanced development and diversification of economic activities.[9]

The fourth NDP, from 1981 to 1985, had the following objectives:

1. increase in the real income of the average citizen;
2. more even distribution of income among individuals and socioeconomic groups;
3. reduction in the level of unemployment and underemployment;
4. increase in the supply of skilled manpower;
5. reduction of the dependence of the economy on the narrow range of economic activities;
6. increased participation by the citizens in the ownership and management of productive enterprises;
7. greater self-reliance, that is, increased dependence on local resources in seeking to achieve the various objectives of society;
8. development of technology;
9. increased productivity; and
10. the promotion of a new national orientation conducive to greater discipline, better attitude to work, and cleaner environment.[10]

Quite a handful, but it is an indication of the obsession of the government with fast-tracking national development.

A fifth NDP was designed to address the following:

1. diversification of the nation's economy from the monocultural one to which it has been pushed by the fortunes of the oil sector
2. revitalization of the agricultural sector with a view to achieve thorough integrated rural development programs;
3. domestic production of raw materials for local industries; and
4. promotion of employment opportunities in order to arrest the deteriorating mass unemployment.[11]

Interestingly, the main concern of the plan was to address the structural defects in the economy and build a more self-reliant economy with less government control.

The imposition of the structural adjustment program (SAP) toward the end of 1986 effectively truncated the fifth NDP and took the initiative of development planning out of the hands of the Nigerian state with the Bretton Woods institutions taking over.

After the NDPS were jettisoned, between 1990 and 1998, the three-year rolling plans were adopted as a strategy for development planning while the government of President Olusegun Obasanjo established the National Economic Empowerment and Development Strategy (NEEDS) as the framework for national development.

Although this chapter will not go into full analysis of the various NDPs, it is just enough to say that their objectives are well captured in the MDGs. As such, if Nigeria remains backward, it is not because of lack of effort. Rather, it is because of the lack of deep-rooted commitment to genuine national development and well-being of the masses of the people by the operators of the state apparatus as well as their groveling subservience to international finance capital. The crises of underdevelopment in Nigeria has been dealt with elsewhere,[12] thus a brief overview will suffice here.

Right from precolonial times, the entity that is now called Nigeria has been operating as an appendage of the international capitalist system. Consequently, like most "developing" countries, Nigeria has lost the development initiative to the advanced capitalist countries of Western Europe and North America, as well as multilateral and bilateral institutions under their control. According to Martin Khor,

> National policies (. . .) that until recently were under the jurisdiction of States and people within a country have increasingly come under the influence of international agencies and processes or (*sic*) of big private corporations or economic/financial players. This has led to the erosion of national sovereignty and narrowed the ability of governments, and people to make choices from options in economic, social and cultural policies.[13]

Khalil Timamy's argument is similar to the above. For him:

> Since the imposition of structural adjustment policies on sub-Saharan Africa in the early 1980s, the freedom of many states to shape their own destinies in accordance with national development aspirations and welfare objectives has been severely compromised, if not hijacked altogether, by the Bretton Woods institutions and their backers. As a matter of fact, the policies designed by these powerful global players have become the policies of African governments. While the principle of sovereignty would, in moral terms, have armed

> African states with an effective weapon to fob off any attempts at interference, the truth is that their capacity for potential resistance has been neutralized by two dynamic constraints: the propensity for corrupt and self-interested African leaders to exploit, in a beneficially partisan manner, any potential opportunities that PSD initiatives might offer in their wake; and the erosive and blackmailing capacity of the conditionality-ridden diplomacy of the Bretton Woods twins in smothering a state's potential to invoke the sovereignty principle to any decisive and practical effect.[14]

The reality today is that the leadership of the Nigerian economy has been in the suffocating hands of outsiders. The direction of the development process, initially economic and lately political, has been dictated by such institutions controlled by the Western world, notably the World Bank and the International Monetary Fund. As such, it can be argued that if Nigeria is not well developed today, it is not necessarily because of the absence of the wherewithal; rather it is partly due to the fact that resources of the country, both human and material, are being diverted to develop other countries of the industrialized world (through unequal trade, debt trap, brain drain, etc.).

THE MDGS AND THE LIMITS OF EXTERNALLY DRIVEN DEVELOPMENT PLANNING

As well publicized by the United Nations, the eight goals set for the Millennium Developments are:

1. eradicate extreme poverty and hunger;
2. achieve universal primary education;
3. promote gender equality and empower women;
4. reduce child mortality;
5. improve maternal health;
6. combat HIV/AIDS, malaria, and other diseases;
7. ensure environmental sustainability; and
8. develop a global partnership for development.

Specific targets were also set for each of the goals.[15]

It is enough for the purpose of this chapter to note that apart from the last two goals, any responsible government does not have to be told before it addresses these concerns. Of course, as mentioned earlier, the NDPs individually severally and jointly have addressed most of the concerns raised by the MDGs. If development strides are not recorded, it is more because the paradigms adopted so far are not appropriate, particularly as they are not people-centered.

In addition, the MDGs are not the first time that the UN would address development concerns worldwide. In the past, attention was focused on women, children, youth, and water. The standing of Nigeria on the HDI is an indication that there is a need to look beyond the MDGs to address the plight of the masses of the people who are becoming increasingly endangered. It becomes imperative therefore to seek an alternative framework to address the development debacle in Nigeria. Even the official report on the progress made on the MDGs suggests that none of the set goals was met.[16] In any case, given the character of the Nigerian society and the paradigm of development adopted, even if the target date is shifted by decades, nothing much would be achieved.

Gavin Williams, Toyin Falola, and Julius Ihonvbere argue that the neocolonial relations of production and accumulation that were imposed on Nigeria at independence have ensured that the Nigerian state acts as the regulator of the interests of foreign capital while the indigenous comprador bourgeoisies that are in control of the neocolonial state themselves depend on foreign capital and act as the link between foreign interest and the local economy for survival.[17] In some cases, they look up to the state as sources of capital and contract.

The series of crises that have riddled the Nigerian economy since independence are better explained in light of this pattern of development foisted on the country at independence. It also explains the failure of various policy options and austerity measures that were designed to resolve the fundamental problems of the Nigerian economy. There is also the lopsided nature of the Nigerian economy, which is both a reflection of the shortsightedness of the indigenous ruling class as well as the distortions engendered by the neocolonial economic structure.

The gross mismanagement of the economy by successive administrations contributed in worsening the economic crises. This is manifested in massive stealing of public funds, excessive contract inflation, corrupt kickbacks, and excessive borrowing at home and abroad,[18] as well as lack of budgetary discipline and financial accountability.[19]

Deriving from the above, it is important to state that in order to address the failure of development and consolidate democratic governance in Nigeria, the active and meaningful involvement of all Nigerians in every facet of national life, ranging from the polity through the economy to the sociocultural, must be guaranteed. This involvement should transcend the casting of votes during election, the results of which are open to manipulation. In the period between elections, there should be avenues for electors to engage and interact with their representatives to ensure that policies and projects are those that would benefit the generality of the people.

LOCAL GOVERNANCE AND THE CHALLENGE OF PEOPLE-CENTERED DEVELOPMENT

It is common knowledge that for too long, governance had been a monopoly of professional politicians in conjunction with their public service partners. In the language of the World Bank, the result of this is "the appropriation of the machinery of government by the elite to serve their own interests."[20] In 2011, for example, it was reported that the federal and the thirty-six state governments had a total number of 1,411 cabinet members at a cost of N63.9 billion.[21] This is a further confirmation of both the selfishness and profligacy of the political class in Nigeria.

Development projects in Nigeria have always been implemented without any kind of contribution by its supposed beneficiaries, the civil society. Indeed, projects embarked upon by politicians were rarely in congruence with the needs of the populace or their reality. On the contrary, they were a way of assuaging the politician's appetite for corruption through embezzlement of public funds. Where developmental projects offered benefits to the civil society, an occurrence that was not too common, the citizenry felt obligated to be grateful to the government for fulfilling its obligation to the people.

In addition, governance has been excessively personalized in Nigeria, such that elected officials have turned themselves into tin gods who wield excessive power of patronage. At the federal and state levels, both the president and governors enjoy near absolute control over the political parties that sponsored them for elections! Also, as a result of the excessive power they wield, elected office holders, such as local government chairpersons, state governors, and the president, almost always impose their will on the rest of society. Even the legislature that is expected to act as a check in a democracy is not expected to question the proposal sent to it by the executive!

Furthermore, government projects are presented as if they are personally sponsored by the office holder as a benevolent act for which the society ought to be grateful. Another extreme is the practice by which wives of the president and state governors, without constitutional backing, create offices for themselves with all the state paraphernalia, and embark on seemingly humanitarian projects using public funds. Apart from the fact that such projects can be accommodated within various government departments, most of them hardly survive beyond the tenures of the incumbents. In reality, such projects are just convenient excuses for diverting scarce public resources into private hands.

RECOMMENDATIONS

Personalization of governance necessarily leads to lack of accountability. Its elimination is a *sine qua non* for progress and the realization of the benefits of developmental programs by the citizenry. In light of this, this chapter makes the recommendations below.

In the first place, development policy formulation, planning, implementation, monitoring, and evaluation must involve the target beneficiaries at all times. In other words, people themselves must identify their development needs and how to go about meeting them. Of course, what is available in terms of resources should be made known to the people in order to help this process. This approach is likely to have the salutary effect of putting a stop to a situation in which projects that have no immediate relevance to the people are foisted upon them. At present, programming and budgeting are, at best, bilateral relationships between the executive and legislative arms of government even though the executive is wrongly resisting the attempts of the legislature to make inputs. In addition, budget preparation and program planning are almost shrouded in utmost secrecy, becoming public knowledge only at the point of public presentation. This lack of popular participation in all aspects of governance encourages lack of transparency and accountability. It is in line with Sidiq Rasheed's view that:

> Without the effective involvement and participation of the poor in the design, implementation and monitoring of the policies, programmes and projects that are targeted and meant to eradicate poverty and enhance their contribution to overall national development, one can hardly expect these efforts to bear fruit.[22]

There can be no excuse for the lack of popular involvement in a democratic polity. At every level, people, especially target beneficiaries, must be part of policy/program/project design, planning, implementation, monitoring, and evaluation. This is the essence of the development process, which is in line with the spirit and letters of the African Charter for Popular Participation in Development and Transformation.[23]

Deriving from the above is the need to localize the process of policy formulation and move away from a situation where people's development needs are determined far away from the locale of development projects, and at times, by the so-called development partners. That was how the millennium development goals came about. Thus, the UN need not dictate to the people their own basic needs. For the purpose of development planning, then, at the level of the local government, each electoral ward can be constituted into a development zone through which people articulate their development needs and prioritize them in light of available financial resources and ultimately offer input into development plans from the local government up to the federal levels.

Second, beyond project planning, there must be institution created to monitor project implementation in order to ensure successful outcome. Similar institutions should exist at the state and federal levels. State and federal constituencies, then, constitute development zones that must work in congruence with the ward development committees. Once the framework is agreed upon, the people themselves should have the liberty to choose their own representatives. If people can secure the development agenda at the grassroots level, the chances that they would profit from the development process are higher. Also, the local government allocation for developmental projects would be judiciously spent for the good benefit of the people. At the very minimum, elected representatives at all governmental levels should be given the responsibility of presenting the government's budget and development proposals to the people before final debate and approval by the various legislatures. The final approved budget must be made public, with all approved projects and their locations clearly spelled out. This would allow members of the public who may not belong to monitoring bodies to know the program projects being proposed by the government over a specific period of time.

In order to ensure transparency and accountability in respect of public finances, the full statement of expenditure should be made public indicating the projects executed, total costs of execution, and the parties responsible for execution. If such expenditure profiles are provided, people are better placed to judge the prudence (or otherwise) of the government. This becomes necessary in light of the high costs of government projects, which are not unconnected with deliberate overinvoicing and inflation of costs. Making such statements of expenditure public will put people in a better position to contest the government's claims in respect to projects costs, which in turn might mark the beginning of saving a lot money used to enrich individuals.

In the final analysis, an avenue should be created for the civil society to have unconstrained access to information about government activities as well as a right to probe public affairs management by state officials. This would enrich their input into policy issues while enriching their participation, not just in the political process, but also in the development process. In all this, the point to note is that governance, particularly democratic, is a social contract between the government and the citizenry. This much is implied in the amended 1999 constitution. Among the socioeconomic rights guaranteed are:

a. equal and adequate educational opportunities (S.18);
b. provision of fair opportunity for all to secure adequate means of livelihood and adequate opportunity to secure suitable employment (S.17(3)(a));
c. health, safety, and welfare of all persons in employment (S.17(3)(c)); and

d. provision of suitable and adequate food, old age care and pensions, unemployment, sick benefits, and welfare of the disabled (S.16(2)(d)).[24]

Incidentally, these are the concerns captured by the MDGs. It means that any responsible government exists for the common good and has a duty to meet the basic needs of the people; otherwise, its legitimacy is threatened. If the government is not living up to its responsibility, the society has an obligation to compel it to do the right thing. Society has a duty to engage the process of governance as active participants in order that they are not short-changed by those who claim to represent them.

Also, active civil society organizations (CSOs) and nongovernmental organizations (NGOs) need to go beyond mere rhetoric; they must transcend the agenda of donors who often are part of the problems militating against people-centered development and the well-being of the poor and the disadvantaged in the society. This was precisely Rasheed's point when he stated that:

> Thus, CSOs and NGOs have a historic role to educate the poor about their democratic rights, convince them of the value and benefits of exercising these rights—particularly the linkage between political and economic gains—and assist them in practising these rights.[25]

Progressive intellectuals and scholars, particularly social scientists, should join hands with CSOs in speaking and working with the people in enthroning real democratic governance in which the good of the majority constitutes the *raison d'être* of government. For relevance, and in order to remove suspicion on the part of the people who have fast become victims of development, the CSOs should consider addressing themselves to the issues raised above.

CONCLUSION

Development process has hardly benefited the vast majority of the Nigerian populace. This chapter thus proposes a new approach to the management of development process in which the people themselves play an active role. Democracy, rightly defined, entails popular participation and representation; thus, it is imperative that the governed have the right to be active participants in how they are governed, particularly in the development process. Thus, citizen involvement is a basic minimum for democratic governance to thrive. In the final analysis, it is not enough to get the people to cast their votes and ensure free and fair elections. It is more important to ensure that elected political office holders deliver on their promises and live up to the demands of their offices. Once we adopt a governance framework that factors in popular participation, it becomes easier to put in place a development paradigm that puts people, and not markets, at the center of development. All available structures should be used to promote popular participation in governance and citizens' engagement with the development process. This popular participation would go a long way in reducing the tension within the polity that constitutes a major threat to national unity and cohesion.

NOTES

1. Economic Commission for Africa, *African Governance Report II* (New York: Oxford University Press, 2009), 9.

2. Figures are cited in United Nations Development Programme (UNDP), "Human Development Report 2015" (New York: United Nations Development Programme, 2015), January 9, 2018, http://hdr.undp.org/sites/default/files/2015_human_development_report.pdf.

3. Ojetunji Aboyade, *Issues in the Development of Tropical Africa* (Ibadan: Ibadan University Press, 1976), 16.

4. World Bank, *World Development Report 1997: The State in a Changing World* (New York: Oxford University Press, 1997), http://documents.worldbank.org/curated/en/518341468315316376/World-development-report-1997-the-state-in-a-changing-world.

5. The National Development Plan, 1970–74, Federal Republic of Nigeria, Lagos, (1970), 32.

6. See, for instance, E. N. Iheanacho, "National Development Planning in Nigeria: An Endless Search for Appropriate Development Strategy," *International Journal of Economic Development, Research and Investment* 5, no. 2 (2014), accessed January 10, 2017, https://www.icidr.org/ijedri-vol5-no2/National%20Development%20Planning%20in%20Nigeria-An%20Endless%20Search%20for%20Appropriate%20Development%20Strategy.pdf.

7. Ibid., 51–52.

8. 1979 Constitution of the Federal Republic of Nigeria, Part II, 7–10, accessed January 10, 2018, http://www.constitutionnet.org/sites/default/files/nig_const_79.pdf.

9. See Olufemi Lewis, "Nigeria's Third National Development Plan, 1975–80: An Appraisal of Objectives and Policy Frame," *The Developing Economies* 15 no. 1 (March 2007): 60–79.

10. See, Federal Republic of Nigeria, *Fourth National Development Plan, 1981–1985* (Lagos: Federal Ministry of Planning, 1981.

11. See Federal Republic of Nigeria, *The Fifth National Development Plan (2008–2011): Implementing the Seven-Point Agenda for Accelerated Economic Growth and Poverty Education* (Abuja: National Planning Commission, 2008).

12. See, for instance, Funmi Adewumi, "Industrial Relations, Economic Development and Democracy: A Preliminary Note," in *Challenges Facing Industrial Relations in Nigeria in the Context of Emerging New World Economic and Political*

Order, ed. E. E Osuji (Ibadan: University of Ibadan Press, 1992), 59–82; and Funmi Adewumi, "Structure Adjustment, Mass Poverty and Urban Violence in Nigeria," in *Urban Management and Urban Violence in Africa,* eds. Isaac Olawale Albert, et al. (Ibadan: Institute for French Research in Africa, 1994).

13. Martin Khor, *Globalisation and the South. Some Critical Issues* (Ibadan, Nigeria: Spectrum Books, 2000), 4–5.

14. M. H. Khalil Timamy, *The Political Economy of Technological Underdevelopment in Africa: Renaissance Prospects, Global Tyranny, and Organized Spoliation* (Lagos: Centre for Black and African Arts and Civilisation, 2007), 363–364.

15. See, Federal Government of Nigeria, *Millennium Development Goals, 2013 Report* (Abuja: The Presidency, 2013), accessed March 15, 2017, http://www.ng.undp.org/content/dam/nigeria/docs/MDGs/UNDP_NG_MDGsReport2013.pdf

16. Ibid.

17. Gavin Williams, "Nigeria: The Neo-Colonial Political Economy," in *Political Economy of Africa*, eds. D. L. Cohen and J. Daniel (London and New York: Longman Group, 1981); and Toyin Falola and Julius Ihonvbere, *The Rise and Fall of Nigeria's Second Republic, 1979–84* (London: Zed Books, 1985).

18. Bade Onimode, "Structural Adjustment Programme and Its Implications for Nigerian Workers. An Independent View," a paper presented at the Annual Industrial Relations Conference of the Department of Adult Education, University of Ibadan, Ibadan, Nigeria, 1987.

19. Segun Osoba, "Nigeria's Debt Crisis and the Nation's Stability," a paper presented at a seminar organised by the Academic Staff Union of Universities, University of Ilorin Branch, 1992.

20. Cited in Julius Ihonvbere, *Economic Crisis, Civil Society and Democratisation: The Case of Zambia* (Trenton, NJ: Africa World Press, 1995), 9.

21. Editorial comment, *The Punch*, Aug. 4, 2011.

22. Sadiq Rasheed, *Development, Participation and Democracy in Africa. Four Essays* (Johannesburg & Pretoria: Foundation for Global Dialogue & Africa Institute of South Africa, 1996), 62.

23. See African Charter for Popular Participation in Development and Transformation, Article 13, Arusha, Tanzania, 1990, accessed January 11, 2018, https://oldsite.issafrica.org/uploads/POPULARPPARTCHARTER.PDF.

24. The Constitution of the Federal Republic of Nigeria, (1999), Preamble and Chapter II on Fundamental Objectives and Directive Principles of State Policy, See Bamidele Aturu, *A Handbook of Nigerian Labour Laws* (Lagos: Friedrich Ebert Stiftung, 2001), 634–635.

25. Sadiq Rasheed, *Development, Participation and Democracy in Africa*, 64.

Chapter 5

Fallacy of Development in Africa

Sunday Layi Oladipupo

INTRODUCTION

Development is desirous and needed in all human facets, especially in the contemporary era where humanity seems to thrive on new innovations. Each country in the world is trying to raise its development base beyond what it was in the past. Hence, one can argue that we are in an era of geoeconomic competition between countries, regions, and continents. Several parts of the world have made tremendous gains in socioeconomic development in an era of competition and globalization. Despite this trend, however, Africa as a continent seems to be at the receiving end of the struggle for development among other continents. Why and how this became the state of Africa is a fundamental minus that needs serious attention. In an attempt to address the challenges of development, various scholars have offered their philosophical and scholastic input in the form of different solutions, yet issues of underdevelopment still proliferate in the continent of Africa.

Given that the question of development is a recurring phenomenon in Africa, this chapter sets to interrogate the propensity of development in the advancement of the continent. The argument is centered on the need to deconstruct the popular opinion that colonialism is the bane of development in Africa. Thus, the discourse herein showcases the place of culture in attaining desired goals that could transmute into viable development, for no society in the world is living outside of its culture. In a way, the chapter attempts to provide an African worldview of development to equip those that are saddled with the responsibility of recreating Africa to experience the desired development in the twenty-first century.

Suffice to say, this chapter tends to advance a proactive revisiting of Africa's past in affecting the present with a view to projecting the future.

It is within the ambit of this discourse that the chapter argues that development is not the same as Westernization, as a majority of Africans seem to think. This chapter, using a philosophical method of analysis, sets to demystify the age long belief of both the West and Africa that unless Africa or Africans adopt the Eurocentric approach, development will continue to be a mirage in the desert. Against this backdrop, the chapter calls for a shift from the "blame game" where colonization has been viewed and accepted as the cause of underdevelopment in Africa; holding on to this belief will only amount to fallacious fact and factual fallacy.

In this chapter, the meaning and nature of development are discussed with a glimpse into different theories of development. This is followed by a discussion about what is actually needed to enhance development in Africa. The chapter concludes on the note that for any society to overcome its developmental challenges, the culture of such society must be considered in relation to contemporary realities instead of looking to the past and on other cultures as models.

CONCEPTUALIZING DEVELOPMENT

Development is an open-ended concept; it has been viewed by scholars of different orientations from diverse worldviews, ranging from economic, social, political, to infrastructural perspectives, just to mention a few. Development is conceived as a multifaceted concept; it could be progressive or retrogressive, upward or downward, forward or backward. It is assumed to be positive when it is progressive, upward, and forward in nature, while it is considered to be negative if it is retrogressive, downward, and backward in nature. It follows that development is an upshot of human desire to improve their lots. Kolawole Ogundowole explains this when he posits that, "development must begin with the desire to improve our lot through our efforts."[1] The implication of this is that development cannot be achieved on a platter of gold; it must be a conscious desire by the people. It is divergent from growth that is natural; it is a desire that motivates human beings to strive for better lives and standards of living.

Apart from the above view, others conceive development from the standpoint of freedom and independence. This idea of development is commonly associated with Walter Rodney and Claude Ake. Both are of the view that development becomes meaningful only if people are free to pursue the objectives they have set for themselves in their own interest and by means of their resources.[2] Thus, one is inclined to subscribe to Behrooz Marvaridi idea that "development requires the removal of major sources of suppression and inequality; poverty, tyranny, lack of economic opportunities, systematic social deprivation, neglect of public facilities, and intolerance or over activity of repressive states."[3] The logic behind this conception of development seems to preach social justice and the possible eradication of poverty in the society. By this, it is imperative to mention that the central aim of development is for the advancement of the total well-being of the people that constitute a given society. It is suffice to say that development is people-centric.

To further widen the conceptual clarification of development, it becomes imperative to adopt theoretical approaches that have been used by scholars in explaining the concept of development. These theories explain different dimensions of development. For instance, the modernist understanding of development presents it as "expansion of infrastructure or a general project of industrialization that brings about access to such facilities as good roads, health system, and portable water, among others."[4] This idea of development establishes a nexus between development and availability of human basic needs. It is against this backdrop that "development begins to take place when it is consciously desired, that is, when it has become part and parcel of the daily need process of a people, when it has become in truth a part of the habit of a people."[5] So in the modernist sense, development is that which is consciously desired by humans for the purpose of making life bearable for them.

Dependency theory is another fundamental theory of development. The central focus of this theory is that development is something that could be achieved based on the unequal exchange of relationships between the developed and the developing nation. The advocates of this theory are of the view that the challenges of development confronting the developing nations are created by neocolonialism. To them, the problem of development continues in the developing nations as a result of the neoliberalist's agenda of perpetual subjugation of the developing nations in the form of master-servant relationship. Thus, while the developed nations are considered the master, the developing nations are viewed as slaves despite their attainment of independence. This theory is well articulated in Walter Rodney's book titled *How Europe Underdeveloped Africa*.[6] According to the proponents of this theory, underdeveloped countries continue to be poor and underdeveloped because of their overdependence on the developed countries and the belief that their own development can only be attained when it is modeled or programmed in line with the developed countries' models of development.

Cultural theory, on the other hand, stands akin to both modernist and dependency theories of development. The advocates of this theory are in sharp contrast with the modernist and dependency theories as they argue that development must be based on the belief system of the society that desires development. The implication of this is that development should be internally construed as against its external posture obtained in modernist and dependency theories. Development in the view of the cultural theorist is all encompassing; that is, development is beyond economic growth and political freedom. It is suffice to say that according to this theory of development, culture could not be ruled out in attaining and sustaining development; rather it is like the popular saying "charity begins at home." Hence, for development to be meaningfully attained, the culture of those that desire such development must be the base/foundation. It should not be built on pseudo-developmental hype orchestrated in the belief that development must follow the Western-centric and/or euro-centric models, as no society can survive outside its own culture. M. L. Igbafen captured the argument of the cultural theorists of development when he posits that:

> The unifying argument of the cultural theorists is the preposition that development in third world countries is retarded not because the resources, human or material, have been taken away but fundamentally because the cultural roots necessary for the production of the totality of resources have been removed.[7]

Derivable from the argument of the cultural theorists of development is the fact that culture is inevitable in emplacing a viable developmental agenda. Given this reality, following Kolawole Ogundowole, "we can therefore say that development is not so much a matter of what we have, but of what we do with what we have; how we do it and well."[8] This in a way will guide against committing an *assumptive fallacy of development.* It is on this note that it behooves us to consider what the continent of Africa needs to overcome underdevelopment and assume its rightful place in the comity of developed nations of the world. Hence, a revisit of African culture for development, which can be referred to as the *indigenous* pursuance of development, is essential.

REVISITING AFRICAN CULTURE FOR DEVELOPMENT

The main point of this chapter is to get rid of self-deception and the illusion that African underdevelopment is an aftermath of colonization. It argues for a revisit of African culture as that which is paramount to enhance developmental projects in the face of the challenges of the twenty-first century. Though it may not be totally possible for Africa and Africans to go back to their old ways (traditional heritage and customs), as cultural values are not static, Africa as a continent stands to lose nothing going back to its indigenous culture and value systems to achieve development even though there is a belief that such return amounts to primitivism. This idea is well captured in Kwasi Wiredu's words:

> The idea of identity usually comes into the focus of earnest discussion when there is a crisis of self-identity. In Africa the crisis has been the after-effect of our previous subjection to colonisation. Colonialism subjugated our people both culturally and politically. It is true that independence brought us some gains. But still our achievements in the decolonisation of various aspects of our life leave much to be desired. We need to examine or re-examine those aspects to find out which bespeak undue influence of the colonial past.[9]

It is apparent from Wiredu's position that Africa needs to revisit its origin to retrace and reaffirm its identity, especially because some of the states that constitute the continent are of a colonial creation. This reveals the reality of African heritages as nations amalgamated together to form a country often share nothing in common, but rather divergent linguistic affiliation and a collective form of cultural make up. It follows, therefore, that to understand the issue of development in Africa, the question of ethnic interrelationship is a fundamental issue to be addressed. This is because some of the countries that make up the African continent are often groups of people with different historical and cultural heritages. This was borne out of the fact that African multinational states were of a colonial creation in which African(s) were not consulted or in attendance when its destiny was decided by European powers. The continent of African was colonized on distinct nationality levels, but when modern states were created, these different nationalities were joined together without considering the consequences. The fallacy is that the amalgamation or merging is on the basis of administrative convenience, but we also know that it was based on economic exploitation on the part of the Europeans. The inability to put cultural factors into consideration continues to be another issue that African underdevelopment can be situated.

It is troublesome to comprehend that in order to fulfill the selfish interest of the European colonial masters, Europeans merged and submerged different African communities together to their detriment without thinking of the aftermath of such actions. Martin Meredith captured this in the following way: "In other cases, Europe's new colonial territories enclosed hundreds of diverse and independent groups, with no common history, culture, language or religion. Nigeria, for example, contained as many as 250 ethnolinguistic groups."[10] The diversity of culture, language, and religion as adduced to by Meredith must be understood before the continent of Africa experiences meaningful development. This needs to be addressed in order to determine the uniqueness of each culture toward the needed development. When this is achieved, the incessant crises that rattle the continent because of religious and cultural conflict, which often leads to violence that metamorphose into disruption of the developmental agenda of the continent, would be addressed. This would help African nations use their diversity and common history of colonial territories, confronted with similar challenges and difficulties, to promote and attain development in the real sense of it.

Beyond this, Africa must continue to pursue its total freedom from the shackles of imperialism. It must advance beyond the current abridged political and socioeconomic freedom that has reduced the continent to second fiddle. This agitation should go beyond the assumptive logic behind the agitation of the earlier nationalists whose campaign for emancipation was beclouded with the long stay of the colonial masters in their homeland. The past African heroes seem to have zealously fought for political freedom with or without the knowledge that political freedom alone cannot do the magic, as it is only an iceberg of what could enhance self-determination and development of the continent. Some of their actions are informed by fallacious thinking that the occupation of their homeland and heritage without them being in charge was a great disservice to humanity and the African continent. Good as this could have been then, the present realities that confront African people have shown that until the current crop of African leaders are ready to embrace the patriotic spirit with which the pioneer nationalists fought for African liberation from the shackles of colonial masters, Africa will only continue to chase the shadow of development.

Thus, the need to usurp the political and economic power from the visionless and corrupt leaders is necessary if Africa is to witness and experience development in the real sense of it. Those who seize the mantle of leadership in Africa must possess the mental magnitude that appeals to reason more than force. It is suggested, therefore, that to abridge and harness Africa's development beyond its fallacious outlook that there is a need to launch a strong and positive revolution through which the entire old older will be overthrown with a mission and vision to bring to bear new order that will galvanize meaningful development in Africa. Africa should change itself from being a howling monster threatening to wreck the whole continent where political office holders do all that is possible to promote their relatives, community interests, and seek kickbacks from contractors, businessmen, political associates, and civil servants in exchange for undue protection and benefits. Hence, even though the majority of countries in the world embrace democracy, democracy does not seem to be the best form of government, especially on the African continent. This is because the attitudes of governments in Africa do not reflect the preconditions of older democracies. Instead of confronting the challenges of bad governance and democracy, many African governments are eager to imitate the development of the West, overlooking the fact that development depends upon good governance.

Beyond this, for Africa to develop, both the leaders and citizens need to display commitment to their belief systems beyond mere talk. Action is needed to embrace indigenous practices that place value on humanity against the holistic adoption of the modern legacy that deprives the less privileged of their humanity, for development can only be meaningful if and only if the people are developed. One of such indigenous practices is the adoption of African languages instead of foreign languages in administration and instruction. Olufemi Taiwo seems to capture the inadequacy of foreign language toward promoting development. He states, "we have kept the inherited languages of our colonisers because we are simply too lazy to develop our indigenous languages for twenty-first century tasks, including those of science and theoretical engagement."[11] This is explicative of the essence of mother tongue in the pursuance of meaningful development. In essence, when the language of people is not adequately understood, their development will be debased; one of the ways to deny people their originality is to take away their language from them. Perhaps, it is suggestive that to get out of the present developmental quagmire that besieges the African continent, African languages should assume their proper place as the language of choice against the present scenario where European languages dominate the system. This is because language is a tool for conceptualizing reality and purposeful thinking. If this cannot be achieved, then we may not have learned from the Kenyan renowned writer, Ngũgĩ wa Thiong'o, that "each language, no matter how small, carries its memory of the world. Suppressing and diminishing the languages of the colonized also meant marginalizing the memory they carried and elevating to a desirable universality the memory carried by the language of the conqueror."[12] Thus, the native language that is well understood by the natives needs to be acculturated in pushing for Africa's emancipation from the polemics of development that rattles the continent. Africans should borrow a lesson from the Chinese, who adopted the Chinese language at every level of their social, economic, and technological interactions. If Africa continues to suppress and/or allow its languages to be suppressed by foreign languages, the problem of development will persist, as reflected in the lack of proper understanding of foreign languages. This deficit in development is important because of the relative understanding of foreign languages adopted in African countries: the moment the language of a people is captured, then such people will be perpetually prejudiced against by others.

Despite the arguments on the efficacy or otherwise of the adoption of mother tongue for instructional purpose, it is believed that its adoption will give room for better understanding and interpretation of issues that seem difficult under the confines of second languages currently in vogue. It is believed that when the mother tongue is adopted, development will be more elaborate. Tunde Babawale of the Centre for Black and African Arts and Civilisation

(CBAAC) attempts to canvass African parents to Africanise their children and argues that:

> Children who speak their local languages very well are known to be more proficient in other foreign languages. And they can communicate better. This has been proved to be true over the years. It is because we have neglected our duty to train the children and show them how and where to go that we are in this mess today.[13]

Impressive was Ngũgĩ's decision to deliver a conference keynote address in his mother tongue before giving its English translation.[14] Indeed, allowing the mother tongue to go into extinction will not only spell doom for the continent but also will deny and deprive Africa and Africans of their heritage and identity because the "direct consequences of language extinction mean the loss of a people and their world, history, cultural heritage, their understanding and testimonial of the world and the loss of scientific, botanical and medical knowledge."[15]

The implication of this is that African culture, which represents its total ways of life, cannot be supplanted in the name of globalization and modernization in expectation of protective and proactive development. Undoubtedly, we cannot shy away from the propensity of the claim that the forces of colonialism and globalization enhance development; however, it is fundamental that it has eroded and alienated the ambiance of African culture that is cloaked with humanity. Thus, Africans cultural values need to be resuscitated, for values are an aspect of culture that not only impact all other aspects but also stand as a driving force for development in any human society. Without dignifying a human being, development to some extent will be a façade, and if critically examined, it could be deduced that some of Africa's cultural values are humanistic in nature as they stress the dignity of a human being and communal living. These values promote a sense of belonging that members of one big family need to guide their human existence. The crux of the argument, therefore, is that Africa does not need to be Westernized to be considered a developed continent while jettisoning its own cultural heritages, but rather, develop its modernity based on its cultural heritages.

Though the rate at which the African continent experiences Western incursion could not be denied in advancing a course, however, despite the desire for modernity, Africa and Africans should always make recourse to their source. Hence, it is apposite to suggest that such desire, when it becomes inevitable, should be moderated by African historical experiences for "the individual is required to subject everything, especially beliefs, to the light of reason and embrace only those that survive reason's harsh and unforgiving searchlight. Appeals to authority, tradition or revelation, are not forbidden but they are all inferior to reason's judgement."[16]

Thus, while it is imperative for Africa to build its development around its historical past, it is equally necessary for a critical reflection to guide against dogmatic acceptance of beliefs without subjecting such to reason. This will help guide against appealing to tradition in pursuing development without recourse to present realities. Therefore, Africans need to domesticate modernity to recreate their world and guide against what is termed "the difference theory." Difference theory is a derivate of superiority and inferiority complex. Africans should see and believe themselves as equal and not different from the rest of humanity. When this is attained, then Africa and Africans will transcend their current dumping ground posture where they receive more than give.[17] Olufemi Taiwo captures this reality when he states, "if we would compare ourselves from them, we might be shamed into action that will move us forward with the rest of humanity."[18] By this, African scholars should advance African indigenous modes of knowledge instead of promoting it offshore where scholars are requested to publish their research finding in international journals forgetting that such journals are also local journals where they are published or located.

The prevalence of viewing modernity as development is cumbersome. Africa must desist from assuming that modernity equals development. Development is what is created of the people, by the people, and for the people. Hence, the kind of knowledge production that is needed to promote the African developmental agenda must be one that is "primarily for us, by us, about us, and near us. It will be driven by awareness that, on balance, a knowledge society is its own reward."[19] The implication of Taiwo's submission is to revive the already relisted African ways of life in as much as no society can develop outside its culture and tradition.

It therefore behoves us to argue that in order to foreclose the quagmire of underdevelopment and get out of the challenges that the fallacies of development bestow on Africa, both the leaders and followers in Africa must see the necessity of Nelson Mandela's view as cited by Martin Meredith that:

> We must face the matter squarely that where there is something wrong in how we govern ourselves, it must be said that the fault is not in our stars but in ourselves that we are ill-governed. The time has now come for 'a new birth,' he said "we know that we have it in ourselves, as Africans, to change all this. We must assert our will to do so. We must say that there is no obstacle big enough to stop us from bringing about an African renaissance.[20]

The inability of leaders to understand the psychic of their followers needs to be halted by attitudinal changes of the followers. In curbing this absurdity, it is incumbent on the followers to always see themselves as end in themselves and not means to an end. It is hoped that when this is done, politicians who have the responsibility of bringing about development will be compelled to doing the right things that will enhance common good. Thus, it will become very difficult, if not impossible, for politicians and political office holders to see the citizen as either tools or enemies.

It is important that African elites break their slavish devotion to Western ethos in viewing their own reality and engage in life rooted in the African belief systems and culture. It is not gainsaying to mention that what we find in Africa today is more than a clash of cultures. It is rather a cultural denigration where African culture has been thrown to an abyss in acceptance of Western culture. In fact, the rate at which Western culture finds its way to Africa is far beyond comprehension and as such cannot be quantified with the rate at which Africans are migrating to the Western world. Thus, while the brains needed in actualizing Africa's development are moving to Europe and other Western nations, what Africa gets is self-imposition of Western culture without proper understanding of what could promote its development. It is, therefore, high time Africa and Africans stopped imagining its development from without. Africa can be comfortable with indigenous development; however, the adoption of African system and culture does not mean their uncritical acceptance.

The implication of the above is that for Africa to experience real development devoid of resentment and to navigate through the fallacious enthronement of development under the pretence of modernization, it must look beyond seeking development aid from the Western world and monetary institutions like World Bank, the International Monetary Fund (IMF), and the International Trade Organization. This is because African countries are poor and underdeveloped precisely because of dependence on such aid; in reality, this neocolonial paradigm makes the poor continent poorer and slows the pace of its growth and development. Dambisa Moyo captured this reality when she argues:

> The notion that aid can alleviate systemic poverty, and has done so, is a myth. Millions of Africans are poorer today because of aid; misery and poverty have not ended but have increased. Aid has been, and continues to be, an unmitigated political, economic, and humanitarian disaster for most parts of the developing world.[21]

The relevance of Moyo's position cannot be glossed over to take Africa out of its fictitious chase for development based on the acceptance of aid from foreign donors, especially, monetary cash donations. The reality is that foreign aid is not judiciously handled, hence the essence of it is often time defeated. It is important to borrow a leaf from some other countries or regions who have developed their countries or regions looking inward to build systemic and functional policies that sustained them such as China and the other

Asian countries instead of allowing the billion dollar loans and aids that hindered Africa's development. Other African nations should embrace the bold step taken by Botswana, which stopped building its hope for development on aid. In fact, it is apposite to mention that the conditionalities attached to aid by the donor nations are more perilous than helpful. The dangers posed by aid to development are evident, for the donors often tie aid to procurement in such a way that the recipient spends such aid to procure specific goods and services from donor countries. The donor also reserves the right to prescribe the sector and/or project that the aid would support while the continuation of such aid is often attached to the acceptance of the receiving nation a set of economic and political policies prescribed by the donor.[22]

Given these then, the receiving nation that the African continent represents will always be at the receiving end of the European counterpart, which provides such aid and can only develop at the pace of the donor country and not at its own desires. Therefore, it would not be absurd to suggest that the continent of Africa should desist from accepting aid and if it becomes inevitable, it should be solicited purely on humanitarian ground without all the conditionalities attached to foreign aid.

Thus, this chapter shares in the sentiment of Toyin Falola that instead of adopting the Western developmental paradigm, "what we should rather do is to celebrate the essence of *Africanity*, to politicize an African identity as a deliberate strategy of curtaining the excesses of globalization."[23] By extension, Africans should present their worldview in a way that will show its relevance to Africa and the world at large. Africa should stop the colonial mentality that is suggestive of African worldview as primitive, such that African achievements, discoveries, and creations could not sustain its betterment unless it has affinity with Western tradition. This old tradition and narrative need to be re-examined in order to move away from the past in such a way that cognizance must be taken to correct the erroneous acceptance of the narratives of the past that Africa is a mere effect.

CONCLUSION

This chapter advances an argument for the need to revisit Africa's past in affecting the present with a bid to projecting what is needed for the continent of Africa to experience development in the real sense of it. It reveals that development is not the same as Westernization, as the majority of Africans seem to think, and urges that there is a need for a paradigm shift from the "blame game" where colonization has been viewed and accepted as the cause of underdevelopment in Africa. Holding on to such beliefs will only amount to a fallacious fact and factual fallacy and thereby hinder development.

Furthermore, this chapter argues that modernization does not equal development and concludes that any attempt at tenaciously holding on to the view that European ways of doing things should be the template on which the African continent can be developed, devoid of African culture and belief system, is nothing but a fallacious assumption. As such, it suggests that for African development, Africans should start thinking of African civilizations. This thought will enhance the thinking of Africans toward rejuvenating African cultural heritage as a veritable catalyst for its civilization instead of the overblotted Western civilization that has pervaded the continent of Africa in recent times.

NOTES

1. Kolawole E. Ogundowole, *Self-Reliancism: Philosophy of a New Order: Alternative Development Strategy for the New States* (Ikeja: John West Publications Ltd., 1988), 91.
2. See Walter Rodney, *How Europe Underdeveloped Africa* (London: Bogle-Louverture, 1972); Claude Ake, *Social Science as Imperialism: Theory of Political Development* (Ibadan: Ibadan University Press, 1979).
3. Behrooz Marvaridi as cited by M. L. Igbafen, *Core Issues and Theories in Philosophy of Development* (Ekpoma: A. Inno Printing Press, 2014), 3.
4. Igbafen, *Core Issues and Theories*, 1–2.
5. Kwasi Wiredu, cf. Olusegun Oladipo, "Nigeria in the Twenty-First Century, Challenges of Freedom and Development," in *Core Issues in African Philosophy*, ed. Olusegun Oladipo (Ibadan: Hope Publications, 2000), 121.
6. Rodney, *How Europe Underdeveloped Africa.*
7. Igbafen, *Core Issues and Theories,* 45.
8. See Ogundowole, *Self-Reliancism,* 91.
9. Kwasi Wiredu, "The Humanities and the Idea of National Identity," in *Identity Meets Nationality: Voices from the Humanities*, eds. Helen Lauer, Nana Aba Appaiah Amfo, and Jemima Asabea Anderson (Legon-Accra: Sub-Saharan Publishers, 2011), 1.
10. Martins Meredith, *The State of Africa: A History of Fifty Years of Independence,* (London: Free Press, 2006), 1–2.
11. Olufemi Taiwo, *Africa Must be Modern: A Manifesto* (Ibadan: Bookcraft, 2011), 17.
12. Ngũgĩ wa Thiong'o, "Europhone or African Memory: The Challenge of the Pan-Africanist Intellectual in the Era of Colonization," in *African Intellectuals: Rethinking Politics, Language, Gender and Development,* ed. Thandika Mkandawire (Dakar and London: CODESRIA Books & Zed Books, 2005), 158.
13. Cited in Adekunle Yusuf, "Help, Nigerian Languages are Disappearing!" in *The Nation,* November 13, 2013, accessed May 28, 2018, http://thenationonlineng.net/help-nigerian-languages-disappearing.

14. Ngũgĩ wa Thiong'o, "Revisiting the First International Congress of Africanists in a Global World," Keynote Address the International Conference on African Studies, University of Ghana, Legon, October 26, 2013.

15. Yusuf, "Help, Nigerian Languages are Disappearing!"

16. Taiwo, Africa *Must be Modern,* 60.

17. Ibid., 77.

18. Ibid.

19. Ibid., 119.

20. Meredith, *The State of Africa: A history of Fifty Years of Independence,* 676.

21. Moyo Dambisa, *Dead Aid: Why Aid is Not Working and How There is A Better way for Africa* (New York: Furrar, Straus and Giroux, 2009), xix.

22. Ibid., 39.

23. Toyin Falola, "Nationalizing Africa, Culturalizing the West, and Reformulating the Humanities in Africa," in *Rethinking the Humanities in Africa,* ed. Sola Akinrinmade et al (Nigeria: Cedar Production, 2007), 31.

Chapter 6

Political Economy of Postcolonial Rail Transportation Management in Africa

Tokunbo A. Ayoola

INTRODUCTION

This chapter aims to examine closely how the colonial railroads inherited by postindependence African leaders were managed in the postcolonial era. Further, it seeks to provide answers to the following questions: To what extent have these leaders, policy makers, and managers been able to develop and successfully manage these transport infrastructures? What subsequent restructuring did they carry out on them? How has the state-led strategy adopted to manage African economies failed to further develop African railroads for the benefit of the continent and its people? Why did many African governments decide in the 1990s to privatize their railroads? Finally, what is the current state of railroad management in Africa?

Before the nineteenth century, when European imperial powers started to invade and encroach on Africa, Africans were using different modes of transportation to convey goods and passengers. The types of transportation systems used in any part of the continent depended on the terrain therein. However, human porterage and pack-animals (donkeys, hinnies, horses, camels, oxen, and mules) were used over very wide areas.[1] These modes were commonly used in the savannah, Sahel, and Sahara Desert regions.[2] On the other hand, water transportation systems were developed in regions with navigable waters—lakes, rivers, deltas, streams, and lagoons. Dugout canoes and small boats were used on the East African lakes (Victoria, Nyasa, and Tanganyika) and on Rivers Nile, Niger, Congo, Senegal, and Zambezi.[3] Furthermore, along the East African coast, Arabs, Africans, and others used small boats—*dhow*—to convey goods and people, and to connect communities and city-states.[4]

In the late nineteenth century, European imperial powers, as part of their countries' deliberate attempts to exploit the continent's resources, embarked on the construction of new transportation infrastructures: seaports, waterways, canals, railways, and roads. During this time, European colonial officials, merchants, and missionaries in Africa, Asia, Latin America, and North America represented and promoted railway transportation and technology as the great "engines of change" and harbinger of "modernity" and economic growth.[5] Although railways constructed and managed in Africa from the late nineteenth century up until the 1960s (when a large number of African countries became independent), were grossly inadequate and very old, nevertheless, they formed the foundation of modern European transportation systems in Africa.[6]

This chapter therefore seeks to answer those key questions posed above, by first examining the development and management of railways in postcolonial Africa. It argues that the neoliberal policies and strategies adopted in the late 1980s and early 1990s designed to resolve the inherent contradictions and mismanagement of Africa's railways simply compounded them instead.

RAILWAY DEVELOPMENTS IN COLONIAL AFRICA

The primary development of railways in Africa occurred principally between the 1850s and 1930s.[7] From the mid-1930s to the late 1950s, however, only a few railway extensions were constructed and added to the continent's rail network. This was a result of lack of capital, the effects of the Great Depression of the 1930s, and the impact of the Second World War.[8] However, from the late 1950s to the 1970s, there were new railway constructions in many African colonial territories and independent countries, including Nigeria, Gabon, Kenya, Angola, Mozambique, Ghana, Democratic Republic of the Congo, Tanzania, and Uganda.[9] Paradoxically, it was during this period that rail transportation started facing stiff competition from its road counterpart, particularly in passenger service and short-distance light freight service.[10] Nevertheless, rail transportation remained the dominant means for transporting bulky agricultural products and mineral resources over long distances up to the middle of the postcolonial period in Africa.

Overall, the development of rail transportation in Africa brought about many changes: efficiency and economy in the transportation of passengers and goods; a new capitalist economy; creation of large national markets; increased agricultural and mineral production; greater ethnic and sociocultural interactions and integration of Africans; and great movements of people within colonial territories and across the continent. Other changes included the transfer of railroad technology to Africa; introduction of skilled and wage labor; expansion of existing towns and cities and the emergence of new ones; provision of employment for Africans; and transmission and exchange of ideas, cultures, and diseases.[11]

Equally, the development of railroads on the continent brought about problems. First, capitalism, a new mode of production was introduced which greatly undermined precolonial African economies and brought many developmental challenges to the continent.[12] There were also the problems of regional inequalities, the undermining of peasant agriculture, huge foreign debts arising from massive loans taken from abroad to construct the railroads, and economic and technological dependence on the West for practically every material needed in managing the railways (i.e., locomotives, wagons, coaches, and spare parts). Other problems included promotion of exploitative wage labor system; facilitation, extension, and solidification of long-distance migratory labor to construction sites of railroads, railroad stations, operational bases, mines, and agricultural plantations; creation of cheap labor reserves; and creation of urban ghettos.[13]

On the other side of the coin, it is fair to submit that Africa's colonial railroads were substandard and inferior to those of Western Europe, North America, and some parts of Asia. With the exception of those in Southern and Northern Africa, other railroads on the continent were no-frills infrastructure built on the cheap.[14] According to Udo, railroads in Sub-Saharan Africa were "circuitous [rail] routes . . . chosen to avoid the bridging of many rivers. In some stretches, the gradients were so steep that the load which the train could carry was greatly limited."[15] Furthermore, most of these railroads were made up of single and narrow tracks that could only carry light freight at very slow speeds. In addition, Africa's "commodity railroads"[16] were of different gauges. Different European colonial powers introduced different railroad gauges; for example, some colonial territories like Nigeria and Sierra Leone, there were more than one type of railroad gauge. By the late 1950s, there were nine different railroad gauges in Africa. These ranged from 1 feet 11 5/8 inches (600 mm) (in Morocco, Congo, Angola, parts of South Africa) to 2 ft (610 mm) and 3 ft, 1 3/8 inches (950 mm) (Eritrea) to 3 ft, 33/8 inches (1,000 mm) (in Kenya and Uganda) to 3 ft, 6 inches (1,067 mm) (in Nigeria, Ghana, Sudan, and Zambia), and so on.[17] Thus, after the attainment of independence, integration of African railroads became a herculean task, particularly in Sub-Saharan Africa.

POSTCOLONIAL RAILROAD DEVELOPMENTS

The African colonial and postcolonial economies were essentially enclave ones,[18] effectively disarticulated from the traditional economy of most

Africans.[19] Thus, transport infrastructures developed to assist these economies were lop-sided and inadequate. As a result, at independence there were no interstate, interregional, and continent-wide trade links on the continent. Consequently, effective economic and social integration became a mirage. Notwithstanding these negative legacies, in the first two decades of independence, African governments failed to pay necessary attention to the fundamental restructuring and modernization of their railroad industries. This lack of upkeep could not have been due to lack of capital, at least that was not the case with some countries like Nigeria, the Democratic Republic of Congo, Gabon, Ghana, Kenya, and Zambia, which were comparatively rich and could afford to spend on their railroads. Rather, the neglect of the railroads by African leaders at that time can only be attributed to the obsession they had with catching up with the Western industrialized nations in industrialization and modernization. Given this mentality, at independence, they launched straight into industrialization, employing the rather detrimental import-substitution strategy as the way forward.[20] By the late 1970s, however, most of the industries set up with costly foreign bank loans had become unprofitable white elephant projects.[21]

To compound an already dire situation, from the mid-1970s on, there were progressive reductions in Africa's external earnings, a practical result of depression in the prices of Africa's primary commodities. Notwithstanding the negative turn of African economies, most African governments continued to spend higher proportions of their limited resources on the provision of corruption-riddled welfare services, including massive urban road constructions, free education, free health care, and highly subsidized transportation, housing, and imported food. Paralleled to these developments was the fact that Africa's transportation systems, at this time, could not cope with the increasing new demands on them.[22] Although no fundamental transformations were carried out in the transport sector by most African countries in the postcolonial period, nevertheless, there were some developments in the *rail transport* sector. But before examining the actual management of postcolonial African railroads, it is apposite to first highlight some of the postcolonial railroad developments before the late 1970s and early 1980s, when the International Monetary Fund/World Bank sponsored Structural Adjustment Programs (SAP) brought about the privatization of not only African economies but also their railroad industries. It is to the postcolonial railroad developments we should now turn our searchlight.

As in other parts of the world, from the 1940s and 1950s onward, rail transport in Africa started losing ground to road and air transports. This was because the former could not cope with the economic boom engendered by the Second World War. As a result of increased production and exportation of agricultural and mineral resources after the imperialist war, there were great increases in foreign exchange earnings for African countries. However, in the midst of this boom, Africa's rail transport systems could not carry all the available freights. There was therefore an urgent need to either restructure the entire existing transportation systems and patterns, or add new extensions to the old structures inherited from the colonial authorities.[23] In the railroad sector, no less than 9,000 kilometers of new lines were constructed.[24] The longest of these lines was the 650-kilometer Nouadhibou to F'Derik and Tazadit iron mines, which opened for operations in 1963.[25] In the same year, another "iron ore railroad," the Buchanan to Mount Nimba (Liberia), was opened. In Sudan, which prior to the 1960s had very poor road networks, new railroads were constructed, particularly to its southern region in the early 1960s. This would appear to be a belated act on the part of the colonial master, Britain, to prepare the Sudanese economy on the one hand for political independence, and on the other, to guarantee its continuous control of the commanding heights of the economy.

In West Africa in 1964, Nigeria added to its existing network the 635-kilometer Kuru-Bauchi-Maiduguri line to tap the abundant peanuts in its northeast region.[26] Similarly, two important railroads were constructed in Gabon in order to mine and export manganese. The first was from Pointe Noire to Brazzaville and to Mbinda to transport timber from the hinterland to the coast. Between 1974 and 1986, the second manganese railway, the 684-kilometer standard gauge *Transgabonais* line was constructed from Owendo Port, very close to Libreville, to Franceville, in the interior. For many years after it was constructed, more than 65 percent of the line's traffic was manganese and timber.[27] In East Africa, the purpose of constructing more postcolonial railroads was not different, being mainly for the transportation of mineral resources. Thus, for the effective mining and transportation of copper in Kilembe, new railroad extensions were added to the existing Kasese and Pakwach lines in Uganda and Kenya, respectively.[28]

In the Portuguese colonies of Angola and Mozambique, there was an even greater need for more railroad constructions. In Angola, the Mocamedes line was extended from Lubango to Menongue. Later, a branch line was built from the Lubango line to the Cassinga iron mines. Furthermore, in 1962, an extension was constructed off the Benguela railroad to Cuima, just as an agricultural line was constructed from Luanda, the capital of Angola, to Uige Plateau. Similarly, to exploit agricultural resources in Mozambique, a rail line was built from the Nacala port in the Indian Ocean into the interior, to Vila Cabral. Subsequently, a branch of the same line was extended into Malawi, to relieve traffic concentrated on the port of Beira.[29]

As the development of railroads *within* African nation-states continued after independence, it appears that a clear realization that genuine development would continue to elude the continent if concerted efforts were not made to construct lateral (within nation-states) and transnational railroads to assist in the effective integration of African markets. One example of the transnational railroads that were constructed during this period to achieve such aim was that which linked Tanzania's railroads with those of Kenya and Uganda to form the East African Railways and Harbours (EARH). As a result of political wrangling among the three states, however, the union of railroads was dissolved in 1977.[30]

Perhaps, the most important of the transnational railroads built in Africa in the 1970s was the 1,860-kilometer Kapiri Mposhi (in Zambia's copper producing belt) to Dar-es-Salaam (Tanzania). This line was first conceived as an important transportation link between Tanzania and Zambia during the colonial period, but due to lack of capital and justifiable economic reasons in the East African region, it was not constructed until the 1970s, in the postcolonial period. But why was the project revived in the latter period? In 1965, Mr. Ian Smith, the leader of the racist white minority settlers in Rhodesia (Zimbabwe), issued a Unilateral Declaration of Independence (UDI) of the colonial territory from Britain, the colonial power, and then proceeded to block the movement of goods to and from landlocked Zambia to Zimbabwean ports.[31] This was because the governments of the two nations not only condemned the UDI, but started supporting Zimbabwean nationalists opposed to the Smith regime. The blockade adversely affected Zambia's main export commodity and foreign exchange earner, copper.

Given the foregoing developments, landlocked Zambia was forced to seek an alternative, expensive, and a much longer route to the sea. This decision, however, was not without its own implication. To finance this option, Zambia and Tanzania first approached the World Bank and some Western European nations for loans and technical assistance for the construction of a railroad from Zambia to the Indian Ocean port of Dar-es-Salaam in Tanzania. The two parties turned down the request on the grounds that the proposed project was not economical feasible.[32] Not deterred, the two African nations approached China, which without delay, provided a U.S. $400 million loan for the construction. China was contracted to build the line that was later called "TANZAM."[33] The construction of the railroad started in 1970 and was completed in 1975.[34] In all, by the end of the twentieth century, Africa had a total of 97,030 kilometers of railroads in thirty-eight countries. Of this total, South Africa alone had almost 30 percent, 31,400 kilometers.[35] Obviously, from this data, Africa, which is about 30,221,532 square kilometers in size, is inadequately served by railroads.

POSTCOLONIAL RAILROAD ADMINISTRATION AND MANAGEMENT

During colonial rule in Africa, European imperial powers, merchants, and firms from their countries developed limited capitalist production on the continent that was limited to European dominated enclave economies composed of banking, insurance, shipping, import and export commerce, mining, plantation agriculture, limited import substitution industrialization, civil bureaucracy, and in the decolonization period, some public enterprises.[36] In the postindependence period, however, these externally oriented economies needed to be radically transformed if the developmental aspirations of the majority of Africans were ever to be realized. Indeed, African nationalists who struggled for and "won" independence had made such a possibility the foundation of their mobilization and agitation for freedom. They promised that after independence, they would radically change the colonial economies to meet the basic needs of the people.[37]

Thus, from the 1960s onward when African states and governments had in theory attained the commanding heights of their economies, the key point of their "statist development strategies" was the consolidation of the management of the existing state enterprises and corporations, and the creation of many others.[38] Earlier in the 1940s and 1950s, African colonial governments decided to establish statutory and public corporations, which transformed how some governmental activities and services were being delivered.[39] One of the key reasons given for the change of government departments into public corporations was that services such as railroads, ports, inland waterways, marine services, coal, electricity, produce buying and selling, and so on, that were administered by the civil services in the colonies and were commercial in outlook and nature, were being unnecessarily stifled by excessive rules and regulations.[40] But how did the original administrative mechanism used in delivering services by the civil services come about in the first instance?

To begin with, the civil service started administering the above mentioned services because private enterprises—European and others—were deliberately bared from constructing and owning such at the time. A good example was the development of railroads in West Africa, where, embarrassed by the railroad loan guarantee scheme scandals in colonial India, the British colonial government acting at the behest of London, successfully resisted pressure from Western capital to finance, construct, and own railroads in the subregion. Second, some other private entrepreneurs did not want to venture into capital-intensive sectors of the economy because they feared they might not be able to make profits.[41] Some of the sectors of African colonies' economies that most Western companies shied away from included electricity and power, railroads, housing, agriculture (food production), waterways, cooperatives, and manufacturing.

In essence, at independence African governments adopted this state-led economic strategy to manage their economies. This choice has been attributed to a number of reasons including lack of capital and entrepreneurial skills on the part of indigenous private business; lack of indigenous private sector capable of building and managing public utilities (ports, electricity, railroads, telecommunications, waterways, and canals); and underdeveloped capitalist production. The strategy has also been explained in other terms including the need to generate adequate revenue from government investments in public corporations; reduce, and possibly eliminate dependence on foreign goods expertise and over bearing multinational corporations; effective controlling strategic high points of the economy; effectively implement development plans—tools for economic management in the early postcolonial period; and providing jobs for Africans, especially at a time when the private sector was not offering many job opportunities.[42]

Other justifications for the adoption of state capitalism in postcolonial Africa included the need to nationalize the economy, especially in socialist states such as Guinea, Ghana, Mali, Tanzania, Zambia, and Algeria; institute economic nationalism (especially by governments that had lost credibility with their people) in order to gain political legitimacy; and utilize public corporations and state-owned companies for political patronage such as creating jobs for supporters and hangers-on.[43]

Among the public corporations owned and managed by African governments[44] up until the mid-1980s when, at the instance of the IMF and the World Bank, they were commercialized or privatized, were African railroad corporations. These have included the Nigerian Railway Corporation; East African Railways and Harbour Corporation, which in 1977 was broken into Kenyan Railway Corporation, Uganda Railway Corporation, and Tanzania Railway Corporation; Sudan Railway Corporation; and the Ghana Railway Corporation. These and other public institutions were managed by the governments indirectly through designated ministries that supervised individual corporation's policy boards.[45] On the other hand, members of these boards were directly appointed by the central governments. The boards' responsibilities included setting policies for the corporations' management, approving their budgets, monitoring their performance, protecting them from external interference, and transmitting their needs and achievements to the governments.[46]

In the first decade of independence in Africa, most of the boards and management of Africa's public corporations seem to have done their best to manage these public institutions as efficiently as possible, but matters soon took a turn for the worse. Since many members of the boards of directors were appointed from the ranks of politicians from the ruling political parties and military juntas, when the latter seized power across the continent, the corporations inevitably became major sources of political patronage and for handing out of largesse and favors to associates and supporters. Many examples of such practices can be cited from Nigeria, Ghana, Kenya, Sudan, Tanzania,

Egypt, and Zambia. These turns of events should not, however, surprise keen observers of Africa. At independence, when African ruling elites or members of the nascent bourgeoisie took over political power, their economic base was very weak. This was the result of the deliberate exclusion of African educated elites from participation in the key sectors of colonial economies: banking, mining, shipping, and plantation agriculture.[47] Therefore, to remedy this dire and "embarrassing" economic position, and in order to exercise effective political power in their newly independent nations, members of the African bourgeoisie belatedly came to the realization that the best way to build themselves up economically could only be achieved through the control and manipulation of postcolonial state. Consequently, African political leaders latched on to state apparatus and organs, using them as platforms for primitive accumulation for self-reproduction. All this was achieved through further extension of the tentacles of the state into production and commerce along with the creation of an unprecedented number of public corporations.[48]

It was in this general context that some political appointees on the boards of African railroad corporations undermined the latter by, for example, enriching themselves and their political parties through awards of contracts and embezzlement of funds allocated and meant for the development of these organizations.[49] Furthermore, in some cases, the political appointees were directly responsible for mass employment of staff, including family members, friends, political loyalists, supporters, and associates.[50] The implication of such overstaffing of railway corporations can be clearly seen in the example of the management of the Abidjan-Ouagadougou railroads[51] and the Nigerian Railway Corporation, which by the late 1970s, had about 35,000 workers to manage a network that was less than 3,600 kilometers and controlled less than 15 percent share of transport traffic in Nigeria.[52] In addition, board members engaged in ethnic and religious rivalries to gain economic advantages over each other at the expense of the unity of purpose, direction, and cohesiveness of the railroad corporations.[53]

Also, the quality of board members and management staff left much to be desired. Since the basic appointment criteria was perpetually being tilted in the direction of political, ethnic, and religious partisanship and not requisite experience, qualifications, expertise, and skills, the quality of policy formation, decision making, and management of Africa's railroad industries was poor. The situation was further compounded by the hasty implementation of the "Africanization" policy, or the indigenization of the upper and middle management levels of railroad personnel. It should be remembered that throughout the colonial period, Europeans, some of whom were not qualified, exclusively held most of the important positions in railroad establishments.[54] Since the railroad industry is a highly technical field, the replacement of expatriates with Africans should have been carefully carried out. To start with, it should have been preceded by training programs and succession planning. Rather unfortunately, this was not the case. Instead, African staff "were put in positions for which they were inadequately trained, which resulted in increased problems of operation, a higher accident rate, and greater maintenance requirements."[55] It is therefore not surprising to observers that throughout the 1960s and 1970s, there was decreasingly poor output from Africa's railroad workshops and the concomitantly declining revenues from the operations of the continent's railroad organizations.[56]

As if to compound an already dire situation, in the 1970s, the African railroad organizations' management was further challenged by two developments. First, the United Nations, the World Bank, and other donor agencies, as a matter of policy, started moving away from funding some specific infrastructure such as railroads. It was in this context that these bodies advised African governments to emphasize less on the construction of new railroads. Rather, African countries should concentrate on the construction of more roads in the urban and rural areas.[57] This was in order to assist in the effective and efficient transportation of Africa's primary commodities, for which the continent was said to have "comparative advantage" in producing and exporting.

About the existing railroads, African governments were advised to concentrate available resources only their maintenance.[58] This policy direction had the effect of diverting considerable resources away from rail transport to road and air transport development.[59] Thus, with the reduced budgets of most African railroad corporations, with the exception of those in South Africa and Northern Africa, most could not procure the requisite number of locomotives, rolling stocks, machinery, and spare parts. Neither were they able to hire and retain quality staff.[60] As a result of this, Africa's railroad industry was not only saddled with old equipment inherited from the colonial period, but was also forced, by the new circumstances they found themselves in, to offer unreliable, inefficient, and worsening passenger and freight services. Consequent upon the advantages conferred on road transport[61] and the discriminatory government policies in its favor, by the early 1980s, rail transportation in Africa had lost a lot of ground to its major rival, road transport, especially in passenger and short-haul freight traffic.[62]

Second, by the mid-1980s, Africa was in serious economic crises, which the World Bank and the International Monetary Fund attributed to many contradictions inherent in African economies. These contradictions were identified as excessive state regulation, inefficiency and corruption of state owned companies, overvaluation of African currencies, state regulation of import licensing regimes, subsidization of many sectors of the economies, serious balance of payment deficits, excessive import dependency, cronyism, corruption, embezzlement by state officials, and huge foreign debts.[63] In the case of foreign debts, in 1970, Africa South of the Sahara owed $6 billion, and a decade later these had reached $60.9 billion. In 1990, they reached $176.9 billion, and in 2003, they totaled $231.4 billion.[64] Completely missing from this long list of the problems confronting African economies is the most critical of them all: the fact that these economies were and are still dependent capitalist and were built on the foundation of exporting primary products and importing consumer goods, machineries, and technical expertise.

Set against the backdrop of the two IFIs' diagnoses, the two financial institutions then went ahead to prescribe measures that they believed would cure the maladies identified above. The IFIs therefore came up with the "Structural Adjustment Programs (SAPs)" under which many African governments and leaders were requested to start implementing specific economic and social reforms. These included the liberalization of the economies, removal of tariffs and controls on imports and exports; devaluation of national currencies, so that African export commodities would be cheaper and imports from abroad would be very expensive to buy; commercialization and privatization of state institutions and corporations, including those managing railroads; drastic reduction of the role of the state in the management of African economies and in its stead the mechanism and operation of market forces; reduction of public expenditure; removal of subsidies on consumers goods; and an increase in bank rates ostensibly to encourage savings and build up local investment capital.[65]

These reforms had many consequences for Africa's railroad industry. First, because of reduction in public expenditures, there was massive reduction in the funding of railroad corporations by governments, their sole financiers. One of the immediate consequences of this was that railroad systems in Guinea, Sierra Leone, in the northeast sector of the network in the Democratic Republic of Congo, and some short railway lines in Angola simply collapsed.[66] Furthermore, as a result of the devaluation of African currencies under the SAP, the importation of machinery, spare parts, locomotives, rolling stocks, steel rails, and communication equipment became rather costly to import from abroad, where all railroad materials and equipment had been imported since the late nineteenth century when European colonizers started developing most African railroads. Thus, by the 1990s, many African national and transnational railroad networks were saddled with obsolete equipment. Consequently, the networks fell into serious state of disrepair.[67]

The foregoing economic and operational problems were, in some cases, compounded by political conflicts. Some of the continent's railroads were destroyed by civil, ethnic, and religious conflicts.[68] From 1975 to the late 1990s, the Benguela railway in Angola, one of the most commercially viable on the continent, was closed down because of prolonged civil war in that mineral rich country.[69] In the 1980s, rebels of the Mozambican National Resistance (RENAMO) supported by Apartheid South Africa blocked the railroads linking Malawi, Zambia, and Zimbabwe with ports in Maputo, Beira, and Ncala in Mozambique.[70] Furthermore, in Liberia, Sudan, Ethiopia, Eritrea, and Uganda, civil unrests severely damaged installed railroad infrastructures.[71] Therefore, in the early 1990s, Africa's railroad networks were clearly in serious trouble.

NEOLIBERALISM AND AFRICAN RAILROADS

Given the bleak prospect of Africa's railroads in the 1980s and 1990s, some government officials began speculating that the golden age of railroad on the continent was truly over. However, with the acceleration of economic globalization from the 1980s onward, coupled with intense pressure from the IFIs on African governments to sell off all state-owned enterprises (including railroad assets), there was new hope for railroad revivals across Africa. The possibility of finally turning state railroad corporations over to the private sector to manage set in motion a tantalizing vision of a second African railroad renaissance. Thus, from the late 1980s on, many railroad privatization regimes started to appear on the scene in Africa, and after many debates as to specific forms of privatization to be adopted, most African governments settled for concessioning of their railways to mostly Western European private companies. Some of these companies were Sitarail (Côte d'Ivoire/BurkinaFaso), Transrail (Senegal/Mali), CANAC/WACEM (Togo), Camrail (Cameroon), *Transgabonais* (Gabon), RSZ (Zambia) BBR (Zimbabwe), Ressano Garcia, CCFB, and CDN (Mozambique), Madarail (Madagascar), CEAR (Malawi), TRC (Tanzania), RVRC (Kenya/Uganda), and Sizarail (Democratic Republic of Congo).[72] A good example of a concession agreement was that between Camrail and the government of Cameroon. This was a twenty-year rolling concession, which permitted Camrail "to operate, maintain, and improve the railway infrastructure and to manage the railway property, which may be extended for five years at every five years."[73] The concession also provided government's retention of "the legal ownership of the fixed assets."[74]

The first privatization of a railway in Africa started in 1995 with the concessioning of the Abidjan (Côte d'Ivoire)-Ouagadougou (Burkina Faso) railroad to Sitarail of France.[75] Subsequently, fifteen other agreements were signed between some of the above-mentioned concessionaires and governments of Gabon, Cameroon, Madagascar, Malawi, Zambia, Zimbabwe, Mozambique, Senegal, Mali, and others.[76] Meanwhile, the South African railroad company, Spoornet, was not left out of the scramble for Africa's public railroads in acting as a concessionaire. It invested in East and Southern African railroad companies and signed a railroad management contract with the government of the Democratic Republic of Congo. On the other hand, Canadian investors, the East African Railway Development Corporation, signed railroad management agreements with Tanzania, Kenya, Uganda, and Zambia.[77]

In the new century, Nigeria undertook many studies to determine which form of privatization would best suit its beleaguered railroad industry. No concession agreements however, resulted from those studies. However, in late 2006, Nigeria embarked on a twenty-five-year railway reorganization and modernization program under which double-track standard gauge rail lines were planned to be constructed to replace the existing narrow-gauge network. The first phase of the project, the construction of the 1,010-kilometer line from Lagos to Kano, was supposed to start in November 2006. The project was estimated to cost U.S. $8.3 billion and was to be financed with loans from the Chinese government and other foreign investors. However, in late 2007, the government of President Umaru Yar'Adua abandoned the entire project because, according to it, the previous Obasanjo government did not follow proper procedures for awarding such contracts.[78] It should here be noted that, Nigeria had not yet succeeded in either privatizing or commercializing its railroad industry. This is due to vested political and economic interests in Nigeria, which have invested heavily in road transport and therefore do not want to see the revival of the railroad transport industry.[79]

EVALUATION OF RAILROAD PRIVATIZATION IN AFRICA

In 2002, precisely seven years after the first railroad concessionary agreement in Africa went into effect, a gulf had already developed between the expectation and reality of privatized railroad industry on the continent. Contrary to the high expectations for the exercise, the levels and worth of foreign investments in privatized railroads were generally low. It would appear that Western companies and banks suddenly developed cold feet in financing the schemes. This was perhaps due to the terrible state of African railroads. Set against this backdrop, concessionaires that initially displayed interest in the privatization programs were only comfortable investing in small and specific *parts* of the railroad networks that would be profitable to them. For instance, CAMRAIL, in Cameroon, that had been expected to start investing immediately when its concession began in 1998, did not start doing so until four years later. Even then, by late 2005, it had only invested $92 million.[80] Overall, in the first five years of granting rail concessions in Africa, not more than $562 million had been invested in eight railroad concessions in Africa.[81]

As a result of the reluctance of Western European companies and banks to fully commit themselves to African railroad privatization, African countries were invariably forced to grant some incentives and breaks, or "sweeteners," to the former in order to encourage their active participation in the concession programs.[82] In the few cases where foreign capital could not initially invest in the renewal and rebuilding of rail tracks and workshops, African governments had to continue financing such projects, and to do this effectively, some of them had to borrow money from the IFIs. Such borrowed money was, in turn, made available to the concessionaires as loans at very low interest rates.[83] These arrangements remind us of the colonial period in Africa, when state authorities often underwrote the economic liabilities and activities of European firms. Some African governments had to intervene financially this way because the concessionaries were very cautious in committing their capital.

Meanwhile, even with such generous financial assistance, more often than not, the railroad concessionaires still decided to focus their attention primarily on managing the day-to-day railroad operations while leaving the more demanding aspects such as financing and rebuilding of rail tracks to the governments. Third, most of the existing concession agreements were for short terms of five years, which could later be rolled over the next twenty-five years. The implication of these kinds of arrangements is that at the end of these short-term agreements, the fate of the railroads concerned is subject to uncertainties. Furthermore, virtually all the existing concessions are gradually evolving into monopolistic structures, totally dominant over the lucrative aspects of railroad operations they have cleverly cornered for themselves. These new "monopolies" are no different from those that existed before the 1990s, when the post-colonial state railroad corporations completely dominated the transportation sector, thereby effectively shutting out participation by both local and foreign private companies. The new monopoly power appears to have granted the concessionaires the exclusive right to fix tariffs as they like. This obviously unintended development has arisen in part due to African governments' unwillingness and incapacity to effectively regulate the concessionaires.[84]

Additionally, the concessionaires have deliberately shied away from competing against road transporters, especially, the truck operators. As a result of their slow movement in rehabilitating and modernizing railroad infrastructures, the concessionaires have not been able to provide faster, cheaper, and alternative means of transporting passengers and goods. It is only in the long distance bulky freight service, where they had comparative advantage over road transport, that they have made progress.[85] They have thus allowed road transporters to continue to determine the nature of competition between the two modes. The concessionaires' argument is that road transportation in Africa is highly subsidized by the government, and therefore have been requesting that African governments impose more charges on road transporters for their continuous use of state constructed and maintained roads.[86]

Furthermore, the concessionaires have been reluctant to take on and pay debts owed by the defunct state railroad corporations. Consequently, the governments have continued to carry the debt burden of the privatized railroad industries—as if privatization never happened. Similarly, they have shied away from being directly responsible for the "loss-making" passenger services, except where African governments were prepared to grant subsidies for those services. For instance, between 1999 and 2004, the Cameroonian government paid the Camrail \$11.1 million in passenger subsidies.[87] Although right from the colonial period, rail passenger services have been unprofitable and have always attracted subsidies from the governments, Africans looked forward to a situation under the privatization programs where these services would still be maintained and greatly improved upon. In some other countries, such services have actually been terminated, while in yet others where services are still running, they have been epileptic.[88]

It is, however, not all gloom and doom for privatized African railroads. Indeed, there have been positive changes in some of the concessioned railroad industries. As can be seen in Table 6.1 below, there have been reductions in the excessive number of workers in the privatized railroad corporations, giving rise to labor and assets productivity. Also, there has been some growth in freight traffic, revenue and staff productivity (Table 6.1). All this is amply demonstrated by the example of the Mali-Senegal railroad performance. Prior to privatization, safety was a major concern for African railroad managers, and up until the early 1990s, most of the rail network tracks on the continent were in serious state of disrepair. One of the key reasons for this situation was the lack of spare parts and equipment to repair and maintain tracks, locomotives, and signal equipment. Consequently, there were many locomotive and train derailments. However, with the infusion of some capital and equipment under the privatization regimes, safety records have improved. Revenues of some of the concessionaires, especially those that have been operating more than five years, such as Sitarail and Camrail, have greatly increased (Table 6.1).

A good example is the TRC. In its first year of railroad concession in Tanzania, freight revenue stood at about \$75 million, but four years later, it rose to about \$136 million. Similarly, revenue profile rose for the KRC's Kenya-Uganda railroad concession from a modest \$79 million to \$132 million within four years (Table 6.1). Concessionaires have thus been able to contribute modestly to governments' coffers through concession fees, value added tax, company taxes, profits, and personnel income taxes. All these data, it must be noted, comes from a very slender portfolio of freight services. Finally,

Table 6.1 Operational and Financial Features of Eight Railroad Concessions in Africa, 1995–2000

		Freight Revenue (in U.S. $ millions)		*Actual Debt Burden by Fifth Year as a Multiple of Fifth Year Revenue*	*Freight Traffic (Tkm millions)*		*Number of Employees*		*Freight Staff Productivity*	
Country	*Concessionaire*	*Year 1*	*Year 5*		*Year 1*	*Year 5*	*Year 1*	*Year 5*	*Year 1*	*Year 5*
Tanzania	TRC	75	136	0.5	1,616	2,819	5,233	5,008	308,000	563,000
Mozambique	CCFB (Beira)	6	72	2.1	285	1,274	na	na	na	na
Kenya-Uganda	URC	24	30	0.6	271	391	1,190	1,190	228,000	328,000
—do—	KRC	79	132	0.3	1,694	2,642	3,700	3,800	458,000	690,000
Zambia	RSZ	35	51	0.3	686	878	1,710	1,232	401,000	712,000
Cameroon	Camrail	58	72	1.8	880	1,114	2,808	2,524	390,000	442,000
Madagascar	Madarail	7	28	0.5	62	185	915	900	68,000	206,000
Burkina Faso-Côte d'Ivoire		21	30	0.2	451	528	1,815	1,650	248,000	320,000
Mali-Senegal	Transrail	32.9	51.7	1.4	382	727	1,550	1,388	246,000	523,000

Source: Adapted from the World Bank, *Sub-Saharan Africa-Review of Selected Railway Concessions*, (Washington, DC: World Bank, 2006), Annex D 4.

the concessionaires have succeeded in lifting the level of rail services and have attracted new traffic.

CONCLUSION

Transportation has always been an important factor in the development of Africa. Conscious of this important fact, European colonialists did not waste time in constructing new and "modern" transportation systems on the continent. Although these new transportation networks were constructed primarily to serve the narrow economic interests of the colonialists, they brought about changes in the social, political, economic, and cultural life of the continent. Although the colonial railroads constructed between the late nineteenth and mid-twentieth century were no-frills functional infrastructures, nevertheless, at independence, they formed the bedrock of the continent's postcolonial transportation systems. Unfortunately, in the early postcolonial period, the inherited railroad infrastructures were mismanaged, and in some cases, they actually run aground. Hence, by the 1990s, most African railroads were in serious trouble. Under economic pressure at home and financial pressure from abroad, particularly from the International Financial Institutions (IFIs), the African governments decided to privatize their railroad industries.

Since the foreign railroad concessionaires that decided to participate in the railroad privatization programs were not philanthropists, but hard-nosed and shrewd business people, they were very selective of those aspects of the African railroad industries in which they were prepared to invest. Consequently, the envisaged changes, social and economic benefits that African governments and people looked forward to achieving have been very modest. Coupled with the frustration arising from the negligible results of the privatization programs is the great burden of the continuous financing of major parts of the privatized railroads, including repayment of debts, rebuilding of tracks, and the provision of communication equipment. Thus, it is fair to conclude that the railroad privatization programs, rather than helping the continent's railroads to become profitable, effective, and efficient, have rather become veritable avenues through which African governments are subsidizing foreign railroad concessionaires' operations in Africa. This appears to be a classic case of "railway neocolonialism" in Africa.

Although, railroad privatization in Africa has brought some improvements in freight services, a large segment of the industry remains unaffected by the injection of new capital. Indeed, many railroads have been abandoned and allowed to go to ruins because foreign private capital is unwilling to invest in the entire rail networks. Yet, Africa should not be content with only small pockets of performing "freight railroads," but should equally be concerned with the more important short-haul and passenger services.

NOTES

1. Willie F. Page, *Encyclopedia of Africa History and Culture. African Kingdoms, 500-1500 Volume II* (New York: The Learning Source Book, 2001), 214; S. D. Neumark, "Transportation in Sub-Saharan Africa," in *An Economic History of Tropical Africa Vol. II: The Colonial Period,* eds. Z. A. Konczacki and J. M. Konczacki (London: Frank Cass and Co. Ltd, 1977), 39.

2. Ibid; Paul Tiyambe Zeleza, *A Modern Economic History of Africa Vol. 1: The Nineteenth Century* (Dakar: Codesria, 1993), 264.

3. Ibid; S. D. Neumark, "Transportation in Sub-Saharan Africa," 40–41.

4. Erik Gilbert and T. Jonathan Reynolds, *Africa in World History from Prehistory to the Present* (New Jersey: Pearson Prentice Hall, 2008), 293.

5. J. Forbes Munro, *Africa and the International Economy, 1800-1960* (New Jersey: Rowman and Littlefield, 1976), 92.

6. Ralph Austen, *African Economic History* (London: James Currey and Heinemann, 1987), 126–129.

7. A. J. Christopher, *Colonial Africa* (London & Canberra: Croom Helm, 1984), 75; C. C. Wrigley, "Aspects of Economic History," in *The Colonial Movement in Africa Essays on the Movement of Minds and Materials,* ed. Andrew Roberts (Cambridge; Cambridge University Press, 1992), 80 ; Neumark, "Transportation in Sub-Saharan Africa," 39–41; Robert Shenton, *The of Capitalism in Northern Nigeria* (Toronto: University of Toronto Press, 1986), 57; William A. Hance, *African Economic Development* (New York: Praeger, 1967), 107; Reuben K. Udo, *The Human Geography of Tropical Africa* (London: Heinemann Educational Books, 1987), 181–182.

8. Wrigley, "Aspects of Economic History," 84.

9. A.M. O'Connor, *The Geography of Tropical African Development* (Oxford: Pergamon Press, 1978), 146–153.

10. Ibid., 154.

11. Erik Gilbert, "The Economic Impact of Colonialism," in *Africa Volume 3: Colonial Africa, 1885-1939*, ed. Toyin Falola (Durham, NC: Carolina Academic Press, 2002), 112–115; Austen, *African Economic History*, 122–125; J. O. C. Onyemelukwe and M. O. Filani, *Economic Geography of West Africa* (London: Longman, 1983), 106–109; David R. Devereux, "Transportation Infrastructure," in *Encyclopedia of African History, Vol. 3*, ed. Kevin Shillington (New York: Fitzroy Dearborn, 2005), 1581; John Sender and Sheila Smith, *The Development of Capitalism in Africa* (New York: Methuen & Co. Ltd, 1977), 14–17.

12. Gordon H. Pirie, "The Decivilizing Rails: Railways and Underdevelopment of Southern Africa," *Tijdschrift voor Economische en Sociale Geografie* 73, no. 4 (August 1982): 222–228; David Slater, "Underdevelopment and Spatial Inequality: Approaches to the Problems of Regional Planning in the Third World," *Progress in Planning* 4, no. 2 (1975): 97–167.

13. Ibid; Austen, African *Economic History*, 126–129.

14. Patrick O. Ohadike, *Development in Africa* (Legon: Regional Institute for Population Studies, University of Ghana, 1988), 322.

15. Udo, *The Human Geography of Tropical Africa*, 181–182.

16. Claude Ake, *A Political Economy of Africa* (Harlow, Essex: Longman Group Ltd. 1981), 44.

17. Guy Arnold, *A Guide to African Political and Economic Development* (London and Chicago: Fitzroy Dearborn Publishers, 2001).

18. David Simon, *Transport and Development in the Third World* (London: Routledge, 1996), 49.

19. Ake, *A Political Economy of Africa*, 44; Gilbert and Reynolds, *Africa in World History*, 287–290; K. Shillington, *History of Africa* (New York: Palgrave Macmillan, 2005), 332–338.

20. Virginia Dehancey, "The Economies of Africa," in *Understanding Contemporary Africa*, eds. April A. Gordon and Donald L. Gordon (London: Lynne Rienner Publishers, 2007), 115.

21. Ibid.

22. Ieuan L. I. Griffiths, *The African Inheritance* (London: Routledge, 1995), 190.

23. O'Connor, *The Geography of Tropical African Development*, 146–148. Ibid., 154.

24. John Howe, "The Future of Surface Transport in Africa," *African Affairs,* 74, no. 296 (1975): 314.

25. O'Connor, *The Geography of Tropical African Development*, 148.

26. Tokunbo A. Ayoola, "Political Economy of Rail Transportation in Nigeria, 1945-1985" (PhD Dissertation, University of Manchester. 2004), 146–201.

27. Richard Bullock, *The Results of Railway Privatisation in Africa* (Washington, DC: The World Bank, 2005), 11–13.

28. Ibid., 40.

29. Ibid., 26, 39.

30. Ibid., 40.

31. Griffiths, *The African Inheritance*, 185.

32. Arnold, *A Guide to African Political and Economic Development*, 138; and Jamie Monson, *Africa's Freedom Railway* (Bloomington: Indiana University Press, 2009), 35–70.

33. Ibid.

34. Ibid.

35. Ibid., 133.

36. Kevin R. Cox and Rohit Negi, "The State and the Question of Development in Sub-Saharan Africa," *Review of African Political Economy* 27, no. 123 (March 2010): 89; Ake, *A Political Economy of Africa*, 40–44.

37. Alex Thompson, *An Introduction to African Politics* (New York: Routledge, 2007), 32–49.

38. Ibid., 175–183.

39. Amishadai L. Adu, *The Civil Service in New African States* (London: George Allen & Unwin Ltd., 1965), 213–214.

40. Ibid.

41. Ibid.; Hance, *African Economic Development*, 130.

42. Ladipo Adamolekun, *Public Administration, A Nigerian and Comparative Perspective* (Harlow: Longman Group Ltd., 1983), 47–48; and Mouftaou Laleye,

"Public Enterprises," in *Public Administration in Africa: Main Issues and Selected Country Studies*, ed. Ladipo Adamolekun (Boulder, CO: Westview Press, 1999), 35–37.

43. Ibid.

44. Alice Galenson, and Louis S. Thompson, "Forms of Private Sector Participation in Railways," World Bank Infrastructure Notes Transport No RW-5, (June 1993): 1.

45. Ibid.

46. Laleye, "Public Enterprises," 39.

47. Ayoola, "Political Economy of Rail Transportation," 204–210.

48. At independence, Nigeria for example had 50 public enterprises, but by 1970, the number had jumped to 200. By 1987, there were about 1,500.

49. Adamolekun, *Public Administration,* 50.

50. Poul Ove Pedersen, "The Changing Structure of Transport under Trade Liberalization and Globalization and its Impact on African Development." Working Paper Sub-series on Globalization and Economic Restructuring in Africa no vii, Centre for Development Research, Copenhagen, Working Paper 00.1 January 2000, 13.

51. Brigitta Mitchell and Karim-Jacques Budin, "The Abidjan-Ouagadougou Railway Concession," in *Africa Transport Technical Note Railway Restructuring* Sub-Saharan Africa Transport Policy Program (SSATP) Note 13 Washington DC: UNECA A and The World Bank, June 1998, 1.

52. Ayoola, "Political Economy of Rail Transportation."

53. Ibid.

54. Hance, *African Economic Development*, 129.

55. Ibid.

56. African Union, "State of Transport Sector Development in Africa," *Report of the Conference of African Ministers of Transport, 21-25 April* (Addis Ababa: African Union, 2008), 10.

57. United Nations, *UN Transport and Communications Decade for Africa 1978-88 Vol. 1: Global Strategy and Plan of Action, First Phase, 1980-1983* (Addis Ababa, Ethiopia, May. 1979).

58. Ibid.

59. Pradip K. Ghosh, ed., *Developing Africa: A Modern Perspective* (Westport, CT: Greenwood Press, 1984), 125.

60. United Nations Economic and Social Council, Economic Commission for Africa, "The Transport Situation in Africa," Addis Ababa, 2009, 9.

61. Ibid.

62. Pedersen, "The Changing Structure of Transport."

63. Jeremiah1. Dibua, "Journey to Nowhere: Neo-liberalism and Africa's Development Crisis," *Comparative Studies of South Asia, Africa and Middle East* 18, no. 2, (1998): 120–121; Neo Simutanyi, *Neo-Liberalism and the Relevance of Marxism to Africa: The Case of Zambia*, Paper presented to the 3rd International Conference on 'The Works of Karl Marx and the Challenges of the 21st Century,' Havana, Cuba, May 3–6, 2006, 3–4; Tony Killick, ed., *The Quest for Economic Stabilization: the IMF and the Third World* (London: Heinemann, 1984).

64. Virginia Dehancey, "The Economies of Africa," 128.

65. John S. Saul and Colin Leys, "Sub-Saharan Africa in Global Capitalism," *Monthly Review* (July–August 1999): 19–20.

66. Bullock, *The Results of Railway Privatisation in Africa*, 2.

67. Pedersen, "The Changing Structure of Transport," 13.

68. Guy Arnold, *A Guide to African Political and Economic Development*, 139.

69. Ibid.

70. Ibid.

71. Bullock, *The Results of Railway Privatisation in Africa*, 2.

72. Ibid., 4.

73. Ibid., 10.

74. Ibid.

75. Ibid., 6–9.

76. Pedersen, "The Changing Structure of Transport," 14; Brendan Martin, "The World Bank, Railway Privatisation and Trades Unions," Friedrich Ebert Stiftung Global Trade Union Program Briefing Paper No. 4 (2007): 3.

77. Ibid.

78. Shehu Abubakar, "Unease in Transport Ministry over N=12.3b railway to CCECC," *Sunday Trust*, November 22, 2009, http://Sunday.dailytrust.com/index.php?option=com; Editorial, "Reviving Rail Transport System," *Nigerian Compass*, June 4, 2010, http://compassnewspaper.com/NG/index.php? Option=com.

79. Ayoola, "Political Economy of Rail Transportation," 204–210.

80. Bullock, *The Results of Railway Privatisation in Africa*, 11.

81. Pierre Pozzo di Borgo, et al., "Review of Selected Railway Concessions in Sub-Saharan Africa," (Washington DC: World Bank, 2006), 22–25.

82. Ibid., 3.

83. The first external loan secured after Sitarail took over the management of the railway between Burkina Faso and Côte d'Ivoire was for $63.3 million. Of this amount, only $6.6 million was directly borrowed by the concessionaire. The balance, $56.7 million, was borrowed in the name of the two African governments involved.

84. di Borgo, et al., "Review of Selected Railway Concessions," 22–25.

85. For instance, it took four years in Cameroon and five years in Mozambique (Ncala railroad concession) before the concessionaires started investing in infrastructures.

86. di Borgo, et al., "Review of Selected Railway Concessions," 22–25.

87. Ibid., 30.

88. Paul Amos and Richard Bullock, "The Financial Performance of Non-Urban Services," Transport Paper 14, World Bank, Washington, DC.

Part II

DEMOCRATIZATION, DEMOCRATIC INSTITUTIONS, AND UNEVEN REGIONAL DEVELOPMENT

Chapter 7

The Legislature and Tenure Elongation in African Presidential Democracies

Joseph Yinka Fashagba and Rotimi Ajayi

INTRODUCTION

Quite a number of African countries returned to democracy from the late 1980s to the 1990s.[1] Both within and outside the continent, there was great euphoria as many states returned to democracy. However, not all the new democracies in Africa have made steady progress toward consolidation. Indeed, while periodic elections have been held as a symbol of democracy, constitutional breaches on tenure of office among incumbent presidents to elongate their stay in power have been very common. Under the current wave of democracy, this has become an emerging phenomenon, spreading very fast with an undermining effect on democracy in Africa.

This phenomenon put some new African democracies under threat of reversal or instigated political instability, taking place under the watch, or sometimes with, the active connivance of the legislative institutions of some states. However, while in some states, the legislatures have served as bulwark for the constitution thereby averting constitutional breach, in others, the legislatures demonstrated incapability in checking the executive from having its way. Consequently, in the latter assemblies, the legislatures in fact became willing tools for the subversion of the national constitution.

The development epitomized the fact that something is either fundamentally wrong with either the constitution or the legislative institution of which the symptom is the weakness of the institution. It could also be that some other extraneous factors with weighty impact on legislative behavior are at work. Steven Fish, in his work, argued that a strong legislature provides a buffer for democracy and in the absence of a strong legislative institution, democracy responds to the vagaries of the centrifugal pressure that may ultimately terminate it.[2] In a recent study of some national legislatures in Africa vis-à-vis the constitutions of the countries, some scholars noted that there exists a significant variation in the powers given to the various legislatures by the new constitutions of the new African democracies.[3] Although the work is essentially and unnecessarily legalistic as well as bereft of empirical quality, it nevertheless helped us to understand that certain constitutional provisions exist in Africa that did not help the legislature to be a strong institution.

Under the new African democracies, the reality has been that the legislative institutions, working under different institutional, constitutional, structural/operational conditions, environments, and constraints appeared to have a different capacity to resist any executive action geared toward undermining the national constitution. Thus, while some assemblies were able to resist executive interference in their internal business, others appear to be very vulnerable to the extent that their executives succeeded in using them to approve tenure elongation without any resistance.

It is against this background that one finds it compelling to interrogate the factors underlying the variation in legislative capacity to resist the executive in amending the national constitutions to suit their own personal and narrow ambition (which undermines the very constitution under which they gained power). To achieve this, the chapter takes a look at four African states, namely Nigeria, Malawi, Burundi, and Rwanda. In the four states, until the incumbent presidents manipulated the political process or attempted to make the parliaments amend their respective national constitutions, all four constitutions provided for a maximum of two terms for the president. However, in both Nigeria and Malawi, the legislatures were able to resist executive pressure, thereby making it impossible for the executive president to continue in office after the constitutionally permitted two terms. Indeed, the two presidents failed in their attempt to elongate their tenure. On the other hand, the legislature in Rwanda caved in to presidential pressure to amend the constitution to elongate the tenure of the president. In the case of Burundi, although the legislature resisted the attempt to elongate the tenure of the president, the president still had his way by using the court. In view of this, this chapter attempts to clarify what therefore accounted for the ability of some states to resist the pressure to change their rules while others failed. This is the major question that this chapter seeks to answer. The data for the study was sourced from the secondary sources. Where necessary, we utilized some descriptive statistics, but our major analytic technique comprised both the explanatory and comparative analysis. In the next section, we undertake a brief review of the literature on the state of legislature in new presidential democracies in Africa.

THE LEGISLATURES IN NEW AFRICAN PRESIDENTIAL DEMOCRACIES

The rebirth of the multiparty-based legislative institution in new African democracies is a recent development. In different countries, legislative hiatus was a significant and conspicuous feature. In some countries, some authoritarian regimes maintained what could be called a shadow of the legislative institution. Unlike in some other forms of government, democratic constitutions not only create, but also specify the role of the legislature and its relationships with the executive or government.[4]

Thus, just like any other major institutions of government, the legislature derives its existence, power, and functions from the constitution. However, the degree of power exercised by each legislature is sometimes both a function of the constitutional provisions and some institutional, operational, and political factors within and outside the legislature. The implication is that the capacity of a legislature to carry out both its constitutionally prescribed roles and institutionally generated responsibilities vary from one country to the other.

On the basis of the foregoing, and for the purpose of our analysis in this study, we will classify the African legislatures into two—namely, the strong and weak. There are the legislatures that appear to demonstrate that they are strong enough to shape government policy, carry out the oversight of the executive, and check executive excesses. This they do whether there is power alternation or not. The second category of legislatures are those who are considered to be weak. Yet, in this category, there are those characterized by inconsistency in terms of the power they wield vis-à-vis the executive. Such legislature may appear to be strong at one point, but such demonstration of strength often fades away from time to time, leaving the executive with much discretion in determining the direction of policy and governance in general. The second variant of the weak type is the one which lacks the power to challenge the executive in policy or law making, oversight, and other areas. This categorization is implicitly evident in the work of Joel Barkan. Consequently, with reference to Africa, Joel Barkan and Fred Matiangi averred that in a number of countries, the legislatures have exhibited weakness, while in others, they have been assertive in checking the excesses of government.[5]

In the first category, among the countries identified to possess strong legislatures are Kenya and South Africa. To be sure, in the areas of budget-making, administrative scrutiny, and policy-making, the Kenyan National Assembly has demonstrated a significant level of assertiveness.[6] In the countries belonging to this category, legislative assertiveness in the form of blocking government proposed legislation, introducing substantial amendments to executive bills, scrutiny of administration, as well as overriding executive veto have been witnessed in one country or the other since the restoration of democracy in the latest wave of democratization across the continent. The power of the executive has been sometimes severely curtailed in a manner that helped to protect the national constitution. This has been witnessed in Nigeria under a National Assembly dominated by the ruling People's Democratic Party (PDP). The Nigerian central legislature has largely remained autonomous in exercising its powers, thereby curtailing executive excesses in the most glaring manner since 1999.[7] Executive discretion is therefore restrained or curtailed, especially when and where the exercise of such power could cause a breach of the constitution. In addition, in such assemblies there is a robust and well-organized opposition presence. The latter feature helps to ensure executive accountability, or at least exposes any untoward executive action. Ken Opalo has argued that the executive often dominates the legislature when the ruling party has a majority,[8] as in Nigeria where the PDP dominated the legislature for sixteen years. But this did not translate into legislating the opposition out of contention. Rather, there is evidence to prove that, at different times, the National Assembly challenged the executive on certain national issues and legislations, with the active involvement of the opposition. This was sometimes done with a deep embarrassing effect on the ruling PDP. Indeed, in order to protect democracy and the national constitution, the legislature that is strong and assertive remains the only institution of state invested with power to keep executives in check and answerable to the people.

The second category of legislatures, as earlier noted, is further subdivided into two. The first subcategory is of the legislatures who demonstrate strength and assertiveness, but only in an unsustainable manner. Some writers believe that while South Africa and Kenya belong to the class of countries with strong assemblies, the legislatures in the second category are those whose powers are largely volatile and sometimes determined by the executive's mood. The Ugandan legislature comes under this category. A number of works on the Ugandan National Assembly show that from 1986, under the no-party legislative system, the assembly was weak and incapable of challenging the executive. This was largely so because the legislators were very often the nominees of the president, while the use of patronage was effectively deployed to ensure that the president maintained a firm grip on the assembly.[9] Opalo equally noted that the significant control that the president wields over legislative elections, especially of incumbents' reelection bids, sometimes affects the prospect for sustained legislative assertiveness in some countries. Thus, in countries where the president holds strong control over the legislative career of new members and incumbents the legislature may be incapable of exercising sustained assertiveness against the executive.[10]

The second subcategory under the weak legislatures is of those who are considered to be lacking the power to challenge the executive, modify legislations, or carry out any major oversight function. Under this category are legislatures of Benin and Ghana.[11] The legislature of Ghana suffers from certain constitutional provisions that gave disproportionate power to the executive vis-à-vis the legislature. Similarly, the members of assembly of Benin are very well aware of their helplessness in both oversight and policy-making, thus leaving the executive with a huge preponderant power. Conversely, a significant discretional power is vested in the president of Ghana, which either intentionally or unintentionally erodes legislative influence and power in certain areas of governance. Indeed, the discretional power of the president of Ghana incapacitates the legislature from exercising effective control over government.

Having attempted to categorize African legislatures on the basis of the degree of influence, power, and relevance in policy and law making and oversight of administration (unlike some works that adopted the constitution as the basis for classification), we now focus our next attention on our case study. This is important, because it will help us understand the political dynamics of executive power play in the African states and investigate why some national legislatures were able to resist the pressure to undermine their national constitutions for the extension of the tenure of their respective presidents beyond the terms while others were not.

THE LEGISLATURE AND TENURE ELONGATION

From the section above, it was made clear that legislatures on the continent of Africa vary in terms of their power and capacity in relations to the executive. The variation in their power consequently shapes their relationship with the executive, especially in regard to their ability to check executive excesses and to serve as a bulwark for the national constitution. It is on this note that this section examines the rationale behind the inability of some legislatures to vote against the proposal to change the rules and thereby extend the presidential tenure beyond what was originally provided for under the constitution in which the president was elected and took oath of office. Specifically, our focus here is Rwanda. Similarly, we interrogate the factors that made it impossible for the executive to change the rule using the legislatures in Nigeria and Malawi, where tenure elongation's bid of the presidents failed in the assembly. Finally, we examine Burundi, where despite the negative vote on the executive proposal to amend the relevant law to extend his tenure, the president still succeeded in securing a third term using the court.

Nigeria's presidential constitution of 1999, which has now been amended three times, no doubt provided for limited terms. Each term, according to the constitution, is four years. Indeed, the constitution provided for a maximum of two consecutive terms for any president that wins a second term. The likely purposes of the provisions are not far-fetched. The tendency for a president to become lax after staying in power for a long time is always a possibility.[12] In addition, fresh or alternative ideas that may be required in government over time may be denied if an individual perpetually remains at the helm of affairs. Consequently, most national constitutions often provide for term limits, with some countries making it impossible for an incumbent to seek reelection immediately after the expiration of the first term. In Nigeria, a provision for two terms of four years each was added to the amended 1999 constitution to ensure that no dictator or unresponsive institutions were created by a sit-tight president.

Despite the clear position of the amended 1999 constitution, an attempt was made under President Olusegun Obasanjo's presidency to change the two terms rules halfway into his second term in office. As a clever man, he was not personally involved, but his political aides, ministers, state governors, and politicians who benefitted from federal patronage became the major proponents, sponsors, and anchors of the "presidential agenda" to give the president a third term of four years. However, giving the president an extension of terms is a constitutional matter; mere wishing and canvassing for it may not get the job done. Consequently, beyond the various individuals engaged outside the National Assembly, some key members of the National Assembly were coopted into the "campaign" for tenure elongation for the president. To be sure, the deputy senate president, Ibrahim Mantu, became the anchorman for the tenure elongation agenda in the National Assembly. His involvement in the project would not have been taken seriously but for his position as the chairman of the "all important" committee on the amendment of the 1999 constitution between 2003 and 2007.

Considering the strategic position of Mantu in the Senate between 1999 and 2007, first as the deputy Senate president and later as the chairman of Constitution Review Committee, and third, his antecedent based on allegation of graft made against him by the then minister of FCT in 2003, most members of the National Assembly who did not support the agenda as well as members of the public who were opposed to the tenure elongation attempt mobilized to neutralize the efforts of the pro-third-term members of the National Assembly.[13] Indeed, some members of the National Assembly were alleged to have compromised by receiving gratification in attempts to broaden and strengthen the support base of the agenda within the National Assembly through the coordinating effort of the deputy Senate president. This latter development resulted in the polarization of the assembly.

Despite the tension generated both within the assembly and the larger society, the leadership of the National Assembly (especially the president of Senate and the speaker of the House of Representatives) was calm while members became polarized. Indeed, in a 2015 interview with *Vanguard*, a popular Nigerian daily, Adolphus Wabara, Senate president from 2003 to 2005, pointed out that his refusal to support President Obasanjo's third-term agenda when approached by the president's close associates and friends was what led to his forced resignation from office, not an alleged bribery scandal.[14]

The debate over the third-term agenda polarized the society along pro-third and antithird term. With the massive negative public and media opinions against the tenure elongation agenda, it became clear that the National Assembly was facing the greatest test of the republic. Thus, while the review exercise made significant progress and all appeared set to give the president his wish, the bill on constitutional amendment was given a technical death. This was achieved in the Senate by mentioning the bill the very day the main sponsor was absent from the chamber and when less than one third of the members who would have formed quorum were not in attendance.[15] Based on the rule on the Senate, any bill so mentioned dies. Thus, the bill was given a befitting burial, thereby putting an end to the tenure elongation ambition of the president.

It has been very evident under the fourth republic that the two chambers of the National Assembly exhibited a significant level of assertiveness and independence, despite the fact that the ruling PDP also controlled the majority in the two chambers from 1999 to 2015. It controlled at least 60 percent between 1999 and 2013. Its dominance of the National Assembly was reduced following the mass defection from the PDP to the newly formed All Progressive Congress (APC) in 2013. This reduced the members' grip and strength of the ruling PDP in the National Assembly. We should note that party switching has been a major feature of the legislature at both federal and state levels in Nigeria since 1999.[16] The fact that the ruling PDP controlled the two chambers of the National Assembly did not translate to a blind support for a president trying to breach the constitution that the president swore to defend and protect. Asking for an extension of tenure from an institution that the president had all the while treated with disdain appeared to be a major indiscretion on the part of the president. Similarly, considering the nature of ethnic fragmentation and politics in Nigeria, the northerners were bent on taking over power after the two terms of Obasanjo and would not have given the necessary support to get the constitution amended for the third-term project.[17] In the next section, we will be focusing on Malawi, an East African state which aborted the attempt of the president to elongate his terms.

Malawi is another country where an attempt to undermine the constitution was made by the president in 2003. Like Nigeria, the Malawian National Constitution provided for two terms for the president. However, unlike Nigeria, the president enjoys the grace of two terms of five years each provided he is reelcected after the first term. However, not wanting to be different from other leaders with the sit-tight mentality prevalent among African leaders, the president of Malawi, Bakili Muluzi, sought to elongate his tenure in 2003. Although Muluzi controlled the government as well as having a majority in parliament, he was faced with a deeply divided society along pro-third and antithird term. In addition, his own party was deeply divided over his ambition. Perhaps the president underestimated the resolve of the opposition against his ambition, largely because he was aware of the significance attached to patronage among members of parliament.[18] To be sure, while Malawi's economy was, and is, not too strong (as it largely depends on donors to fund its development budget), the government has been able to establish a patronage regime in the form of both appointment and monetary reward to sway parliamentary outcome to its favor from time to time.

Perhaps, because of the role of patronage, not only did an opposition member on the platform of the Alliance for Democracy (AD) introduce the tenure elongation amendment proposal in the legislature, but also twenty-nine members of opposition and an independent member voted in support of the proposal to amend the constitution to meet the ambition of the president for a third term.[19] Fifty-nine members of the opposition, however, voted against the proposed amendment. Indeed, the president would have succeeded had he not lost the vote to extend his tenure narrowly by three votes. If the three votes had gone to him, that would have given him the required two-thirds majority to pass the proposed amendment to the constitution. In our next discussion, we shall examine the case of Burundi.

Burundi's transition to the current democratic government was anything but smooth.[20] The civil war that ravaged the country was the basis of the negotiation between the parties to the conflict. On a mutual post-war agreement, a two-term presidency was agreed upon and provided for in the constitution. However, like many of his colleagues on the continent, as the end of the second term of President Pierre Nkurunziza of Burundi beckoned, the urge to stay beyond the two terms stipulated in the country's law appeared to become irresistible for him. Indeed, rather than starting to prepare for life after office, the president changed his country's constitution to elongate his tenure—this became the president's major preoccupation. Perhaps the overwhelming majority status of his party in the legislature gave him the false hope that he would secure the required two thirds for the passage of the proposed constitutional amendment making him eligible to participate in an election that would have given a third term in office.

Although the president's ambition was obvious, it appeared that he was bereft of any support from all critical stakeholders and every segment of the society, including his own party and the civil society, among others. To be sure, while the president submitted a proposal to the legislature in which his ruling party controlled the majority required to get his proposal passed, it was evident that apart from some members of opposition, some members of the president's ruling party were not in support of his attempt to circumvent the constitution. Consequently, all those opposed to the third-term bid from both the ruling and minority party voted against the proposal to kill it. Consequently, President Nkurunziza of Burundi narrowly lost the 2015 parliamentary vote that would have altered the constitution to make him eligible to run for a third term in office.[21]

Although Nkurunziza lost in parliament, that was not sufficient enough to discourage him. Perhaps emboldened by the way President Samuel Nujoma of Namibia circumvented his country's constitution to secure an extension after two terms in office through the court, Nkurunziza approached the constitutional court in Burundi, and with harassment and intimidation, he secured the court's approval.[22] The pronouncement of the court facilitated his participation and eventual "victory" in the 2015 presidential election.

Another African country where a successful attempt was made to alter the constitution to create room for the president to continue in office beyond second term in office was Rwanda. Unlike in Nigeria, Burundi, and Malawi, the Rwandan National Assembly exhibited lack of political will and gut to vote against the third-term bid of President Paul Kagame. Indeed, the action of the legislature in terms of the way the voting on the constitutional amendment went suggest that the legislature was a pliant institution. No point proves this better than the voting patterns; out of the twenty-four members of the Senate, all twenty-four voted for the amendment to permit a third term for the president. In the parliament, the second chamber of Rwanda, seventy-nine of the eighty members also voted in support of the amendment to accommodate a third term to enable the president to run again for a new term of seven years in 2017.

Some or a combination of reasons could have accounted for such voting pattern. First, executive intimidation or subtle threat could have forced members to support the amendment blindly; second, the president might have employed patronage or outright monetary inducement to sway legislators; third, the legislators might have responded to popular opinion among the public demanding an extension of tenure for the president for the stability of the state; fourth, the alleged intolerance of opposition by the ruling party could have suffocated all forms of dissent, thereby paving the way for total support among the ruling party members of parliament; fifth, the small size of the assembly makes it possible to engage and handle the legislators individually. In fact, in all, there are 104 legislators which makes it quite easy to ensure compliance in voting; and sixth, the fact that majority of members are women makes the assembly more likely to follow presidential lead. By 2013, 65 percent of members were women. This does not mean that in other male-dominated assemblies in Africa the presidents do not have their way. Indeed, in many countries, male-dominated members voted in favor of altering their constitutions to allow for a third term for presidents.

Although we cannot say with certainty the extent to which each of the factors shaped legislative voting on the third-term bid of the president, we cannot rule out that a combination of two or more of the factors could have delivered such a vote in both the Senate and Parliament. Nevertheless, there was an allegation against the ruling party to the effect that it stifled opposition in Rwanda.[23]

However, the fact that members of the public were allowed to participate through referendum and the majority voted in support of the amendment shows that the legislature also sought to reflect the will of the people in supporting the proposed third term. Consequently, the president has successfully secured the constitutional approval to contest the presidential election for the third term in 2017 through legislative voting, legitimated or approved by the public through referendum. Thus, Rwanda remained one of the African countries where the legislatures did fail to muster the necessary political will to stop the president from adjusting the rules in the middle of the game.

CONCLUSION

Starting from 1999, the PDP has been the majority in the Nigerian Legislature at the national level. The dominance continued until the major implosion that decimated it in 2013. The legislative elections of 2003 shows that the PDP won 223 of the 360 seats in the House of Representatives. The then main opposition party, the All Nigerian People's Party (ANPP) received ninety-six seats, the Alliance for Democracy won thirty-six seats, the United Nigeria People's Party (UNPP) had two seats, the National Democratic Party (NDP) got one, the All Progressive Grand Alliance (APGA) won two seats, the People's Redemption Party (PRP) got one, and others one. By this, the PDP, which was also the ruling party, had 61.94 percent of seats in the House of Representatives between 2003 and 2007, leaving the opposition with about 38 percent of seats in the chamber.[25] Similarly, in the Senate, the 2003 elections showed that the PDP won 76 seats out of the 109 seats of the chamber, the ANPP got 27, while the AD received 6 seats. By this, the PDP controlled 69.72 of the seat.[24] With this background, the president of Nigeria must have developed false hope and an expectation without reckoning the disdain with which he had treated the institution he would someday look up to for a favor to alter the constitution to actualize his inordinate third-term bid.

Unlike the Nigerian president, whose party controlled about 70 percent of members of Senate and 61 percent of the House of Representatives in the National Assembly during which time an attempt was made to change the constitution, the Malawian ruling United Democratic Front (UDF) controlled 95 (49.48 percent) of the 192 seats in parliament. This appeared to place him at the mercy of the opposition members who took advantage of their numerical strength to nail the ambition of the president. While the president needed thirty-three votes from members of opposition in the parliament to realize his ambition, he was only able to muster thirty, while fifty-nine opposition members voted against him. This demonstrated the role and importance of a virile legislative minority in entrenching democracy in a society where executive lawlessness and rascality is the norm.[25] Although all members of the ruling party voted for the amendment, the initial disadvantage in number of members could not be offset by the votes of the thirty opposition members who teamed up with them.

However, in Nigeria, despite the fact that the ruling party controlled more than the two-thirds majority required to pass the amendment bill to make the president eligible for a third term, the majority members of the party working in concert with the president of the Senate ensured that the bill was given a technical knockout. The step appeared to be the best option for the members of the ruling party in the national assembly. To be sure, despite the provision for separation of powers in the 1999 Constitution and even after its alteration in 2010, the Nigerian president constantly meddled in the internal business of the two-chamber National Assembly and, in fact, masterminded the impeachment or forced resignation of two Senate presidents in 2000 and 2005. Considering the way and manner the president constantly interfered with the internal business of the National Assembly, he only succeeded in making many enemies for himself from the institution. The antagonistic relationship resulting from the meddlesomeness of the Obasanjo Administration in the National Assembly was, perhaps, a major reason why members embarrassed him by killing the bill with which he sought to extend his term beyond the two permitted under the 1999 Constitution. What this goes to suggest is that, whatever the motivating factor for legislative action, the Nigerian Legislature and others in Africa could serve as the protector of the general will of their constituents by mustering the required political will to protect the constitutions, irrespective of the pressure that the presidents may mount on the institution.

With respect to Malawi, while the popular view in the literature on comparative politics is that the Malawi Assembly is vulnerable, due to the invisible hand of patronage, the significant presence of members of opposition, who voted in line with their conscience, appeared to be important in off-setting the role of patronage in giving the president a firm grip at all time. Perhaps it is safe to argue that issues over which patronage may play a key role vary according to the issue at stake, the interests of the elites, as well as the civil society and the public. And in the case of the third-term ambition of President Muluzi, the groundswell of opposition from the public must have emboldened the fifty-nine (30.7 percent) members of opposition who failed to succumb to executive pressure to undermine the national constitution.

Unlike in Malawi where every member of the ruling party in Parliament voted in favor of a third term for the president, despite controlling the majority of members in their respective national assemblies, the presidents of Burundi in 2015 and Nigeria in 2006 did not enjoy even the support of all members of their parties on the unconstitutional moves of the presidents to change their countries' constitutions in favor of the ambition of the presidents. Indeed, although patronage is known to be a major political tool to build an elite coalition in Nigeria, it did not help the ambition of the Nigerian president to have a third term in 2006. This contrasted with the legislative voting in Rwanda, where 99 percent of members voted in support of the proposal to extend the tenure of the president.

Curiously, while a large segment of the public in Nigeria, Burundi, and Malawi kicked against the proposed extension for their presidents and succeeded in seeing to the failure of the bid in parliament (although sometimes with a very narrow margin), the support of the people of Rwanda and some segment of the international community for the proposed change to the constitution to allow third terms perhaps played a role in the outcome of the legislative voting that subsequently received the support of the people in referendum in Rwanda in 2015.

Indeed, what has become evident in Africa so far in this study is that while we cannot rule out the possibility of a president making an effort to alter the constitution to extend their stay in power, much depends on the legislature to muster the necessary political will to stop such undemocratic ambition. Similarly, the role of a viable and uncompromising opposition is inevitable in taming this third-term virus, which has proved to be very contagious, from desecrating the presidential democracy and constitutional term limit in Africa. Yet, the actions of the media, the civil society, and the general public in Nigeria, Malawi, and Burundi have demonstrated how public support can spur the legislature into serving as a bulwark for the constitution.

NOTES

1. Nicolas van de Walle, "Presidentialism and Clientelism in Africa's Emerging Party Systems," *Journal of Modern African Studies* 41, no. 2 (2003): 297–321.
2. M. Steven Fish, "Stronger Legislatures, Stronger Democracies," *British Journal of Politics* 17, no. 1 (2006): 5–20.

3. Lia Nijzink, Shaheen Mozaffar, and Elisabete Azevedo, "Can Parliaments Enhance the Quality of Democracy on the Continent? An Analysis of the Institutional Capacity and Public Perceptions," Center for Social Science Research Working Paper, no. 160 (2006).

4. Ian Lienert, "Role of the Legislature in Budget Processes," Technical Notes and Manuals, International Monetary Fund, 2010.

5. Joel D. Barkan and Fred Matiangi, "Kenya's Tortuous Path to Successful Legislative Development," in *Legislative Power in Emerging African Democracies*, ed. Joel D. Barkan (London, Lynne Rienner Publishers, 2009), 33–72.

6. Ibid.

7. Joseph Yinka Fashagba, "Legislative Oversight under the Nigerian Presidential System," *The Journal of Legislative Studies* 15, no. 4 (2009): 539–559.

8. Ken. O. Opalo. "African Elections: Two Divergent Trends," *Journal of Democracy* 23, no 3 (2012): 80–93.

9. Nelson Kasfir and Steven Hippo Twebaze, "The Rise and Ebb of Uganda's No-Party Parliament," in Barkan, *Legislative Power*, 73–108.

10. Opalo "African Elections," 2012.

11. Adamolekun, L. Ladipo and M. Laleye, "Benin: Legislative Development in Africa's First Democratizer," in Barkan, *Legislative Power,* 109–145.

12. Read Opalo, "African elections," 2012.

13. Fashagba, "Legislative Oversight, 539–559.

14. Emmanuel Aziken, "Defection: Why Tambuwal Should Step Down—Wabara," *Vanguard*, November 3, 2014, https://www.vanguardngr.com/2014/11/defection-tambuwal-step-wabara.

15. Fashagba, "Legislative Oversight."

16. Joseph Yinka Fashagba, "Party Switching in the Nigerian Senate under the Fourth Republic," *The Journal of Legislative Studies* 20, no 4 (2014): 516–541.

17. See Fashagba, "Legislative Oversight."

18. Daniel J. Young, "An Initial look into Party Switching in Africa: Evidence from Malawi," *Political Party* 18, no 2 (2012): 1–21.

19. Daniel N. Posner and Daniel J. Young, "The Institutionalization of Political Power in Africa," *Journal of Democracy* 18, no 3 (2007): 126–140.

20. Opalo "African Elections," 2012.

21. Posner and Young, "The Institutionalization of Political Power," 2007.

22. "Burundi Court Backs President Nkurunziza on Third-Term, *BBC Africa*, May 5, 2015, https://www.bbc.com/news/world-africa-32588658.

23. "Africa, 99% of Rwanda Lawmakers Vote for Changes to Allow Kagame Extend his 15 Years in Power," *Mail and Guardian,* July 14, 2015.

24. Emmanuel Remi Aiyede and Emeka Njoku, "The Nigerian Senate," in *The Legislature in Nigeria Vol 1*, eds. Emmanuel O. Ojo and Julius Shola Omotola (Ibadan: John Archer Publishers Ltd., 2014), 142–162.

25. Joseph Yinka Fashagba, "The Nigerian House of Representatives," in Ojo and Omotola, *The Legislature in Nigeria*, 163–184.

Chapter 8

The African Diaspora and the Quest for Democracy in Africa

Revisiting the June 12, 1993, Presidential Election in Nigeria

Udida A. Undiyaundeye

INTRODUCTION

Frustrated by the sorry plight of his fellow Blacks in the United States, in 1859 a prominent African American, a physician, an abolitionist, and an officer in the U.S. military, Martin R. Delany, visited Abeokuta, in Yorubaland, in present-day Nigeria, where he signed a treaty with its chiefs for the settlement of African Americans wishing to relocate to the African homeland. Delany envisioned that this settlement would be the vanguard of a prosperous state he hoped to establish in Africa.[1] This state, he hoped, would not only be the pride of Black people, but would also command the fear and respect of other races of the world. The matter was never explored beyond the initial visit to Abeokuta, apparently as a result of the conditions Delany had to contend with on his return home and because of the onset of the civil war in 1865. While nothing much came out of this attempt, this idea remained and was resurrected by Marcus A. Garvey nearly eighty years later. A Jamaican who later became a great orator and one of the greatest campaigners for Black political emancipation, Garvey campaigned, not only for the restoration of Black pride and dignity and the amelioration of the economic situation of the African Americans, but also for the establishment of a strong and powerful nation that would command world respect and be a rallying point for the struggle for the attainment of the aspirations of Black people all over the world.[2]

Nigeria literally took the bull by the horns when it warned against the denigration of African Americans in its maiden speech at the United Nations in New York, in October 1960. This speech was delivered by the newly independent state's foreign minister, Jaja Wachuku, in October 1960, to the loud applause of African Americans. Nigeria's size and its human and natural resources predisposed the country to lead the crusade for uplifting the Black race. As for the African American community, it constitutes the largest pool of black industrial, technological, financial, and scientific elite that could partner with Nigeria to work toward the mutual benefit of black people.[3] It was in this context that African Americans were keen followers of the transition to civil rule in Nigeria instituted by General Ibrahim B. Babangida, when he became Nigeria's military president in 1985.[4] African Americans, through the Congressional Black Caucus (CBC) which had members on both the House and Senate Foreign Relations Committees, exemplified this keen interest when it set up a task force under the chairmanship of Congressman William J. Jefferson, from Louisiana, to monitor the presidential election in which M.K.O. Abiola was one of two candidates.[5] Even before the election, Abiola had cultivated a very robust relationship with the African American leadership. The CBC task force came out of the desire to promote democracy in Africa. The Caucus felt that if democracy could take roots and thrive in Nigeria, Africa's most populous nation, the future of democracy in Africa would be bright. As a result of the robust relations between Abiola and the Black leadership in the United States, he was endorsed and supported for the June 1993 presidential election.

The presidential election, which concluded the transition to civilian rule that Nigerians had patiently waited for took place on June 12, conducted by the National Electoral Commission (NEC), chaired by Humphrey Nwosu. Although actual voting was done secretly, votes were counted in the open in the presence of NEC officials and party representatives. The election, at its conclusion, was declared peaceful, free, and fair. The release of the election results, awaited with high hopes by Nigerians, began on June 15. The first results, from fourteen states and the Federal Capital Territory (FCT) showed that the Social Democratic Party (SDP) candidates Abiola and Baba Gana Kingibe had a substantial lead. They won 8,341,309 votes (58.36 percent) out of the 14,296,396 votes cast, while Alhaji Bashir Othman Tofa of the National Republican Convention (NRC) won 5,952,086 (41.64 percent) votes.[6] The next day an Abuja High Court ordered a halt to further announcement of results, much to the chagrin of Nigerians.[7]

Abiola's victory was unprecedented because it was only in two of the thirty states—Sokoto and Kebbi—that he failed to obtain the mandatory one-third of votes cast.[8] Abiola was very successful because he was seen as a candidate of change, a means of easing out the military as there seemed to be no candidate that was capable of challenging it. Often associated with Abiola were qualities such as courage, hard work, philanthropy, and altruism. These sterling qualities, especially philanthropy, stood him in good stead. Indeed, his landslide victory could partly be associated with his philanthropic activities.

In fact, this was what brought him to national and international fame. It was on account of his philanthropy that the Congressional Black Caucus issued the following tribute regarding him:

> Because of this man, there is both cause for hope and certainty that the agony and protests of those who suffer injustice shall give way to peace and human dignity. The children of the world shall know the great work of this extraordinary leader and his fervent mission to right wrong, to do justice, and to serve mankind. The enemies which imperil the future of generations to come: poverty, ignorance, disease, hunger, and racism have each seen effects of the valiant work of Chief Abiola. Through him and others like him, never again will freedom rest in the domain of the few. We, the members of the Congressional Black Caucus salute him this day as a hero in the global pursuit to preserve the history and the legacy of the African diaspora."[9]

It was also on account of his philanthropy, which was color, religious, and ethnic blind, that he became a recipient of a host of traditional titles and honorary doctorate degrees from universities within and outside Nigeria. What made his victory such a landmark in Nigerian political history was that religion, which had always been a dominant factor in the country's geopolitics, played no role in the election. Abiola ran on a Muslim/Muslim ticket, which in a normal run, would have been a hard sell in religiously conscious Nigeria.

ANNULMENT OF THE ELECTION

For seven days after the court order to halt the release of the election results, gloom and uncertainty enveloped the country. The silence was broken with a bombshell. Nduka Irabor, press secretary to the Vice President Augustus Aikhomu, circulated what was described as "an unsigned and undated statement on a plain piece of paper without government letterhead or the president's seal."[10] This was the statement that announced the annulment of the election. The statement continued to terminate the eight-year-long transition program and all court proceedings regarding the election. It also repealed the decrees that governed the transition, suspended the electoral commission, and nullified all its acts. The immediate reaction to the annulment was violent demonstration in the Southwest, Abiola's ethnic homeland.

Although, an important figure from the Muslim North, Ibrahim Dasuki, the Sultan of Sokoto and the president general of Supreme Council for Islamic Affairs, issued a statement that ended with an appeal that Abiola's mandate be validated,[11] much of the opposition to the election's annulment came from the Southwest. Yoruba traditional rulers, the obas, also denounced the annulment and called for a reversal and installation of Abiola as president.[12] Former Head of State Olusegun Obasanjo also joined in the outcry against the annulment.[13] Abiola himself protested the annulment, arguing that the courts that granted injunctions to an organization, the Association for a Better Nigeria (ABN), which sought to halt the announcement of the rest of the election results, "deliberately intended to cause the greatest possible confusion."[14]

The international community also condemned the annulment. Nigerians living overseas expressed outrage and some Nigerians living in the United States marched to the Nigerian Embassy in Washington, DC, and vandalized it.[15] The United States not only cancelled its $22.8 million aid package to Nigeria but also expelled the Nigerian military attaché from the country while it recalled its own. The United Kingdom suspended all military assistance to Nigeria and denied visas to Nigerian military personnel. The European Union (EU) and other non-African states condemned the annulment.[16] These condemnations were only tough in words, but lacked the bite in action because, as the military authorities correctly guessed, the West did not have the courage to take the one action that mattered most in the circumstance: oil sanctions that would have hurt it badly.[17] Meanwhile, the federal government had spent a whopping ₦75 billion on the transition program.

But then, why was the annulment so roundly condemned, both within and outside the country? In Abiola's victory was the hope of advancement for Nigeria, a country that had witnessed untold ethnoregional and religious upheavals in its postcolonial history. About the election, it is pertinent to note that a southern politician was accepted as leader by the Hausa-Fulani majority of the North, and that the election was adjudged by observers from all over the world as free, fair, and credible; indeed, the freest the country had ever conducted.[18] The job of unifying Nigeria seemed cut out for Abiola.

On August 3, 1993, Abiola slipped out of Nigeria to the United Kingdom and subsequently to the United States where he was granted audience at the White House. Altogether he spent fifty-two days abroad canvassing support for the validation of his mandate, and returned on September 24.[19] The condemnation and protests that trailed the annulment forced Babangida to step aside, putting in place the Interim National Government (ING), led by the seasoned businessman, Ernest Shonekan, an ethnic compatriot of Abiola. The ING included General Sanni Abacha, a veteran of coup plotting, as defense minister.[20] But Abacha had his own ambitions, which he succeeded in concealing from his military colleagues and Abiola. Indeed, Abiola believed that Abacha would reverse the annulment. *The African Concord,* a daily newspaper owned by Abiola, noted that:

> Abacha has consistently warned his colleagues of the implication of staying beyond 27 August. General Abacha was said to have told a meeting of Army top brass that they (the military) had been voted out of office by the Nigerian people. According to him, he did not intend to stay a day longer than 27 August because he did not want "any small boy" to shoot him out of office.[21]

However, on November 18, Abacha shoved the ING out of office. His maiden speech to the nation made it clear to Nigerians, and Abiola in particular, that the validation of the June 12 presidential election mandate was out of his calculations as he hinted at his own transition program.[22]

Faced with this precarious reality, Abiola decided on what he thought was the next line of action. On the eve of the first anniversary of his election, he made what has become known as the Epetedo Declaration, a statement in which he claimed his mandate and ostensibly declared himself president of Nigeria and commander-in-chief of the Armed Forces.[23] When the state declared him wanted, he promptly went into hiding, but was subsequently arrested on charges of treason.[24]

The arrest and detention of Abiola did not lead to the lowering of tension in the country. In fact, it heightened it. Pro-democracy groups that emerged in the course of this crisis intensified their activity. An umbrella pro-democracy organization, the National Democratic Coalition (NADECO) had, as its cardinal aim, the peaceful resolution of the political crisis rocking the country.

NADECO was well placed, not only to articulate the national problems but also to proffer solutions. It had an external wing, NADECO-Abroad, which was inaugurated in May 1994 when it became clear that Abacha would renege on his promise to convene a constitutional conference with sovereign powers.[25] NADECO was an amalgam of technocrats, retired senior military officers, established politicians, political organizations, and pro-democracy groups who had their eyes on the enthronement of true federalism, the validation of the June 12, 1993 presidential election results, and the formation of a broad-based national government led by Abiola. It also wanted a sovereign national conference to be convened to find solutions to burning national issues.[26]

NADECO-Abroad, with headquarters in Washington, DC, was coordinated by the noted political scientist, Professor Bolaji Akinyemi, who at different times had served as the director-general of the Nigerian Institute of International Affairs (NIIA), and as Nigeria's Foreign Minister. As NADECO's foreign spokesperson, he held consultations with the Congressional Black Caucus. For instance, on September 16, 1994, he addressed the Black Caucus Legislative Conference in Washington, DC, where he called, among other measures, for a strong American intervention in Nigeria with a view to installing Abiola as president.[27]

Apart from Akinyemi, there were other pro-democracy elements living abroad and opposed to Abacha, including intellectuals such as the Nobel laureate Wole Soyinka, Sola Adeyeye, Kayode Fayemi, and Julius Ihonvbere. Also prominent, among this group was Anthony Enahoro, exiled in Virginia. Enahoro was a veteran politician who had been involved in the anticolonial struggle that eventually brought independence to Nigeria in 1960. In fact, he moved the motion for Nigeria's independence in 1953. As one of the main architects of a sovereign Nigeria, Enahoro devoted his later life to ensuring a democratic Nigeria.

Pro-democracy groups operating abroad used the clandestine Radio Democracy, which later became Radio Kudirat (named after Abiola's assassinated wife, Kudirat Abiola) to oppose the military dictatorship at home.[28] Besides NADECO, there were other pro-democracy groups including Campaign for Democracy (CD), Civil Liberties Organization (CLO), and Constitutional Rights Project (CRP).

Pro-democracy agitations gained momentum when it became clear that international condemnation of the annulment was confined only to verbal expression and nothing more. This was despite the fact that NADECO had courted Western countries to slam sanctions on Nigeria. The refusal to impose sanctions could mainly be attributed to an important economic factor. Simply, the United Kingdom and European Union member states could not afford to offend Nigeria, their main market for military hardware and industrial materials, consumer goods, and the like. Indeed, the United Kingdom dominated the service sector of the Nigerian economy. In addition, Western Europe was a safe haven for illicit funds stolen from Nigeria.

For the United States, the situation was dicey as the State Department saw it. First, how would the United States impose sanctions when the Nigerian people themselves were complacent and incapable of presenting serious opposition to the military junta? Second, there were concerns about $4.8 billion worth of investments and welfare of American citizens in Nigeria. Third, America had slammed oil sanctions on Iraq, Libya, and Iran, and so for strategic reasons, it could not add another country to that list.[29] Even though the United States had made, through its National Endowment for Democracy, annual grants of $40,000 for 1995–1996, 1996–1997, and 1977–1998 financial years to NADECO, it became apprehensive of the organizational structure of the organization and stopped the grant.[30] Clearly, all the states that would have applied meaningful sanctions, especially on crude oil on which the military government depended to perpetuate itself in power, declined to do so.

THE AFRICAN DIASPORA INVOLVEMENT

The African Diaspora involvement in Nigerian political crisis was championed by African Americans in the United States. Mike O' Brien, a staff of the U.S. Information Service in Nigeria, set the ball rolling on the eve of the presidential election with his declaration of American "opposition to any postponement of the election," sequel to the June 10, Abuja High Court injunction against the conduct of the poll.[31] Piqued, the Nigerian military authorities withdrew accreditation to the American election monitors including Walter C. Carrington, the U.S. ambassador to Nigeria, an African American.[32] Carrington promptly fell out with the military authorities as he clashed quite often with the Abacha junta following his denunciation of the regime's repression of its political opponents. In retaliation, the Abacha regime demanded that the U.S. government lift Carrington's diplomatic immunity so that he would be interrogated over the spate of bombings going on in the country.[33] Things took a bad turn in September 1997 when, at a party attended by Carrington in the home of a top NADECO leader Ayo Adebanjo, armed security agents stormed the house and threatened to shoot the guests.[34]

Abiola was no stranger to the black community in America. He was an advocate of Pan-Africanism, a concept that had its roots in the African diaspora, at least since the mid-nineteenth century. Abiola had also been a champion of reparations for the slave trade,[35] a campaign that was very well welcomed by the African American community. Prominent African Americans, indeed, took up the challenge to ensure his release from Abacha's gulag and the restoration of democracy in Nigeria. To effect this, they organized a national campaign, which *The New York Times* described as the "first time African-Americans have embarked on a protest of such magnitude against a black African government."[36] This elaborate campaign organized by TransAfrica, a black lobby group for Africa and the Caribbean, was championed by its executive director, Randall Robinson, supported by many notable African Americans across the professional spectrum. They included the famous political figure and civil rights icon Jesse Jackson; the award-winning poets Maya Angelou and Alice Walker; the national television star Bryant Gumbel; the music superstar Quincy Jones; and the boxing champion Sugar Ray Leonard.[37] The group not only campaigned for the restoration of democracy in Nigeria, it also lobbied Washington to achieve this. Abiola was so much in the good stead of Black America that at his death, the Congressional Black Caucus saluted him "as a hero in the global pursuit to preserve the history and the legacy of the African Diaspora."[38]

Abiola was also no stranger to the American political establishment and the press. It was apparently because of this connection that in July 1994, the U.S. House of Representatives unanimously passed a resolution in which it called upon the Abacha Government to release him from detention and restore democracy in the country. Washington followed up this resolution when President Clinton dispatched Jesse Jackson to Nigeria as "special envoy" to help persuade the Nigerian government to release Abiola from detention. The Nigerian pro-democracy leadership, however, doubted if the visit would advance their course. First, as pointed out by Soyinka, one of its leading proponents, a cozy relationship existed between Jackson and Babangida.[39] Second, there was the fear that Abacha would manipulate the visit to further his own ambition to cling to power. In the final analysis, Clinton failed to restrain the Abacha regime. The fact that after Jackson's mission Abacha remained in power for four more years until his death underscored the genuineness of the fears of the pro-democracy leadership.

Indeed, the fears of American inaction were well founded. At the Senate hearings in May 1996, top members of the Congressional Black Caucus helped to defeat a bill, the Nigerian Democracy Act, sponsored by Nancy Kassebaum (Republican KS), which provided for stiffer sanctions to force the Nigerian regime temper its iron fist rule.[40] The call to abandon the sanctions option was unanimous; the members rather preferred rapprochement with the regime. It does not appear that the activities of the pro-democracy leadership abroad, the Congressional Black Caucus, and the African American leadership in general, had any particular influence on the U.S. government. However, it is of note that a street corner in New York City, 44th Street and Second Avenue where the Nigerian Mission is located, was renamed Kudirat Abiola Corner.[41]

Abiola had all the requirements the U.S. government wanted in an aspiring leader of Nigeria. In addition, he had suffered injustice and indignities in the campaign to actualize his electoral mandate. He was in the good books of the African American leadership, and, indeed, the U.S. government had, at least at the initial stages of the pro-democracy agitation, funded NADECO-Abroad.[42] So why was Washington lukewarm toward the validation of Abiola's mandate?

First, the protest against the annulment of the election was basically confined to the Southwest, in the Yoruba ethnic homeland. The Nigerian political class was not unanimous in its opposition to the annulment, thus the apprehension in Washington about backing the democratic movement. Second, the activities of Abacha's lobbyists who hired public relations firms and agents were perhaps effective in polishing the image of the regime. The Chagoury Brothers, Abacha's business allies made a $460,000 donation to Clinton's Democratic Party.[43] Clinton's decision to avoid Nigeria during his 1997 African tour might be attributed to the successful influence of Abacha's allies and agents. Third, with $4.8 billion American investments in Nigeria, the American private sector naturally lobbied in support of Nigeria's military dictatorship and this proved quite effective. Fourth and perhaps most important was the reparation campaign led by Abiola, which was of serious concern to the United States and its Western allies. This campaign, a demand of Western reparations to black people for the enslavement of millions of Africans in the New World, was supported by many in the African American community. But this was seen in the West as capable of causing injury to the Western economy. Thus Abiola's commitment to this cause might have contributed to the refusal of U.S. State Department and the White House to fully support him in his bid to reclaim his mandate.[44] Clearly, the United States preferred as lesser of two evils to support the Abacha dictatorship than to see the democratically elected Abiola assume the presidency of Nigeria, one of the most powerful African states. Consequently, Washington decided to manage the Abacha transition program from the sidelines in the hope that an acceptable candidate would emerge with whom it could do business.

In the final analysis, national interests of the United States and other Western countries dictated the abandonment of Abiola in spite of the merit of his case and the West's vaunted democratic values. So, where did the abandonment of Abiola by the West leave the African American leadership and members of the Congressional Black Caucus? Distraught and powerless to impose their will and fulfill their desire, the African American leadership had no alternative but to join forces in clamoring for Abiola's release from detention. That clamor was terminated by Abiola's rather sudden death soon after Abacha's own equally sudden death, thus closing a negative chapter in Nigeria's political history.

CONCLUSION

The June 12, 1993, presidential election and its aftermath were momentous events in the political history of Nigeria. It is clear from the crises that tailed the annulment of the election that Nigerians failed to speak with one voice and act as a united people wronged. They also failed African Americans who intervened because of historical ties, with some risking their lives to help sort out the crises. African Americans and the Black world were let down by this failure, which was much to the delight of the United States and its Western allies.

NOTES

1. Robert S. Smith, *The Lagos Constipate 1851–1861* (London: The Macmillan Press Ltd., 1978), 108. See also Martin R. Delany, *Official Report of the Niger Valley Exploring Party* (New York: T. Hamilton, 1861).

2. Army Jacques Garvey, *The Philosophy and Opinions of Marcus Garvey on Africa for Africans* (Denver, MA: Majority Press, 1986), 126.

3. For details, see Okon E. Uya, *Diasporas and Homelands: An Emerging Central Theme in African Cultural and Historical Studies* (Lagos: CBAAC, Occasional Mimeograph, 2013).

4. For details, see Max Siollun, *Soldiers of Fortune: Nigerian Politics from Buhari to Babangida*, (Abuja: Cassava Republic Press, 2013), 204–261, and Lai Joseph, *Nigeria: Shadow of a Great Nation*, (Lagos: Dubeo Press Ltd., 1995), 313–320.

5. Larry Diamond, A. Kirk-Greene, and Oyeleya Oyediran, eds., *Transition without End: Nigerian Politics and Civil Society under Babangida* (Boulder, CO: Lynne Rienner Publishers), 289.

6. Ibid.

7. Ibid.

8. Joseph, *Nigeria Shadow,* 443. See tables 11A and 11B, 290–1.

9. NTA, "Remembering June 12 1993: Life and Times of M.K.O. Abiola," June 12, 2017, accessed June 12, 2018, http://www.nta.ng/news/obituary/20170612-remembering-june-12-life-m-k-o-abiola.

10. Siollun, *Soldiers of Fortune*, 246. See full text of the annulment statement on page 291.

11. Ibid.

12. Ibid., 247.

13. Ibid., 247–248.

14. Ibid.

15. Joseph, *Nigeria Shadow*, 466.

16. Siollun, *Soldiers of Fortune*, 247.

17. Ibid.

18. Joseph, *Nigeria Shadow*, 479 and 496.

19. Ibid., 482.

20. Ibid., 398.

21. Siollun, *Soldiers of Fortune*, 251.

22. Joseph, *Nigeria Shadow*, 482.

23. Olawale Oshun, *The Open Grave: Nadeco and the Struggle for Democracy in Nigeria*, (London: Josel, 2002), 258–262.

24. Kunle Amuwo, Daniel C. Bach, and Yann Lebeau, eds., *Nigeria during the Abacha Years: 1993–1998: The Domestic and International Politics of Democratization* (Ibadan: Institut français de recherche en Afrique, 2001), 346.

25. Amuwo et al., *Nigeria during the Abacha Years*, 162.

26. For the mission, vision and purpose of the organization, see NADECO's website at http://nadecousa.org/.

27. Lydia Cherr, "Nigeria's Abiola and Company: A Highly Manipulable Crowd," *EIR News Service*, October 14, 1994, accessed June 8, 2018, http://www.larouchepub.com/eiw/public/1994/eirv21n41-19941014/eirv21n41-19941014_032-nigerias_abiola_and_company_a_hi.pdf.

28. Studies on Kudirat Abiola include, Dapo Olorunyomi, ed., *Kudirat: Steps in Time* (Gbagada: Kudirat Initiative for Democracy, 2004) and Tunde Fagbohungbe, *Heroine of Democracy: The Travails and Triumphs of Kudirat Abiola* (Ikeja, Lagos, Nigeria: Nigerian Lawhouse, 1999). A brief note on Radio Kudirat is provided at "Nigeria Opposition Radio: Kudirat Background," *BBC News*, July 10, 1998, http://news.bbc.co.uk/2/hi/world/monitoring/130200.stm.

29. Amuwo et al., *Nigeria during the Abacha Years*.

30. Ibid., 143.

31. Diamond et al., *Transition without End*, 310.

32. See, “Military Agents End Party for U.S. Envoy at Gunpoint,” *Chicago Tribune*, September 21, 1997, accessed March 7, 2016, http://articles.chicagotribune.com/1997-09-21/news/9709210150_1_gani-fawehinmi-nigeria-security-agents.

33. Ibid.

34. See Howard W. French, “U.S. Envoy to Nigeria Is Given a Stormy Farewell,” *New York Times*, September 26, 1997, accessed June 5, 2018, https://www.nytimes.com/1997/09/26/world/us-envoy-to-nigeria-is-given-a-stormy-farewell.html.

35. Diamond et al., *Transition without End*, 295.

36. Karen De Witt, “Prominent Black Americans Take Aim at Nigeria,” *New York Times*, March 17, 1995, accessed June 6, 2018, https://www.nytimes.com/1995/03/17/world/prominent-black-americans-take-aim-at-nigeria.html.

37. Ibid.

38. See “Biography of M.K.O. Abiola.” *Nigerian Biography*, March 28, 2016, accessed June 5, 2018, http://www.nigerianbiography.com/2016/03/biography-of-mko-abiola.html.

39. See “Rights Groups in Nigeria Fault Jackson,” *New York Times*, July 24, 1994, accessed June 12, 2018, https://www.nytimes.com/1994/07/24/world/rights-groups-in-nigeria-fault-jackson.html.

40. See “S.1419—Nigeria Democracy Act,” 104th Congress (1995-1996), accessed June 12, 2018, https://www.congress.gov/bill/104th-congress/senate-bill/1419.

41. See “Kudirat Abiola Corner: New York Street named After Nigerian Woman, MKO Abiola’s Wife,” *NaijaGists.com*, May 21, 2015, accessed June 10, 2018, https://naijagists.com/kudirat-abiola-corner-new-york-street-named-after-nigerian-woman-mko-abiolas-wife. See also Robert Egbe, “How New York Named Street After Kudirat Abiola,” *The Nation*, May 9, 2018, accessed July 20, 2018, http://thenationonlineng.net/how-new-york-named-street-after-kudirat-abiola/.

42. Oshun, *The Open Grave*, 143.

43. Ibid., 144.

44. Ibid., 142.

Chapter 9

Bill of Rights for Africa

Uneven Regional Development and Indigenous Peoples Protests

Rufus T. Akinyele

INTRODUCTION

To use Tedd Gurr's popular coinage, Africa is home to many "Minorities at Risks."[1] The concept of minority has been defined in various ways. In 1950, the United Nations defined minorities as "those non-dominant groups in a population that possess and wish to preserve ethnic, religious or linguistic traditions, or characteristics markedly different from those of the rest of the population."[2]

Although the concept of minority can be stretched to cover gender and sexual categories, this work is concerned mainly with ethnic minorities. Morton B. King noted that a minority situation exists only where the majority inputs to itself or exhibits the air of inherent superiority or looks down on members of the minority group as inferior.[3] Rodolfo Stavenhagen observed that the uneven and exploitative relationship between the dominant and minority groups could take several forms such as "… unequal regional development or differential access to positions of privilege or power, or of different forms of segregation and discrimination in social, economic, and political life."[4]

While this generally describes the experience of all ethnic minority groups, this is particularly true for a class of minority groups now popularly identified as indigenous peoples. The unique characteristic of this group is not just their small number compared to the other groups in their countries but also their attachment to their primordial ways of life. As Ted Gurr noted, their members mostly "live in peripheral regions, practice subsistence agriculture and herding, and have cultures sharply distinct from the dominant group."[5] Many of these groups also live in resource-rich areas that have become targets for development projects by the State or multinational companies. The net result is that their land is either polluted or that they are forcefully uprooted from their ancestral home, thus making them victims of globalization and modernization. Such groups are found everywhere in Africa. They include the Ogiek of Kenya, the Buela of the Democratic Republic of Congo, the Tonga of Binga District of Zimbabwe, the Ogoni of Nigeria, and the Baka of Cameroon, just to mention a few. The struggle of these groups to maintain their separate identities, particularly through the control of their ancestral land and the practice of their culture and tradition, is the subject of this chapter. The focus is also on the role of the international community as arbiter in the contestations between the marginalized groups and the State at the behest of human rights agencies, brandishing what can best be described as the "Bill of Rights." Four cases are cited in the paper—the Tonga of Zimbabwe, the Ogiek of Kenya, and the Ogoni and Igbo of Nigeria. It is important to note that each of the countries mentioned in this study, Zimbabwe, Kenya, and Nigeria, have constitutional clauses that prohibit discrimination against minority groups. Article 27(4) of the 2010 Kenya's Constitution, Article 23(2) of the current Zimbabwean Constitution, and Chapter 4(42) of the 1999 Constitution of the Federal Republic of Nigeria enshrine the right to freedom from discrimination.[6] While such "negative rights" might ensure the vertical mobility or upward movement of individual members of the minority group, it does not guarantee their group rights. This is why there is a growing demand for a bill of rights as an additional safeguard in a continent where size and population have become important considerations in the power equation and political calculation among ethnic groups in different countries.

UNEVEN REGIONAL DEVELOPMENT AND INDIGENOUS PEOPLES PROTESTS

The Tonga

The Tonga are a partitioned African group found in Zambia (1.38 million), Zimbabwe (137,000) and Botswana.[7] In Zimbabwe, they are found in the northern end of the country. The Tonga are autochthones who probably occupied the Zambezi river valley since the early stone age. Their livelihood revolved around the great river before the advent of colonialism. The river basin provided them with enough game to hunt and fruits to pick. The physical environment also influenced their mode of worship, which centered on a fish like god called Nyaminyami. In spite of the pressure of modernization, the Tonga have remained deeply attached to their culture and tradition.

The fortune of the Tonga took a new turn in 1955 when the government of Zimbabwe decided to build the Kariba Dam across the Zambezi River. There are several stories regarding the ways in which the Tonga were relocated from their ancestral homeland to their present location. The most popular one is that the government deliberately released the water that flooded their homeland in 1957 to make their evacuation look like a humanitarian project. The other is that the Tonga were induced by mouth-watering promises, including the irrigation of their new homes, the provision of government schools, good roads, pipe borne water, and hospitals to abandon the river valley for the upland location.[8] Irrespective of which version is true, the reality is that the Tonga feel completely betrayed and marginalized in their current location. The new homeland experienced low and erratic rainfall and the soil is extremely poor. The Tonga have also been prevented from practicing hunting by the Protection of Wildlife Act, which requires hunters to get a special permit before killing animals. The negative effect of the relocation of the Tonga from their ancestral homeland, as a result of the construction of the Kariba Dam, has been noted by several scholars and minority rights groups. For instance, the Minority Voices Organization wrote:

> The majority of the 250,000 Tonga are now heavily reliant on material and international food aid. Despite the tourism and fishing opportunities of Lake Kariba, the Tonga community did not benefit from the construction of the Kariba Dam and the five-star hotels, resorts and safari camps that were seeing built along the shores of Lake Kariba. Unemployment remains high. They have been robbed of an opportunity to worship their Nyaminyami god, use their language, and are dissociated from their ancestral land.[9]

The marginalization of the Tonga is also echoed by Ivor Marowa who noted that the entire Binga District to which the Tonga principally dwell has only ten secondary schools that are more than sixty kilometers apart. The district also suffers from lack of amenities and infrastructure. Ivor Marowa wrote:

> The dam which caused their displacement is producing electricity but has not benefitted Binga villages. Although it has massed great amount of water, the water does not irrigate their land, and they have continued to endure drought. The boating and fishing have not contributed meaningful developments to Binga, even though they bring in foreign currency. The Tonga have helplessly watched efforts to pump water to Bulawayo while Binga, closer to the dam, has no water even to drink. The Tonga have watched their heritage being usurped by colonialists, both white and black. The Tonga have become frustrated from the impoverished life they lead, and their survival is punctuated by hardships, which the government has failed to address.[10]

The Tonga are listed among the indigenous peoples of the world by the United Nations; the campaign for the improvement in their condition is currently championed by minority right groups whose reference point is the UN Charter on the Protection of Human and Peoples' Rights.

The Ogiek of Kenya

"The Ghost Tribe of Kenya," "the last remaining indigenous peoples living in Kenya," and "people who are too poor to own cattle" are some of the ways the Ogiek of Kenya have been described in literature.[11] The Ogiek arc the most marginalized group in Kenya, and like all minorities, theirs is a story of government exploitation, harassment, and denial of cultural rights. Evidence points to the fact that the Ogiek were the first to settle in the forest of the Central Right Valley area of Kenya. The forest provided them habitat and means of livelihood. Guy Yeoman wrote, "The Dorobo, also known as the Ogiek, are unique people ultimately related to a particular ecosystem. They are incapable of retaining their essential characteristics if that ecosystem is destroyed."[12]

From 1903, the British colonial administrators began to cast a lustful eye on the timber in the Mau forest, the home of the Ogiek. Between 1911 and 1914, the Ogiek were forcefully ejected from that part of their land ostensibly on the basis of the agreement between the British and the Maasai. In 1911, the Maasai renounced their claims to land in Nakuru, Naivasha, and Laikipia for the settlement of white farmers. Unfortunately, most of the land signed away actually belonged to the Ogiek. A second ejection took place in 1918 when African soldiers were drafted to relocate the Ogiek to the more arid region of Narok. Records also indicate that more evictions took place between 1926 and 1927. In 1936, those who had stubbornly remained on the "crown land" were forcefully ejected. The nature of the resistance from the Ogiek led to the setting up of the Kenya Land (Carter) Commission of Enquiry. John Kamau had this to say about the outcome of the enquiry:

> The Kenya Land (Carter) Commission, which was set up to look into land problems in the Kenya colony between 1938–1939, deprived the Ogiek of their tribal status and denied them any claim to ancestral land. The Ogiek were to be moved into tribal reserves of other communities, especially the Nandi, Kipsigis, and Maasai. This proved to be impractical since the Ogiek abandoned the reserves and went back to their homes in the forest where they were seen as squatters.[13]

By 1954, the entire Mau forest had been included in the government official document, the gazette, thus transforming the Ogiek into a "landless" or "ghost" people. The 1957 Forest Act formally sealed the hope of the Ogiek for a return to their homeland. Even though the Act was revisited in 1964, it left the Ogiek exactly where they were. The Ogiek had not fared any better under the independent government of Kenya. In 1977, the Commissioner of Rift Valley Province ordered the invasion of the Mau West Forest. The houses of the Ogiek were torched and many of them were arrested and docked for alleged trespassing. In 1987, the government banned the rearing of livestocks and farming in the forest, thus putting the livelihood of the Ogiek at risk. In 1989, the government also shut down all the schools within the reservation area in a bid to drive out the Ogiek. Since then, the Ogiek have taken their case beyond the courts and government to the international community. The development itself illustrates a common trend in minority agitations in Africa. At first, the Ogiek adopted the method of passive resistance to their forceful ejection under their traditional rulers. For instance, the Ogiek frequently moved from Marioshoni back to Narok under Tiwas until his death in 1947. After that, the Ogiek sent many protest petitions and delegations to the government to complain about their situation. In 1990, for instance, the Elders of the Ogiek sent a memorandum to the Rift Valley Provincial Commissioner, Yusuf Haji, on the gradual loss of their land. Ostensibly in response to this petition, the schools that had been closed were reopened in 1992. Emboldened by the new development, the Ogiek sent a protest letter to the president, Daniel Arap Moi. The Ogiek also saw the need to support the ruling party so that their case could get a favorable hearing.

Their support for the Kenya African National Union (KANU) initially paid off. The Ogiek produced a counselor in the election of February 1993 while Marioshoni, Baraget, and Nessuit, inhabited by the Ogiek, were recognized in the gazette as administrative units. This brought some recognition to Ogiek chiefs. The rumor that the government was about to return part of the Mau Forest to the Ogiek filled them with false hope, especially between 1994 and 1995. Subsequent events show that the government was only willing to return five acres per household. The Ogiek quickly mobilized themselves and travelled all the way to see the president in his country home. Not only were they rebuffed, their problem was compounded by the revelation that some of their neighbors, particularly the Kipsigis, Maasai, and Tugens, had posed as Ogieks to obtain the five acres promised under the new arrangement.[14] Since then, the Ogiek and the government have been on the war path. Many of them have been arrested and imprisoned for taking part in demonstrations and protests.[15] Journalists who visit the Ogieks to collect information are similarly harassed by law enforcement agents.

In November 1996, the Ogiek formed the Ogiek Endorsis Alliance under Daniel Kibet Chesot to fight for their rights. The Ogiek have also instituted several lawsuits to seek redress for their marginalization. The notable ones include the following:

1. Mau East—HCCA No 6351 97 challenging Mauche Scheme and nullification.
2. South West Mau—HCCA No 238/99 Challenging Eviction (descriptive).
3. Songoo Case (Narok)—challenging the grabbing of their ancestral land by a senior government official.[16]

The outcome of the court cases so far has not favored the Ogieks. On one occasion, the Kenya High Court justified the eviction of the Ogiek from the Mau Forest to save the entire country from what it called a possible environmental disaster, which the indiscriminate burning of the forest by the Ogiek would cause. It has also been alleged that some of the judges argued that granting the Ogiek exclusive rights to the Mau Forest would be extending to them the privileges not extended to others. The government would appear to have found a safely net in the opinion held by the court that:

> The real threat to life is not eviction of the Ogieks, but the negative imminent effects of ecological mismanagement in the forest. The Ogieks can still obtain their livelihood from the forest without inhabiting it. Their right to life would still remain intact.[17]

While reacting to this verdict, Muyambi Kiai of the Kenya Human Rights Commission argued that the court failed to guarantee the Ogiek their right to the Tinet Forest habitat because the judiciary was yet to come to terms with or even understood the constitutional protection of minorities.[18]

The hope that the Ogiek will ever get a reprieve from the court is slim, simply because of the alleged involvement of some government officials in illegal tree felling. It was also alleged that the interest of the ex-president Arap Moi, in Timsales Ltd., a company that has been active in the deforestation of the area, made him openly oppose the demands of the Ogiek. He was reported to have boasted that he was not worried about the court cases instituted by the Ogiek saying, "I am the court."[19] Following the turn of events, the Ogiek have increasingly turned to the minority rights groups in Kenya for assistance. As elsewhere, the latter have been invoking the international conventions for the protection of minorities to plead the case of the Ogiek with the government and the international community. Specifically mentioned are the United Nations Declaration on the Rights of Persons Belonging to National or Ethnic, Religious and Linguistic Minorities adopted by General Assembly Resolution 47/135 of 1992, and the African Charter on Human and Peoples' Rights. The activists also noted that although Kenya is a signatory to the International Covenant on Civil and Political Rights, the government is not fulfilling the obligations contained in them. These documents not only forbid discrimination against ethnic, religious, and linguistic minorities, but as John Kamau noted, the covenants also grant them the right to preserve those characteristics they wish to maintain and develop.[20]

On the whole, the fears and demands of the Ogiek are clearly outlined in their memorandum to the Njojo Land Commission appointed in 2000 to look into the land problems in Kenya and suggest the way forward. Concerning the fears of the Ogiek, the relevant portion of the document reads:

> All the Ogiek, wherever they exist, have one common problem, which is disinheritance of their ancestral land, marginalization, and poor or no representation in the existing governments . . . . Although the Ogieks are a numerically small minority who constitute no political threat, they have been subject to negative stereotypes, from denial of rights to segregation. They have also been victims of much mistrust, suspicion, conflict, competition, and rivalry between Kenyan Communities jockeying for power and control over resources. This leaves the Ogiek being no different from the Twa of Rwanda and Burundi, who are victims of both Hutu and Tutsi governments and also of the Ogoni of Nigeria.[21]

The demands of the Ogiek to end their marginalization were also outlined. These include the creation of a trust land where they can assert their customary rights, adequate representation in government, and inclusion in any task force or commission whose decision could affect the welfare of the Ogiek now or in the future.[22]

The Ogoni Crisis

The Ijaw were the first to protest against government neglect of the Niger Delta area of Nigeria.[23] However, it was the Ogoni that pioneered the campaign for environmental justice, corporate social responsibility, and indigenous peoples' rights in Nigeria.[24] The protest of the Ogoni can best be understood in the context of oil exploration and the general neglect of the Niger Delta. The picture of the area painted by David Aworawo is particularly instructive:

> The Niger Delta area is today in crisis. This is reflected in the increasing vibrancy and militancy of the people. At the root of the crisis is the persistent degradation of the environment. Since the rural economy of the people depends on the fertility of the soil and the salubrity of the water system, the intense pollution has threatened the peoples' means of livelihood. The agitation in the area is therefore a struggle for survival. But the oil producing companies operating in the area are more concerned about making profits than about backlog environmental issues, and the Nigerian government too has been more concerned with the royalties that accrues to her. The case of the Niger Delta has therefore become like the biblical vineyard of Naboth.[25]

This phase of the history of the Niger Delta started in 1956 when oil was discovered in commercial quantity at Oloibiri. At different times, the Nigerian government tried to tackle the environmental and developmental problems of the area through the creation of development agencies. In 1959, the government created the Niger Delta Development Board (NDDB) on the recommendation of the Willink Minorities Commission. The politicization of its operation rendered it largely ineffective. This was followed by the Niger Delta Basin Development Authority (NDBDA) that was established in 1976. Like the other river basin development authorities of the same period in Nigeria, the impact of the NDBDA was hardly noticed. The government also established the Oil Mineral Producing Areas Development Commission (OMPADEC) in 1992 in response to the growing demand of the Niger Delta communities for a fair share of the national cake. Records show that OMPADEC left a legacy of "erecting signboards indicating projects that were neither started nor executed."[26] The current intervention, the Nigeria Delta Development Commission, was established by the Obasanjo Administration in 1992. The failure of these government agencies paved the way for the violent agitations in the Niger Delta in which the Ogoni played a leading role.[27]

The Ogoni, whose population has been estimated between 500,000 and 850,000, live in Rivers State of Nigeria.[28] The oil wells in Ogoni land include Bomu, Afam, Korokoro, and Ebibu. The contradiction between the rich resources of the land and the squalor of the area provoked the Ogoni crisis that attracted the attention of many scholars. A milestone in the protest was the formation of the Movement for the Survival of Ogoni People (MOSOP) in 1990 to champion the struggle of the Ogoni for resource control and self-determination. It is important to note that the first major protest of the Ogoni against the Nigerian State was organized on January 4, 1993 in commemoration of the declaration by the United Nations of 1993 as the International Year for the World's Indigenous Peoples. The case of the Ogoni against the Nigerian state was presented in the form of a bill of rights called the Ogoni Bill of Rights (OBR). Articles 15–19 detailed the negative effects of oil exploration in Ogoni land, namely environmental degradation and the transfer of Ogoni wealth exclusively to other parts of the federation. Article 20 outlined the conditions under which the Ogoni would wish to remain a part of the Nigeria State. These are: political control of Ogoni affairs by Ogoni People, the right to control and use "a fair proportion of Ogoni resources for Ogoni development," and the right to protect Ogoni land from further degradation.[29]

The Bill of Rights was sent to the government on October 2, 1990, for urgent consideration and action. Disappointed by the silence form the government, the Ogoni turned their attention to Shell, the company that was polluting their land. The violent confrontation between the Ogoni and Shell forced the company to withdraw from Ogoni land in the first quarter of 1993. The company gradually realized the need to placate the Ogoni and other oil producing communities through the award of contracts and other "settlements." The manner of disbursement of such "awards" invariably pitted the youths against some Ogoni leaders who were described as bribe takers or vultures. The investigation of the murder of four of the leaders on May 21, 1994, resulted in the detention and hanging of Ken Saro-Wiwa and eight others on November 10, 1995. The extra judicial murder of Saro-Wiwa helped to turn the attention of the international community to the situation in the Niger Delta. Human rights activists and environmental protection groups also took up the campaign. For instance, in 1996, the Centre for Constitutional Rights (CCR), Earth Rights International (ERI), and other human right lawyers sued Shell for human rights violation in Ogoni land. Unable to get justice in Nigeria, the legal battle was taken to the United States where Shell was sued under the Allien Tort Statute of 1789. In 2009, Shell made an out-of-court settlement of $15.5 million for the families of the activists executed by the Nigerian government.[30]

At the same time, MOSOP leaders sent petitions to the United Nations, the Commonwealth, and the African Union (AU) urging them to compel Nigeria to respect the rights of the Ogoni as outlined in UN and AU Connections of which Nigeria is a signatory. They also called on the United States and other oil importing countries to boycott the purchase of crude oil from Nigeria because "it is a stolen property." Lastly, they called on the advanced countries of the world to grant asylum to MOSOP leaders and provide facilities such as schools and health centers in Ogoni land. The internationalization of the Ogoni crisis is beginning to yield long term benefit that could change the landscape of Ogoni. In 1997, the United Nations responded to the petition of MOSOP by creating the position of Special Rapporteur on Nigeria. The Rapporteur, Mr. Soli Sorabjee, in his report to the 48th Session of the UN Commission on Human Rights in March 1998, recommended that the Federal Government undertake an independent study of the environmental condition of Ogoni land. This eventually led to the invitation of the United Nations Environmental program (UNEP) in 2006, within the context of Ogoni Shell reconciliatory programme. The report, which was submitted on April 4, 2011, showed that the level of contamination in some area was more than one hundred times the World Health Organization (WHO) standard. On March 2, 2016, the Buhari Administration announced its decision to commence the clean-up of Ogoni land. While praising the president for the good intention, the president of MOSOP, Mr. Legorsi Saro Pyagbara, stated that, "any clean-up and remediation of Ogoniland that is not backed up by a clear and practical development framework, or plan to address other socio-economic issues is not likely to succeed in the long term."[31]

Biafran Agitation

The current agitation of the Indigenous People of Biafra (IPOB) for the creation of an independent State from Nigeria is not in the same category as the three cases already treated. In terms of population and size, the Igbo are widely recognized as one the three largest ethnic groups in Nigeria. The population of the Igbo is estimated at 28 million, which is about 18 percent of the total population of Nigeria.[32] The Igbo have produced the Heads of State, speakers of the National Assembly, and several ministers in line with the principle of Federal Character.[33] The agitation of IPOB can therefore only be explained in the context of the three-cornered hegemonic contest between the Hausa/Fulani, the Yoruba, and the Igbo for the control of the Federal Government. This same struggle resulted in the Nigerian Civil War (1967–1970) that ended with the slogan of "No winner, no Vanquished." Although the Federal Government attempted to reintegrate the Igbo into the Nigerian federation through the program of Rehabilitation, Reconstruction, and Reconciliation, it has been argued that the one-sided nature of the implementation is responsible for the disaffection of the Igbo.[34] Many have also argued that the Igbo were crammed into a fewer number of states to deny them their fair share of the national cake.

Indeed, the Political Bureau instituted by the Babangida Administration recommend the creation of one additional state in 1987 "to reassure the Igbo that they have been fully reintegrated into the Nigerian political scene and thereby end the profound sense of frustration which led to the strident calls for a confederal arrangement by the Igbo."[35] The government turned down the request in the belief that "the mixture of states and population in some meaningful proportion as a criterion for representation or sharing of offices will suffice in giving all Nigerians access to the development opportunities which abound in Nigeria."[36]

The hope that the return to civil rule would bring good tidings for the Igbo soon turned into an illusion. Indeed, many Igbo held the belief, as claimed by an observer, that "the Igbo nation still has a long battle to wage in its struggle to extricate itself from the shackles of marginalization,"[37] as a result of an alleged determination by Nigerian leaders since the end of the Nigeria civil war to make the Igbo pay for the war. Expressing disappointment at the composition of President Olusegun Obasanjo's cabinet of in 1999, the observer noted:

> With Obasanjo's election as President and the Igbos contribution to that reality, the Igbos had thought that the worst days were over. How naïve they are. The president in his very first presidential appointments told the Igbos that yesterday is too fresh to be forgotten as no Igbo in any of the arms of the military was considered fit to be service chief.[38]

This feeling of marginalization led to the creation of the Movement for the Actualization of the Sovereign State of Biafra (MASSOB) under Ralph Uwazurike in the post-1993 era. Disagreement among MASSOB members on the strategy of actualizing the goal resulted in the formation of IPOB in 2012 by Nnamdi Kanu, the founder of Radio Biafra. On February 28, 2015, IPOB opened its first embassy in Victoria, Spain. The goal was to open more embassies in 2016 in Sweden Russia, Canada, and the United States. Kanu was arrested in Lagos on October 14, 2015, and is currently being charged with treason. Although Kanu has argued that the formation of IPOB is in consonance with the United Nations Charter on the Rights of Indigenous Peoples and ratified by African countries including Nigeria, the federal government believes the opposite. The detention of Kanu has raised many issues: Has the condition of the Igbo become bad enough to warrant secession from the country? Is secession the best solution to the perceived marginalization of the Igbo? Opinion differs on these issues.

To start with, President Muhammadu Buhari has argued that no group can legitimately claim that it is marginalized under the existing arrangement of appointing ministers on state basis. During a media chat, the president said:

> Help me define the extent of marginalization. Who is marginalizing them? Why? How? Do you know? The constitution said there must be a minister from each state. Who is the Minister of Petroleum? Is he not Igbo? Who is the Governor of Central Bank? Is he not Igbo? Who is the Minister of Labour? Who is the Minister of Science and Technology? Who is the Junior Minister of Education?[39]

Rev. Father Matthew Kukah argued that the agitation should be seen as a reflection of the socioeconomic problems of the country, a point of view largely shared by Chief Olusegun Obasanjo who interpreted the Biafra protests as “a cry for attention” motivated by the lack of socioeconomic opportunities particularly in Southeastern Nigeria.[40] Chief Ayo Opadokun, the convener of Coalition of Democrats for Electoral Reforms, argued that the creation of a Biafran state is not the solution to the marginalization of the Igbo. In his opinion, marginalization is a national problem which only the practice of true federalism can solve.[41]

Many Nigerians also wondered why the Igbo would wish to cram themselves into an enclave called Biafra when the whole of Nigeria is not even big enough to accommodate them. For this group of Nigerians, the only logical explanation for the protest is the implication of the displacement of the Jonathan Administration on the Igbo ambition to produce the president of the country in 2019. Evidently, many Igbo supported ex-president Goodluck Jonathan in the belief that their association with the People’s Democratic Party (PDP) would pave the way for the emergence of an Igbo president in 2019. This calculation was upturned by the emergence of Buhari as president in the

2015 election through what has been widely interpreted as a Yoruba/Hausa Alliance. The press release by the United State of Biafra (USB) on behalf of IPOB underscored this point:

> The political landscape of Nigeria has been in such a way that Biafrans will never produce Nigeria presidency [*sic*]. The shock emergence of Jonathan as the president of Nigeria after the sudden death of President Yar'adua, disorganized the long held political equation in Nigeria. This 'aberration,' where a Biafran has risen to the topmost position is the major reason for the political tension in Nigeria. The political landscape, which has been dominated by the Hausa-Fulani oligarchy and their Yoruba minions, has deliberately schemed out Biafrans from attaining the topmost position in Nigeria. It is on record that throughout the 53 years of Nigeria's independence, Biafrans have cumulatively held the position for less than 4 years [Aguiyi—Ironsi, 6 months; Goodluck Jonathan—3 years]. The Hausa-Fulani 'owners' of Nigeria are battling to 'correct' the political anomaly, as can be seen from various recent political moves being made in the country. They have made it clear they must take back power by 2015, even without consulting the rest of the population. Therefore, it would be foolhardy for Biafra to remain in such a country where every expression, action, and word is targeted against them and where it is amply clear that they are not regarded as part of the owners of the country, but rather subservient to the Hausa-Fulani oligarchy and their Yoruba lackeys.[42]

The presentation of Goodluck Jonathan as a Biafran indicates that IPOB is claiming the whole of Eastern Nigeria for the Biafran state. The non-Igbos of the region have repeatedly dissociated themselves from the Biafra project. The governors of the Igbo states have similarly distanced themselves from IPOB.[43] The Ohanaeze Ndigbo, the leading pan Igbo organization, has advised that the ghost of Biafra should not be resurrected. The plea of Ohanaeze Ndigbo and prominent Nigerians for the release of Kanu subsequently yielded fruit. Kanu was released on bail by the Federal High Court, Abuja, on April 25, 2017. The stringent bail conditions include the clause that he would not grant any press interviews, address any rallies, and stay away from any gathering of more than ten persons.[44]

The new freedom enjoyed by Kanu seemed to embolden IPOB members and numerous Igbo youths who daily thronged to his residence in Umahia to pay him homage. One consequence of this is the widely reported resolution of IPOB to prevent the holding of the November 18, 2017, election in Anambra State if a referendum on Biafra was not conducted before that date.[45] In response, the coalition of Arewa Youth Groups, a body claiming to represent the voice of the Hausa/Fulani of Northern Nigeria, gave the Igbo living in the North up to October 1, 2017, to quit the region since the action of IPOB has shown that the Igbo are no longer happy to be a part of the country.[46] The quit notice provoked a nation-wide discourse on the restructuring of the Nigeria federation. The dangerous dimension of the political discussion precipitated a wave of reactions. First, the police threatened to rearrest Kanu for violating the conditions of his bail.[47] Second, the All Progressive Congress (APC) ruling party had to publicly explain that its support for the restructuring of the country should not be misinterpreted to mean the endorsement of the dismemberment of the county, but the greater devolution of power to the States and local governments.[48] Third, the vice president, who has been holding fort for the president that is receiving treatment in London, held several meetings with State governors and traditional rulers across the country to inform them that the unity of the country is nonnegotiable.[49] Fourth, the media attention Kanu has enjoyed since April 25, 2017, has widened the crack in the wall of the solidarity of the Igbo over Biafra.

To begin with, the news of the appointment of Kanu as the supreme leader of Biafra by a group known as Biafran Peoples National Council (BPNC) at Afara Ukwu on June 28, 2017, has embittered MASSOB and the Biafran National Youth League (BNYL).[50] While the president of Ohanaeze Ndigbo, Chief John Nnia Nwodo, called on all well-meaning Igbo to distance themselves from the incisive speech of Kanu and his movement, the Buhari Support Group (BSG) denounced Kanu as "a young man of no fixed address in London, who only returns to Nigeria to cause trouble."[51] One political commentator even described Kanu as a megalomaniac, stating that the idea of a supreme or maximum leader is not in consonance with Igbo history or their republican spirit.[52]

As of now, the political tension has cooled off, but the ethnic gladiators are threatening to widen the theatre of the war. The Arewa Youths has threatened to appeal to the United Nations to classify IPOB as a terrorist organization in view of the violence and general insecurity the group has caused.[53] The statement drew the ire of MASSOB, IPOB, and other supporters of Biafra. The spokesman for MASSOB blamed the northerners for the long period of misrule that laid the foundation for the present economic and political crisis in the country. He added that if there is any group that should be labeled a terrorist group in Nigeria, it should be "the Fulani herdsmen who have been going about killing and raping women and destroying peoples' farmlands."[54] Of course, this is not the first time the possibility of externalizing the Biafran case would be contemplated. Earlier on, the Ohanaeze Youth Council (OYC) had threatened to drag the security operatives to the International Court of Justice at Hague for the extra—judicial killings of IPOB protesters.[55] IPOB said it would order its members to carry arms to protect themselves as of Wednesday, February 17, 2016, in line with the relevant Acts and Declarations of the United Nations.[56]

The Inspector General of Police, however, warned IPOB of the consequences of such an action. The hope that the Biafran agitation would receive international support was recently dashed by the European Union's foreign affairs chief, Federica Mogherini, in her response to the letter from Jonathan Levy, the chief administrative officer of the Organization of Emerging African States (O.E.A.S), based in the United States. The organization had asked the E.U. to support the call for a referendum on the creation of Biafra. Mogherini s response was that while human rights protection and respect for fundamental freedoms remain a priority for the E.U., issues of self-determination must be pursued in accordance with international law.[57]

CONCLUSION

It is evident from the four case studies examined in this chapter that uneven regional development is the root cause of the minority agitations. Although the experiences differed, the common denominator is the feeling of being treated as second class citizens in countries that should be composed of free equals. Vital Bambanze, chair of the UN Expert Mechanism on the Rights of Indigenous Peoples, hit the nail on the head when he wrote that:

> One of the overriding threats facing minorities and indigenous peoples in every region of the world is the risk of being driven from their land and natural resources, which are vital for their livelihoods, their culture, and often their identity as a people. Many communities have been closely tied to their territory for centuries. Yet, once their land is targeted for development- mining, oil, and gas, dams, agribusiness, tourism or conservation—they are deftly and often violently evicted with little or no compensation.[58]

Second, the case of Tonga, Ogiek, and Ogoni shows how globalization and modernization can promote uneven development and heighten the fear of domination in developing countries. The economic element of globalization could ignore the socioeconomic and cultural rights of the indigenous peoples, which are well protected or recognized in International Bill of Human Rights (IBHR).

Third, although the struggle of the four groups featured protest petitions, demonstrations, and violence, the main demand is presented in form of a bill of rights, championed by minority and human right activists. Significantly too, all of them cited the United Nations Convention on Human Rights and the African Freedom Charter as legitimate basis for their actions. Article 27 of the International Covenant on Civil and Political Rights (ICCPR) prohibits States from depriving the minorities the right to enjoy their own culture, practice their own religion, or use their own language. Article 1 of the United

Nations Declaration of 1992 on Persons Belonging to National or Ethnic, Religious and Linguistic Minorities (UNDM) recognizes the right of minorities to protect their existence and separate identities. Article 4, paragraph 2 of the same document recognizes their right to develop their culture, language, tradition, and custom within their country. Significantly too, Article 21 of the African Charter on Human and Peoples' Rights adopted in 1981 recognizes the rights of minorities to 'free possession of their riches and natural resources while Article 2 enshrines their right to economic, social, and cultural development in strict respect of their liberty and identity. This pattern of agitation seems to illustrate the new phase of minority agitation in Africa in the twenty-first century.[59]

Fourth, although some of the groups believe they can acquire the justice, which the courts in their countries have denied them for political reasons elsewhere, the focus has always been on Europe and America. We should recall that Saro-Wiwa's plaintiffs took their case to the United States while OYC threatened to drag the law enforcement agents in Nigeria to the International Court of Justice at Hague. It would therefore appear that the African Court for Human and Peoples Rights is not well known. The Court was established by the African Union in January 2004, with the first eleven Judges elected by the Assembly of that continental body two years later. The headquarters is at Arusha, Tanzania. States, NGOs and individuals could bring complaints to the Court.[60] In any case, the only way to stem the tide of minority agitations in Africa is for the governments to promote good governance that will ensure equitable allocation of resources and fairness in the distribution of government appointments.

NOTES

1. See Ted Gurr, *Minorities at Risk: A Global View of Ethnoplitcal Conflicts* (Washington, DC: United State Institute of Peace Press, 1998).
2. A. C Helpburn, *Minorities in History* (London: Edward Arnold, 1978), 2.
3. Morton B. King, "The American Course," *American Sociological Review* 21 (1956): 80–83.
4. Rodolfo Stavenhagen, "The Ethnic Question and the Social Sciences," *Journal of Culture and Ideas,* 1 no. 1 (1983): 122.
5. Gurr, *Minorities at Risk*, 20.
6. See "Constitution of Kenya, 2010," accessed July 20, 2018, http://www.kenyalaw.org/lex/actview.xql?actid=Const2010; "The Zimbabwe's Constitution of 2013," accessed July 20, 2018, https://www.constituteproject.org/constitution/Zimbabwe_2013.pdf; and, "Constitution of the Federal Republic of Nigeria," Abuja, 1999, accessed July 20, 2018, https://publicofficialsfinancialdisclosure.worldbank.org/sites/fdl/files/assets/law-library-files/Nigeria_Constitution_1999_en.pdf.

7. See A. I. Asiwaju, ed., *Partitioned Africans: Ethnic Relations across Africa's International Boundaries, 1884–1984* (London: C. Hurst and Coy, & University of Lagos Press, 1984), 256; see also Fergus Macpherson, *Kenneth Kaunda of Zambia: The Times and the Man* (Nairobi, London, New York, and Oxford University Press, 1974), 23–24 for the arbitrariness of the Zambian border and the relationship between the Tonga people.

8. See Minority Voices Newsroom, "The Tonga People in Zimbabwe: A Forgotten People," accessed July 20, 2018, www.minorityvoices.org/news.php/en/306/the-tonga-people-in-zimbabwe-a-forgotten-people.

9. Ibid.

10. Ivan Marowa, "The Tonga People of Zimbabwe: Historical Memories and Contemporary Challenges of a Minority Society," in *Minorities and the State in Africa*, eds. Michael U. Mbanaso and Chima Korieh (New York: Cambria press, 2010), 191.

11. See Joseph K. Sang, "Kenya: the Ogiek in Mau Forest," April 2001, accessed July 20, 2018, https://www.forestpeoples.org/sites/fpp/files/publication/2010/10/kenyaeng.pdf.

12. Guy Yeoman, *Swara Magazine,* 1979, cited in Towett J. Kimayo *Ogiek Land Cases and Historical Injustices* (Nakuru: Egerton Welfare Council, 2004), http://freeafrica.tripod.com/ogiekland/book.htm.

13. John Kamau, "The Ogiek: An in-depth Report," OGIEK.ORG, accessed July 23, 2018, https://www.ogiek.org>report>ogiek-ch1.

14. The Government only promised to release a portion of the land to Kenyans and not the entire forest.

15. See Kenna Claude, "Ogiek Leaders Now Arrested," *The People,* April 3, 2000, cited in Kamau, "The Ogiek."

16. See Kamau, "The Ogiek," Appendix 1.

17. Ibid.

18. See Indigenous People of the World, "The Ogiek," accessed July 20, 2018, https://intercontinentalcry.org/indigenous-peoples/ogiek/.

19. See Elijah Kinyajui "The day the Ogieks angered President," *The People,* November 26, 1999 cited by Kamau, "The Ogiek."

20. Kamau, "The Ogiek."

21. Memorandum of the Ogiek Community, Submitted to the Njojo Land Commission, 2000 in Appendix 2 of Kamau, "The Ogiek."

22. Ibid.

23. See Rufus T. Akinyele, *Isaac Adaka Boro: Patriarch of Minority Activism in the Niger Delta* (Lagos: University of Lagos, Faculty of Arts Monograph Series 1, 2006).

24. The Ogoni, through Ken Saro-Wiwa, successfully internationalized the struggle.

25. David Aworawo "The Impact of Environmental Degradation on the Rural Economy of the Niger Delta," in *Environmental Problems of the Niger Delta*, ed. Akinjide Osuntokun (Davidson Press, Ibadan), 160–161.

26. The *Guardian,* May 23, 1996. See also *The Guardian*, January 26, 1994, 16–17; *The Guardian*, May 12, 1997, 3.

27. See Claude Welch, "The Ogoni and Self-Determination: Increasing Violence in Nigeria," *Journal of Modern African Studies* 33, no 4 (1995): 635–649; Cyril Obi, "Globalisation and Local Resistance: The Case of Ogoni Versus Shell," *New Political Economic* 2, no. 1 (1997): 137–148; Kayode Soremekun and Cyril Obi, "The Changing Pattern of Private Foreign Investment in Nigeria Oil Industry," *Africa Development* 18, no 3 (1993); Feyi Adeoye, "Language of Terror: Perspectives from the Global South," in *Global Understanding in the Age of Terrorism*, eds. Ayodeji Olukoju and Muyiwa Falaiye (Lagos: University of Lagos Press, 2008), 151–164; Anthony Agbali, "Politics, Rhetoric and Ritual of the Ogoni Movement," in *Nigeria in the Twentieth Century*, ed. Toyin Falola (Durham: Carolina Academic Press, 2002), 505–531; and Ben Naanen, "Oil Producing Minorities and the Restructuring of Nigerian Federalism: The Case of the Ogoni People," *The Journal of Commonwealth and Comparative Politics* 33, no. 1 (1995): 46–78.

28. The population of the Ogoni in 1990 was estimated at 500,000. See Agbali, "Politics, Rhetoric and Ritual," 510.

29. See The Movement for the Survival of the Ogoni People, "The Ogoni Bill of Rights," Oct. 1990, accessed July 21, 2018, http://www.bebor.org/wp-content/uploads/2012/09/Ogoni-Bill-of-Rights.pdf.

30. Leslie Berliant, "Shell Settles Human Rights Case in Nigeria for $15.5 Million," *InsideClimate News*, June 9, 2009, accessed July 21, 2018, https://insideclimatenews.org/news/20090609/shell-settles-human-rights-case-nigeria-155-million.

31. See "Welcome Address by MOSOP President, Mr. Legborsi Saro Pyagbara," Stakeholder Consultative Meeting between the Federal Government and Ogoni on UNEP Report," Peace and Freedom Centre, Bori, March 4, 2016, accessed May 5, 2017, http://www.Ogoninews.com/ogoni/709-full-text-of-welcome-remarks.

32. The Igbo case has added a new dimension to the definition of minorities. I am of the view that what is being alleged is marginalization, which is a common cry of every section of the country.

33. The Federal Character Principle stipulates that every part of the country should be involved in the running of the government. Consequently, the constitution stipulates that each state of the Federation should produce at least a minister. The zoning formula of the different political parties also recognizes the rotation of political posts on zonal basis.

34. See Olukunle Ojeleye, *The Politics of Post-War Demobilsation and Reintegration in Nigeria* (Burlington, VT: Ashgate Surrey, 2010).

35. See *Government Views and Comments on the Recommendations of the Political Bureau* (Lagos: Federal Government Press, Lagos, 1987), 16.

36. See *Daily Times,* September 24, 1987, 11.

37. See "Igbos, It's Still a Long Way to Zion," *Post Express,* June 1, 1999, 32.

38. Ibid.

39. Simeon Ejembi, "Biafra: Kanu Came into Nigeria without any Passport, Says Buhari," *Punch Online*, December 31, 2015, accessed July 25, 2018, https://www.latestnigeriannews.com/news/2406804/biafra-kanu-came-into-nigeria-without-any-passport-buhari.html.

40. Conor Gaffey, "Biafra Protests a 'Cry for Attention', Says Former Nigerian President Obasanjo," *Newsweek*, January 18, 2016, accessed July 25, 2018, https://www.newsweek.com/biafra-protests-cry-attention-former-nigerian-president-416913.

41. Toluwani Eniola, "Biafra Not Solution to Igbo Problems, Says Opadokun," *The Nigerian Blogger*, December 18, 2015, accessed July 25, 2018, http://thenigerianbloggers.blogspot.com/2015/12/biafra-not-solution-to-igbo-problems.html.

42. "Indigenous People of Biafra and the Biafra Republic: Restoration Agenda, Key Facts," United States of Biafra (USB) Facebook, January 12, 2014, accessed July 25, 2018, https://www.facebook.com/Princemeka12/posts/indigenous-people-of-biafra-and/657700930940385.

43. "Biafra: Ohaneze Ndigbo Holds Talks with Presidency over Kanu," *The Nation,* February 27, 2016, 54.

44. Ihuoma Chidozie, "Biafra: Security Agents Lack Grounds to Re-Arrest Kanu, Says IPOB," *Punch* July 1, 2017, 11.

45. See "You Can Stop Anambra Election, Police Tells IPOB," *Punch*, July 2, 2017, 7.

46. See "Anti-Igbo Threat: Yakassa, Junaid Mohammed Call for Calm," *Punch*, June 2, 2017, 7.

47. *Punch*. July 1, 2017, 11.

48. See "We Promised Restructuring Not Break Up—APC," *Punch*, July 2, 2017, 7.

49. See, Olalekan Adetayo, "Nigeria's Unity Not Negotiable, Osinbajo Insists," *Punch*, June 26, 2017, 14.

50. See "Ohanaeze Overules Kanu on Anambra Poll Boycott Order," *Punch*, June 30, 2017, 11; "Biafra Group Pulls out of Coalition, Rejects Kanu as Supreme Leader," *Saturday Telegraph*, July1, 2017, 7.

51. See, Kenneth Ofoma, "Anambra Poll: Buhari Support Group Hails Nwodo on Nnamdi Kanu," *Saturday Telegraph*, July 1, 2017, 42.

52. Azuka Onwuka, "Nnamdi Kanu and the Lure of Megalomania," *Punch*, June 26, 2017, 21.

53. See Ameh Comrade Godwin, "Biafra: You Are Confused, Directionless—MASSOB Fires Northern Youths," July 14, 2017, accessed July 21, 2018, http://dailypost.ng/2017/07/14/%E2%80%8Ebiafra-confused-directionless-massob-fires-back-northern-youths.

54. Ibid.

55. Anayo Okoli, Chimaobi Nwaiwu, and Eric Ugbor, "Biafra: Over 1,000 of Our Members Killed since Kanu's Arrest, Detention—IPOB," Vanguard, February 11, 2016, accessed July 25, 2018, https://www.vanguardngr.com/2016/02/biafra-over-1000-of-our-members-killed-since-kanus-arrest-detention-ipob. See also Jasmine Buari, "Pro-Biafran Supporters to be Docked Tomorrow," NAIJ.Com, accessed July 25, 2018, https://www.naija.ng/669562-13-pro-biafran-supporters-docked-tomorrow.html#669562.

56. "We'll Now Carry Arms in Self-Defense—IPOB," *Daily Trust*, February 15, 2016.

57. Conor Gaffey, "EU Responds to Calls for Biafran Independence," *Newsweek*, January 20, 2016, accessed July 25, 2018, https://www.newsweek.com/eu-responds-calls-biafran-independence-417696.

58. Beth Walker, ed., *State of the World's Minorities and Indigenous Peoples* (London: Minorities Rights Group International, 2012), foreword.

59. For details, see Ibrahima Kane ed., *Protecting the Rights of Minorities in Africa: A Guide for Human Rights Activists and Civil Society Organizations*, (Minorities Rights Group International, 2008), accessed July 21, 2018, https://resourcecentre.savethechildren.net/library/protecting-rights-minorities-africa-guide-human-rights-activists-and-civil-society.

60. Ibid.

Part III

GENDER RELATIONS, HEALTH CARE, AND DEVELOPMENT

Chapter 10

Vanishing or Emerging Voices?

Nigerian Women and Political Participation

Ngozi U. Emeka-Nwobia

INTRODUCTION

On May 29, 2015, Nigeria marked the sixteenth anniversary of uninterrupted democratic rule and fifty-five years of independence. Since its independence, women, who constitute about 50 percent of the country's population, have consistently been alienated from full participation in the democratic process, and where involved, are grossly underrepresented in elective positions and as political office holders. This chapter examines the resilience of women's participation in Nigerian democracy with a critical focus on the Fourth Republic and especially the 2015 general elections. The work explores women's participation in campaigns, political rallies, the electioneering process, and electoral positions as well as their involvement in governance and decision making. Findings reveal that factors such as sociocultural constraints and stereotyped ideologies, lack of internal democracy among the political parties, economic inhibitions, funding, violence, and thuggery have consistently posed a threat to the participation of women in Nigerian democracy, hitherto silencing their voices. The chapter, therefore, argues that the structural factors limiting their participation should be addressed as a means of redressing the phenomenon. It concludes that if women, who constitute half of the population, remain underrepresented in the decision-making process, the true test of democracy will only remain a mirage and cannot truly deliver for all of its citizens.

The place of women in national development is indispensable and pervasive, as their contributions permeate every sphere of a nation. A United Nation's declaration stipulates that the full and complete development of any country hinges on the maximum participation of women in all facets of the country's life, including its political, economic, social, and educational development, to ensure the maximum growth and development of the nation.[1]

This indispensable role of women in national development has not in any way guaranteed their full representation in governance and decision making processes in most countries of the world, Nigeria inclusive.

Women's underrepresentation in the political sphere and in the democratic process is a global concern which is not only prevalent in African countries, but visible across the globe. This stems out of male dominance and inclination toward men over women in some cultures. In many societies in Africa, male dominance starts right from birth, where a male is preferred to a female child. Bearing a male child is assumed to be a form of security for a married woman, as it guarantees her stay in her matrimonial home and a share of inheritance in her marriage.

In some African societies, women are often considered objects of pleasure for men to be used and discarded at will. This negative portrayal of women has lingered over the years, transcending many generations even up to the twenty-first century. The male-dominated society has also imposed some gender-biased cultural norms in favor of the male. Some Nigerian communities subtly approve of such practices as preference for male children, blaming women for childlessness, and being responsible for a child's sex. Other ways of discriminating against women include the practice of female circumcision (female genital mutilation), upholding widowhood practices, denial of inheritance, and giving away immature girls to early marriage without their consent. It has been shown that preference for male children, which is widespread, has generational effects on the female child who is expected to be a homemaker who takes care of her siblings before being married off unlike her brothers, who are sent to school.[2] This has contributed to the level of illiteracy among women in some communities in Africa.

The culture of many ethnolinguistic groups in Nigeria ensures the total dependence of women on men for their viability in the society.[3] Relationships are patterned to incapacitate and render a woman voiceless without a man. That is why women who have reached marriageable age and remain unmarried are regarded as social outcast, quite unlike their male counter parts. This stereotype could, however, be the reason why Nigeria is yet to produce a woman as president, even in the twenty-first century. Despite the fact that women have consistently been relegated and underrepresented in very pervasive ways, especially in human right issues, less attention has been focused on their plight and addressing the issue of underrepresentation.

This incongruity has overtly influenced women's participation in democracy and the decision-making process. The few daring women who seek electoral offices are confronted with the societal imposed restrictions of preference for male candidate by the men, and even by their fellow women who perceive them as good enough only for subservient positions.

Notwithstanding this age long marginalization, the twenty-first century has witnessed a gradual increase in the participation of women in politics and democracy. Women have, against all odds, been involved in several dimensions of political activism, ranging from "being foundation members of political parties to vying for elective positions at the executive and legislative levels."[4]

In the executive branch of the government, women have grossly been underrepresented. Indeed, no woman has successfully emerged as an elected president, and the country is yet to witness the election of a woman as governor in any of the thirty-six states of the federation since the onset of democracy. The best women have enjoyed so far is the deputy governor position. One interesting occurrence that could have resulted in the first woman governor in Nigeria was the short-lived elevation of Dame Virginia Ngozi Etiaba, from deputy governorship to governor. Etiaba had been sworn in as deputy governor in Anambra State on March 17, 2006, making her the first woman deputy governor in the South-East and South-South geopolitical zones. Following the impeachment and removal of the state governor, Peter Obi, by the state legislature for alleged gross misconduct, Etiaba became the governor on November 3, 2006, the first woman to hold that position in Nigeria. Obi's impeachment was later reversed by the Court of Appeal, after which Etiaba duly relinquished the governorship position to him within two hours of the Court of Appeal's judgment on February 9, 2007. Etiaba then reverted to the position of deputy governor, which she held till March 16, 2010.[5]

This chapter explores the democratic process in Nigeria, with the view to explore the level of women's participation in Nigerian politics in the twenty-first century, of which extant literature has decried as underrepresented. This is undertaken through a critical examination of women's involvement in campaigns, political rallies, electioneering process, vis-à-vis their election and participation in the three tiers of government. Through historical evidence, it ascertains the status of women and their level of involvement in Nigerian democracy from 1999 to 2015 in order to determine if their voices are vanishing or emerging. The chapter further probes into some of the factors impeding women's involvement in the democratization process in Nigeria. Although there is no legal justification for limiting women participation in democracy, there have been societal inhibitions imposed by culture, ethnicity, and religion, which all serve as barriers to the actualization of the recommendation of the Beijing Declaration and Platform for Action.[6]

WOMEN AND GOVERNANCE IN NIGERIA

It is imperative to take a historical recourse for a proper understanding of the place of women in the twenty-first-century democratic process in Nigeria. The issue of inadequate representation of women in the fledgling democracy can arguably be attributed to the colonial experience, which empowered men while disempowering women.

Typically, African communities are classified, either as matrilineal and patrilineal;[7] or double-descent, as is the case of Afikpo, an Igbo community in Southeastern Nigeria.[8] In Igbo society, economic changes in colonial times undermined women's status and reduced their political role such that patrilineal tendencies persist today to the detriment of women.[9] The same sentiment is visible in the Kikuyu community in Kenya, where on the eve of the colonial era, women were embedded in gendered constructions of power, authority, and ownership/access to property in a manner that publicly diminished their individual agency. This has affected women's participation in political decision-making, which is mostly peripheral.[10]

In precolonial Nigeria, women played a major role in social and economic activities. Women were politically active and relatively less exclusive in decision-making processes, but this was truncated with the advent of colonial administration, which came up with policies that were antiwomen. This gradually transformed a hitherto politically gender-unbiased society to a predominantly male-dominated political arena. For instance, women were known to have occupied very influential political offices. For instance, prior to the advent of colonialism, Hausa women had high status. Queen Amina's rule in fifteenth-century Zaria is a vivid example. Queen Amina succeeded her father and conquered all the towns around Zamfara and Nupe, dominating these regions for thirty-four years. She also introduced fortifications into the Hausa cities during her reign.[11] The position of Hausa women changed after the conquest of Hausa land by the Fulani in the early nineteenth century. This reduced the participation of women in Hausa politics during the colonial period.

In some Igbo societies, women were not really kings, but queen mothers who wielded much power and control over communities. Some other communities that did not have queens still had women who exercised very strong political influence in their communities through organized bodies like the Umuada Igbo.[12] The influence of these women led to the popular Aba women's protest. Women wielded overwhelming influence in community politics, land disputes, family issues, etc. These women were equally economically independent. They were powerful political forces who occupied very sensitive positions in the overall political and economic hierarchy of their respective communities.

During the colonial period, women still asserted and expressed themselves politically, not being deterred by the colonial policies. Women such as Mrs. Margaret Ekpo of Calabar, Madam Tinubu of Lagos and Egbaland, Mrs. Funmilayo Ransome-Kuti of the Abeokuta Women's Union (AWU), and Hajiya Sawaba Gambo of Northern Element Progressive Union (NEPU) left invaluable foot prints in the political history of Nigeria.[13] Although women enjoyed high political authority in Nigeria in general, men had always been dominant in the political arena with women playing subordinate and complementary roles.[14] Given the male-dominated structure of the society, women saw no reason to agitate the issue of equality of representation in the decision-making and judicial processes.

Women's political fortune dwindled with the advent of the colonial masters, who introduced antiwomen policies, which promoted patriarchalism in Nigerian politics. The colonial policy considered "only men to be active in the public sphere and earn a living to support their families."[15] Men were trained in educational assistance programs under the colonial administration, and thereafter, recruited into colonial civil service and merchant houses. These practices empowered African men and gave the man undue advantage over their female counterparts, leading to the underrepresentation of women in formal agencies of government.

Another antiwoman colonial policy was the restructuring of the African traditional economies and their linkage with the international capitalist economic system. The Nigerian economy was, therefore, transformed to production of primary crops exported to European factories as cheap raw materials. African men hitherto emerged as producers and exporters of crash crops, while their wives were in charge of home management and the production of food crops. This boosted the economic base of men against women, and partly provides the reason why postcolonial Nigerian politics were flooded with men who were economically viable to fund elections into political positions. Women were reduced to the lowest ebb of exclusion from mainstream political participation and were considered not good enough to take up the position of presidency and other sensitive positions. They were portrayed as second fiddles, only fit as deputies and assistants to their male counterparts.

In contemporary Nigeria, women play multiple roles within the family, community, and the society, but there is still a lot of gender discrimination in the public sphere where women are marginalized in the electoral process and are still underrepresented in governance, decision making, and politics in general. The situation in the Northwest geopolitical zone of the country tells much on the level of alienation from active participation of women as a major political bloc. The zone has the largest number of female registered voters in Nigeria, but unfortunately, it has the least number of women in political office at the state and federal levels. The issue at stake is this: how can the number of women voters be translated into a power force? The major impediments to the realization of women's goals have been enumerated by various scholars, including lack of mentoring, poverty, education, and societal imposed role assignment. Over the years, women have been marginalized and commodified in the country, often told what to do and how to do it; how to dress, speak, sit, behave; when to be seen; and when to speak. These subtle societal impositions have largely crept into their subconscious mind and affected their perception of themselves and the society's perception of them. F. C. Enemuo notes that women are regularly exposed to various forms of physical, psychological, sexual, and emotional violence.[16]

WOMEN, DEMOCRACY, AND POLITICAL PARTICIPATION IN NIGERIA

The terms "democratization" and "empowerment" currently abound in global and contemporary discourse geared toward a freer community with equal participation of the citizenry. Their effects are also implied in gender discourse as well. The concept of gender operates as an evolving aspect of women's identities and a medium through which expectations are prescribed, social norms formed, and power relations negotiated.[17] The meaning, perception, and construction of gender as a societal role assignment on the male and female sexes are pivotal paradigms in dimensions of political involvement.

The debate on the involvement of women in politics and democracy has become a veritable part of global and contemporary discourses on development, governance, and democracy. Literature is replete with critique on the inadequate representation of women despite the recommendation of the Beijing Platform of Action (which Nigeria subscribes to) that 35 percent of the seats in government be reserved for women participants.[18]

Women's participation in the democratization process varies across nations. In Nigeria, women constitute over 50 percent of the population and 51 percent of voters in the general election; unfortunately, they do not have equal privileges like their male counterparts.[19] Statistics reveal that women's overall political representation in governance is less than 7 percent.[20] This record projects Nigeria as being far from the Beijing Declaration, which recommended 35 percent seats in government.

Constitutionally, in Nigeria, there is no legal impediment to the participation of women in governance. Voting and standing for election are the democratic right of the citizenry. Section 40 of the 1999 constitution confers on all citizens the right to democratic governance. This grants equal opportunity to all citizens (irrespective of sex) to participate in decision-making and governance.

Nigeria is the most populous African nation with a population of about 180 million people. Of this magnitude, 49 percent are female; some 80.2 million are girls and women. The U.K. Department for International Development records that: "Nigeria's 80.2 million women and girls have significantly worse life chances than men and also their sisters in comparable societies . . . women are Nigeria's hidden resource. Investing in women and girls now will increase productivity in this generation and will promote sustainable growth, peace and better health for the next generation."[21]

In spite of the significant population and contribution of women in Nigeria, they are still generally marginalized and less prominent in democratic involvement. This is because the legislative framework that stipulates at least 30 percent representation of women in government is hardly ever implemented, and as such, the quota of women is not secured.

The transition from military to civilian rule in 1999, which ended after sixteen years of authoritarian rule under military dictatorship in Nigeria, was conceived by many as the advent of new hopes and expectations for the citizenry. The country had battled with endemic corruption, ethnoreligious conflicts, unemployment, poverty, gender inequality, and other maladies, which stunted the process of national development.

Democracy is premised on the game of number where the majority rules. However, number has not translated to votes for women's political leadership and participation. The major concern is where the demographic majority (women) constitute the marginalized and the least represented population in decision-making. There is no democracy if women are not full participants in the democratic process and governance.[22] As Clark has stated,

> Gender equality and women's empowerment are not only human rights; they are also imperative for achieving inclusive, equitable and sustainable development. Women's political participation is central to these goals, and political parties are among the most important institutions for promoting and nurturing such participation. With less than twenty per cent of the world's parliamentary seats occupied by women, it is clear that political parties need to do more—and should be assisted in those efforts—to support women's political empowerment. Globally, although forty to fifty per cent of party members are women, women hold only about ten per cent of the leadership positions within those parties.[23]

True democracy and good governance, indeed, require the representation and participation of the different strata that make up the population.

Inequality is a drag on growth and development; thus, there is a strong relationship between inequality and slow growth in poor countries. The effect of inequality on growth can be seen as a rough indicator of inequality of opportunity and limited social mobility in a particular setting, a phenomenon sometimes also referred to as destructive inequality.

Citizens' Forum for Constitutional Reform captures it thus:

1. It is unjust, illegitimate and undemocratic to exclude women from the political process.
2. The views of 50 percent of the population cannot be ignored.

3. Democracy must be inclusive of the diverse perspectives of the values of women as well as men in arriving to decisions and carrying forward any strategy.
4. Women's political rights are an integral and inseparable part of their human rights.[24]

Nigeria has articulated and signed into law various policy frameworks to guarantee the right and participation of women in politics and the decision-making process. Some of these include section 40 of the 1999 constitution, the National Policy on Women 2000, and the National Gender Policy 2006. Some of these policies exist on paper as the plethora of legislative positions has not propelled them into concrete women's empowerment and effective political participation. It is against this background that Nigerian women have agitated for greater access and representation in politics and decision-making.

WOMEN AND ELECTIONS, 1999–2015

Elections are conducted every four years in Nigeria, thus this chapter draws data from the close of the twentieth century in 1999 to the twenty-first-century Nigeria. This section will examine the participation of women in Nigerian politics from 1999, when the nation returned to democratic rule, until the 2015 general election.

As it is clearly illustrated in table 10.1, there is a greater percentage of women's participation in the lower house than in the upper house. Interestingly, in the upper house (Senate), there is a greater participation of women in 2007, which recorded nine (8.3 percent) senators and twenty-six (7.2 percent) women members of the House of Representatives. 2011 recorded a decline in women participation in politics, with only seven women (6.4 percent) at the senatorial level and twenty-five (6.9 percent) at the lower house. 2015 witnessed an abysmal decline in women participation in politics, as only seven women (6.4 percent) were elected to the House of Assembly, and nineteen (5.2 percent) women to the House of Representatives. This result shows the vanishing voice of women in political participation in the House of Assembly and the House of Representatives.

Going by the data above, the democratic process in Nigeria still falls short of the recommended 30 percent of the Beijing Platform for Action in 1995 and the 35 percent recommendation of National Policy on Women adopted in July 2000. In as much as there are opportunities for women's participation in politics, it is a glaring fact that their involvement in elective and appointive positions is still low, though it is better now than before. The twenty-first century has witnessed the participation of women in every electoral process in the country even though their level of participation has not translated to the expected level of success.

Table 10.1 Gender Participation in Senate, House of Representative, and State Houses of Assembly

Year	*Total No. of Seats*	*Men (%)*	*Women (%)*
Senate			
1999	109	106 (97.2%)	3 (2.8%)
2003	109	105 (96.3%)	4 (3.7%)
2007	109	100 (91.7%)	9 (8.3%)
2011	109	102 (93.6%)	7 (6.4%)
2015	109	101 (92.7%)	8 (7.3%)
House of Representatives			
1999	360	348 (96.7%)	12 (3.3%)
2003	360	337 (93.6%)	23 (6.4%)
2007	360	334 (92.8%)	26 (7.2%)
2011	360	334 (92.8%)	26 (7.2%)
2015	360	346 (96.1%)	14 (3.9%)
State House of Assembly			
1999	978	966 (98.8)	12 (1.2%)
2003	951	912 (96.0)	39 (4.0%)
2007	900	843 (94.2)	54 (5.5%)
2011	900	832 (93.1)	68 (6.9%)
2015	900		

Source: Excerpt from UN Women's Preliminary Analysis of the 2011 General Elections in Nigeria. 2015 Data was compiled by the author from the website of the Independent National Electoral Commission (INEC): www.inecnigeria.org.

History would have been made in Nigeria's electoral process if Aisha Jumai Alhassan (popularly called Mama Taraba), who contested for the governorship position under the platform of All Progressive Congress (APC) in Taraba State, had won to emerge as the first elected female governor in Nigeria. Alhassan was a senator representing the Taraba North constituency of the state, which she won under the platform of the People's Democratic Party (PDP), but later decamped to the APC from where she contested for the 2015 general elections. She would have been the first woman in Nigeria to scale the hurdles of electioneering campaign to become a governor and thus breaking the cycle. However, the result of the election was declared inconclusive by INEC. In the rerun election, Alhassan's hopes were finally dashed when her male rival, Darius Dickson Ishaku, was declared the winner. Alhassan described her opponent's victory as a "daylight robbery" and alleged that the election was characterized by violence, massive rigging, ballot snatching, and the abuse of the card readers in substantial parts of the state. Thus, the end results did not reflect the true wishes of the people of Taraba.

Sarah Jubril's presidential aspirations were another case of preference of the male over the woman, incidentally, even by women themselves. Jubril was the only woman among the three PDP candidates for the 2011 presidential election primaries, with the other two being President Goodluck Jonathan and former Vice President Atiku Abubakar. Her ambition translated to mere wishes, as she did not get more than a lone vote, which she probably cast for herself. In this case, even other women did not consider her worthy of their vote.

The decline in women participation became even more pronounced in the 2015 elections. The few courageous women who participated have always turned out to be losers. This, however, proves that despite having good numbers in terms of political representation, there is not a matching increase in voting patterns of women to women candidates. Women's low performance was not out of lack of turnout by women voters. Rather, it was because the system was skewed against women such that it was difficult for them to win elections. Indeed, the political climate was intolerable of women, but in favor of men. Ebere Ifendu, chair of Women in Politics Forum (WPF), adequately expressed this problem:

> Looking at what is going on in Taraba and Akwa Ibom where women contested, there was so much violence, and unfortunately, we are not going to have as much women as the previous senate. We are not happy with it, but we have to re-strategize and see what we can do to have more women participate. Because as it is, we are just back to square one. Until there is legislation on the 35 percent affirmative action, women will continue to have problems because election is very much monetized, women don't have resources to match men. There is no genuine internal democracy in the political parties and candidates are handpicked, adding that when one scales party primary he or she has scaled the most hurdle.[25]

Women usually flood every political meeting, but unfortunately, they attend primarily as observers and fans and do not contribute to women's political empowerment. Women's role in the Nigerian polity has always been to mobilize for men's electoral success—men who would go on to pursue chiefly a male hegemonic agenda. In essence, women, who constitute the bulk of the voting bloc, are largely marginalized in Nigerian politics such that it has almost been accepted as a norm. In as much as there is no constitutional inhibition on the alienation of women from political participation in Nigeria, there are, however, certain societal imposed stereotypes, economic and religious factors, lack of education, etc., which still exclude them from exercising their right.

WOMEN PARTICIPATION IN THE DEMOCRATIC PROCESS

A number of factors, identified by extant literature, have militated against the full participation of Nigerian women in the democratic process. These factors are the following:

Exclusion from Informal Political Party Networks

This is a major form of discrimination against women politicians. Most nominees for political offices are men, thus constituting discrimination against women. Women are denied access to adequate information, and as Christiana Ogbogu has observed, decision-making is usually the terrain of men while women are generally receivers of instructions on what to do.[26]

Another major hindrance to the full participation of woman is the nocturnal nature of most caucus meetings and political party networking. Most women in Africa may not be predisposed to attend such gathering owing to the multitasked nature of African women. Again, most inner caucus political meetings take place at night and in locations like hotels, which culturally are perceived as places where married women are not supposed to be seen without being in the company of their husbands. Women, for fear of being seen as participants in the 'dirtiness of politics,' may not easily and readily attend such meetings, thus they are thus excluded from vital political decisions (including those that affect them).

Patriarchy and Societally Imposed Norms and Prejudice

Men generally dominate the Nigerian political class. Indeed, men have generally played a dominant role in all areas of human endeavor. This is attributed to the chauvinism and patriarchy that is prevalent in the Nigerian society dictated by culture. In addition to this, there are obnoxious cultural beliefs and practices that deny women access to positions. Such practices include restriction of movement at certain days, early marriage, and discrimination against women under various traditional values and customs. In many African societies, men are perceived as superior to women, which transfers over to the political arena. Politics tend to expose women to close interactions with men, which is considered culturally unacceptable in some cultures in Nigeria. Thus, politics is construed as a dirty game where women politicians are portrayed as wild women who are no longer obedient to their husbands because they abandoned their marital responsibilities. A woman politician in Oyo State, Mosunmola Adeniran, decried the fate of Nigerian women politicians when she said that:

> We face lots of challenges; our men won't allow us to spread our wings and we really want to fly . . . if you are a woman, the marital problem is there where they tag you as a prostitute. People believe that any women in politics is [*sic*] a prostitute, but it is not so. They give us bad names and there is the financial constraint.[27]

The societal misconception about women being involved in politics, which is considered a "dirty game," has to a great extent worked against some women of proven integrity who run for elections. This has thus prevented them from contributing their quota to national development.

Religion

Like most African countries, Nigeria is a highly religious state, and every societal occurrence has a religious interpretation. Most religions advocate that the man is the head while the woman should be subservient to the man. This belief system permeates into the subconsciousness of the Nigerian man, who plays the lordship role over the submissive woman.

God Fatherism

Political godfathers are powerful political figures who not only wield economic power but also use violence and corrupt means to ensure that candidates of their choice emerge as winners in elections by all means. Godfathers are not only financiers of political campaigns as they also exercise power as a result of their ability to control and manipulate national, state, and local political systems in support of candidates of their choice. In Nigerian politics, it is not uncommon to find an elected politician, a godson, that is, a protégé of a godfather, under the strong influence of the later. It is worthy of note that godfathers tend to avoid sponsoring women for fear that they may lose in the election. The absence of godmothers in Nigerian politics is quite revealing.

Finance

Elections are highly monetized in Nigeria. The high cost of financing elections has made it almost impossible for women to match up with the financial might of their male counterparts. Financing elections in Nigeria, from party primaries, campaigns, and declaration of interest, up to the actual contest, which requires enormous financial commitment. Lack of financial wherewithal has contributed to the political alienation of women. Many women politicians simply do not command the necessary resources to match their male counterparts. Also, for the most part, women, do not have the stomach for the violence associated with politics.

Nature of Political Party Formation

Political party formation in Nigeria evolved from clubs and informal meetings initiated by men and business partners. Women are only contacted at a much later stage when party structures are already in place for membership. Thus, women are excluded from participation in the formation stage of political parties. Consequently, they are denied the benefits accruing to foundation membership and collective ownership of the parties. Also, the noninclusion of women in top party hierarchy and structure leads to the absence of women in the mainstream political parties.

Affirmative Action

Nigeria has a lot of policies which sound beautiful on paper, but are hardly implemented. One of such is the nonadoption of affirmative action in the nation's constitution. Political parties' constitution and their manifestos have further widened the gap between women and men's political participation. Nigeria, unlike many African states, lacks a formal quota system which would have served as a mechanism for increased women's participation in politics. This lack of a quota, combined with cultural and structural factors, pose often-insurmountable barriers to women's political participation.[28]

ENHANCING WOMEN PARTICIPATION

The development of any nation depends largely on the representation of all segments of its population in governance and decision making, irrespective of gender, age, or class. There should be consciousness that women have needs that are different from those of men, so only they can tell their own stories; thus, there is the need for women's involvement in governance. The failure of the society to incorporate women, or their underrepresentation in the three tiers of governance, is a major loss to the society as half of its population has been disenfranchised. Men and women have different needs, interests, and priorities, and this makes for disparity. Women can never be adequately represented by men.[29] For instance issues related to family, reproductive health, women and child trafficking, child labor, marriage, widowhood practices, abuses, work-based childcare, violence against women, valuation of unpaid labor, employment policies, HIV/AIDS, etc., can best be addressed by women. Thus, women's political participation provides the opportunity for them to deliberate on issues confronting them. The number of women in the legislative arm can also influence the extent to which women's issues attract attention.

CONCLUSION

There is no true democracy without the representation of half of the country's population. Women constitute the least represented and the most marginalized socially, economically, politically, and materially. There is a nagging question as to whether Nigeria is actually practicing democracy or civilian rule because of the underrepresentation of women in decision-making. The participation of women at all levels of decision-making is crucial in the actualization of true democracy and realization of fundamental women's right. Women have the potential to contribute meaningfully to national development and sustenance of democracy. Indeed, women have historically made immense contribution to national development. For instance, Ngozi Okonjo-Iweala, the former Minister of Finance, utilized her experience and expertise in stabilizing Nigerian's economy while in office. Also, Dora Akunyili, a former boss of National Agency for Food and Drug Administration and Control (NAFDAC), performed exceptionally well in championing the fight against the infiltration of adulterated drugs into the Nigerian pharmaceutical industry. These and other examples show that the role of women in national development is indispensable. For a nation to attain overall meaningful development, the place of women who constitute a large proportion of the population must be secured. Women should not be left out of the issues that especially affect their livelihood. Civil rule cannot be said to be democratic when over half of the civil society is made up of women who are excluded from the democratic process.

NOTES

1. United Nations Entity for Gender Equality and Empowerment of Women, "The Convention on the Elimination of All Forms of Discrimination against Women (CEDAW)," adopted in 1979 by the UN General Assembly, is often described as an international bill of rights for women. It consists of a preamble and thirty articles that define what constitutes discrimination against women. It also set up an agenda for national action to end such discrimination, assessed March 22, 2016, http://www.un.org/womenwatch/daw/cedaw/text/econvention.htm.

2. F. C. Enemuo, "Gender and Women Empowerment," in *Elements of Politics*, eds., Remi Anifowose and Francis Enemuo (Lagos: Sam Iroanusi Publications, 1999), 230.

3. Ngozi U. Emeka-Nwobia and Chinwe Obianika, "Gender Dynamics and Domestic Violence Against Igbo Women of Southeastern Nigeria," in *The Long Struggle: Discourses on Human and Civil Rights in Africa and the African Diaspora*, eds., Adebayo Oyebade and Gashawbeza W. Bekele (Austin, TX: Pan-African University Press, 2017).

4. Titilope Olusegun Olalere, "Women and Nigerian Politics: An Appraisal of 2015 General Elections," accessed on Mach 22, 2016, https://www.inecnigeria.org/wp-content/uploads/.../Conference-Paper-Olalere-Titilope.pdf.

5. "Etiaba, Nigeria's first Female Governor," *Saturday and Sunday Peoples Diary*, January 3–5, 2015.

6. The United Nations, "The Fourth World Conference on Women: Action for Equality, Development, and Peace," Beijing, China, September 14–15, 1995.

7. Jacqueline Adhiambo-Oduol, "Empowerment of Women Throughout the Life Cycle as a Transformative Strategy for Poverty Eradication," Division for the Advancement of Women (DAW), United Nations Expert Group Meeting, New Delhi, India, November 26–29, 2001.

8. Simon Ottenberg, *Double Descent in an African Society; The Afikpo Village-Group* (Seattle: University of Washington Press, 1968), 265.

9. Ifi Amadiume, *Male Daughters, Female Husbands: Gender and Sex in an African Society* (London: Zed Press, 1987).

10. S. A. Khasiani, "Youth Service: The Kenyan Profile," paper prepared at the Ford Foundation Workshop on Youth Involvement as a Strategy for Social, Economic, and Democratic Development, Costa Rica, January 17, 2000.

11. Herbert Richmond Palmer, ed., *Sudanese Memoirs: Being Mainly Translations of a Number of Arabic Manuscripts Relating to the Western and Central Sudan* (3 Volumes) (Lagos: Government Printer, 1967).

12. Ngozi U. Emeka-Nwobia, "Women's Involvement in Peacebuilding and Conflict Resolution among the Igbo of Southeastern Nigeria," *Kujenga Amani*, a publication of the Social Science Research Council, New York, 2015, accessed March 22, 2016, https://kujenga-amani.ssrc.org/2015/05/28/womens-involvement-in-peacebuilding-and-conflict-resolution-among-the-igbo-of-southeastern-nigeria.

13. See Toyin Falola and S. U. Fwatshak, eds., *Beyond Tradition: African Women and Cultural Spaces* (Trenton, NJ: Africa World Press, 2011), 327–344.

14. Titilope Olusegun Olalere, "Women and Nigerian Politics: An Appraisal of 2015 General Elections," accessed March 22, 2016, https://www.inecnigeria.org/wp-content/uploads/.../Conference-Paper-Olalere-Titilope.pdf.; See also, Patrick Kenechukwu Uchendu, *The Role of Nigerian Women in Politics Past and Present* (Nigeria: Fourth Dimension Publishing, 1993), 22.

15. N'Dri Thérèse Assié-Lumumba, "Behind and Beyond Beijing: An African Perspective on the Fourth World Conference on Women," *CODESRIA Bulletin*, 3 (1996): 206.

16. Enemuo, "Gender and Women Empowerment."

17. Bilkis Vissandjee, et al., "Empowerment beyond Numbers: Substantiating Women's Political Participation," *Journal of International Women's Studies* 7, no. 2 (2005): 123–141.

18. Olayode Kehinde, "Women Participation and Gender Mainstreaming in Local Governance in Nigeria," in *Deeper Insight into Nigeria's Public Administration*, ed. Banji Oyeniran Adediji (Bloomington, IN: Author House, 2013), 449–468.

19. I. Ofong, "Women's Participation in Politics in Nigeria," a paper presented at the 8th International Interdisciplinary Congress on Women, Makerere University, Kampala, Uganda, July 21–26, 2002.

20. Damilola Taiye Agbalajobi, "Women's Participation and the Political Process in Nigeria: Problems and Prospects," *African Journal of Political Science and International Relations* 4, no. 2 (2010): 75–82.

21. UK Aid, "Gender in Nigeria Report 2012: Improving the Lives of Girls and Women in Nigeria," *Issues and Policies Action* (British Council, Nigeria, 2012), iii.

22. Maureen A. Azuike, "Women and Governance: Four years of Democracy in Nigeria," in *Democratic Rebirth in Nigeria, Vol. 1*, eds. Aaron Gana and Y. B. Omelle (Abuja: AFRIGOV, 2003).

23. Helen Clark, "Foreword," in*Empowering Women for Stronger Political Parties—A Guide Book to Promote Women's Political Participation*, eds. Julie Ballington, et al. (New York: United Nations Development Programmes and National Democratic Institute, 2012).

24. Citizens' Forum for Constitutional Reform, "Affirmative Action for Women—Memorandum" (Abuja: Center for Democracy and Development, 2005).

25. Ojoma Akor, "How Women Performed in the 2015 General Elections," *Daily Trust*, April 24, 2015, 8.

26. Christiana O. Ogbogu, "The Role of Women in Politics and in the Sustenance of Democracy in Nigeria," *International Journal of Business and Social Science* 3, no. 18 (September 2012): 182–191.

27. Quoted in T. Ligali, "Men Don't Believe We'll Do Anything Right," *Sunday Tribune,* September 28, 2007.

28. Alexandra Z. Safir and Mayesha Alam, "Special Report: The 2015 Nigeria Elections and Violence against Women in Politics," April 2015, accessed March 25, 2016, https://giwps.georgetown.edu/sites/giwps/files/Special%20Report%20-%20 Nigeria.pdf.

29. Lorraine Corner, "Women Participation in Decision-making and Leadership: A Global Perspective," paper presented at the Conference on Women in Decision-Making in Cooperatives, Tagatay City, Philippines, May 7–9, 1997, accessed March 25, 2016, http://iknowpolitics.org/sites/default/files/decision-making26leadership_global.pdf.

Chapter 11

Women, Conflict, and Nigeria's Sustainable Development Agenda

Adaora Osondu-Oti

INTRODUCTION

Within the last few decades to the end of the twentieth century, African countries have had numerous conflicts with devastating consequences. For instance, in East Africa, Burundi faced internal conflict in 1960 resulting in the loss of hundreds of thousands of lives and refugees of over half a million persons.[1] In Somalia, the decades-long civil war claimed hundreds of thousands of lives while there were over 800,000 refugees and over one million internally displaced persons that catapulted the country into a failed state.[2] The ethnic conflict in Rwanda resulted in genocide in 1994 with the killing of over half a million persons from one ethnic group. The continuing conflicts that ravage the African continent represent a heavy social and economic burden.[3] As of 2002, war was estimated to have cost $1 billion per year in Central Africa, without counting the cost of aiding refugees, estimated to be about $500 million in the region.[4] Countries in West Africa such as Sierra Leone and Liberia were not left out of the war brutalities and devastation. In Sudan, where conflict has existed since 1956, more than two million people have lost their lives since the early 1980s,[5] and at the moment, South Sudan (the state that emerged after the 2011 referendum) have been engulfed in serious conflict since 2013, with greater losses of lives, displacement and famine. Today, the United Nations seeks assistance for 1.9 million South Sudanese refugees.

After Nigeria gained independence in 1960, civil war broke out seven years later in 1967 and lasted for three years with great losses of lives and properties. Having gone through many years of military rule, the country returned to democratic rule in 1999. Within the euphoria that came with the country's return to democratic rule, crisis ensued. The return to civilian rule provided some of the aggrieved groups the opportunity to voice out their grievances, as democracy is believed to offer people the avenue to freely express themselves. It is a consensus that democracy helps to protect basic personal liberties such as liberty of speech, and affords citizens the opportunity to claims their rights. Democracy provides the avenue for the demand of justice; even though it has failed to prevent conflict, as seen in the case of the militancy in Niger Delta region of Nigeria, the call for secession from the South East region, and the current Boko Haram insurgency in the northern region of the country.

For example, at the dawn of democracy in Nigeria, due to long years of neglect of the Niger Delta, the people of the region, especially the youths became violent, and in the process resorted to militancy. The subsequent deployment of military troops by the Nigerian government combined to create a theatre of violence in the Niger Delta. Until 2009 when the Nigerian government under the leadership of late Musa Yar'dua granted Amnesty to the militants, both the government forces and the militants engaged in battle, or "noninternational armed conflict."[6]

No doubt, conflict has often taken immeasurable toll on human lives, leaving people dead, maimed, abducted, and displaced internally or some as refugees in other nations. While conflict inflicts suffering on everyone, women are particularly affected by its short and long-term effects.[7] For instance, sexual assault and exploitation are employed as tools of war against women; women are victimized and victimization leads to isolation, alienation, prolonged emotional trauma, and unwanted pregnancies that often result in abandoned children.[8] In large part, women are targeted for rape, abducted by the rebel groups, taken into the army camp, serve as army wives, and more often than men are subject to sexual assault.[9] For example, many cases of rape were reported during the militancy in Niger Delta.[10]

Also, the Boko Haram Group have carried out terrorist activities in many states of the Northern Nigeria, including Niger, Borno, Adamawa, Yobe, Kano, Kaduna, Nassarawa, and even the Federal Capital Territory. Just like the Niger Delta militant group, the Boko Haram insurgency has taken its toll on women and girls. The group have engaged in raping of women and kidnapping of young girls. One clear case is the kidnapping of over 200 Chibok school-girls by Boko Haram Group in April 2014, and at the time of writing not all, the girls have been rescued by the government. In conflict situations (for example, the militancy in Niger Delta and Boko Haram insurgency in the northern region of Nigeria) women are major targets and their security threatened. In many circumstances, the challenges they might face or they face are neglected and unrecognised.

It is clear that the international community's adoption of the Sustainable Development Goals agenda in 2015 was to address the various needs and concerns of humanity, and in that way, make development agenda of nations sustainable. A development that does not improve the conditions of the people is nothing but maldevelopment or no development. The pursuit of development or sustainable development as the case may be is to address the security, well-being, and human rights of the people in both peace times, as well as conflict and postconflict era. While the sustainable development agenda centres on many goals (up to seventeen), including the promotion of gender equality and empowering women (Goal 5, which was the Goal 3 of the Millennium Development Goals), the challenges of women in conflict torn regions and countries emerging from conflicts was not incorporated on the sustainable development goals' agenda.

Thus, for development to be sustainable, it is important to look into those challenges women face or could face not just in peace times, but also in times of conflicts. The post-2015 sustainable development framework has presented a unique opportunity to build on the achievements of the Millennium Development Goals (2000–2015), while also addressing the dimensions that are left behind. According to the UN document, sustainable development is a development that must be able to meet the needs of the present and future generations. It must be holistic and encompassing if African countries (many of whom have experienced conflicts and some are still experiencing conflicts) are to move toward sustainable development. Although not explicitly stated, there are barriers to achieving gender equality for women (Goal 5 of the sustainable development goals). Conflict poses a great threat to women's lives and security and hinders their personal development. Thus, with reference to Nigeria, this chapter examines women, conflict challenges, and the Nigerian government commitments (if any) to gender dimension of the sustainable development agenda. The chapter addresses the importance of recognising the challenges women face in conflict times for the country's achievement of the sustainable development agenda. With the introduction as Section 1, Section 2 is an overview of the UN Sustainable Development Goals. Section 3 analyses women and conflict challenges, and Nigeria's commitment to the gender aspect of the sustainable development agenda. Section 4 is the conclusion and recommendations.

THE UN SUSTAINABLE DEVELOPMENT GOALS

After the UN World Commission Conference on Environment and Development in 1987, the concept of "sustainable development" spread throughout the UN system. Sustainable development became an agenda of the world community, and it was meant to underpin the future development of all nations. The most often cited definition of sustainable development is the one proposed by the UN World Commission on Environment and Development (WCED) otherwise known as the Brundtland Commission. The Commission defined sustainable development as the development that meets the needs of the present without compromising the ability of future generations to meet their own needs. In the WCED analysis of the concept of sustainable development, "development" clearly points to the idea of change; of both directional and progressive change. It is a process of directional change by which a system improves through time in a sustainable way. Lele describes sustainable development as a new way of life and approach to social and economic activities for all societies, rich and poor that is compatible with the preservation of the environment.[11] According to Pearce and Watford, sustainable development describes a process in which the natural resource base is not allowed to deteriorate. Sustainable development emphasizes the hitherto unappreciated role of the environmental quality and environmental inputs in the process of raising real income and quality of life.[12] Beyond the initial environmental preservation emphasis on sustainable development, the concept of sustainable development assumed an important and new dimension within the United Nations in the twenty-first century with member countries canvassing for diverse ways and approaches to make development sustainable. As a result, conferences were organized and decisions reached.

One of the main outcomes of the UN Conference on Sustainable Development (Rio+20) in 2012 was an international agreement to negotiate a new set of global goals to guide the path of sustainable development at the end of the Millennium Development Goals Target in 2015. Thus, in September 2015, world leaders converged at the UN Headquarters in New York to consider and adopt a new and comprehensive development agenda. Sustainable Development Goals (SDGs) were adopted with 169 targets aimed at shifting the world onto a sustainable and resilient development pathway while ensuring that no important area is left behind. The SDGs were put forward for countries to pursue for a period of fifteen years (2015–2030). These goals are seventeen in number.[13] For instance, Goal 1 is to end poverty in all its forms; Goal 2 is to end hunger, achieve food security and nutrition; Goal 3 is to ensure healthy lives and promote well-being; and Goal 5 is to achieve gender equality and empower women. The Sustainable Development Goals (SDGs) went beyond the MDGs and provided a comprehensive vision and framework for action for all countries.

In the realm of the present sustainable development debate, one major issue/question that is considered is: what is to be sustained or to be made sustainable? In providing answer to this, three aspects of sustainable development are recognized: the economic, the social, and the environment. These are further discussed below:

- Economic: An economically sustainable system must be able to produce goods and services on a continuing basis, to maintain manageable levels of government and external debt, and to avoid extreme sectoral imbalances, which damage agricultural or industrial production.

- Social: A socially sustainable system must achieve distributional equity, adequate provision of social services including health and education, gender equity, and political accountability and participation.
- Environmental: An environmentally sustainable system must maintain a stable resource base, avoiding overexploitation of renewable resource systems or environment sink functions, and depleting nonrenewable resources only to the extent that investment is made in adequate substitutes.

While the economic and environmental aspects of sustainable development cannot be excluded in the quest for sustainable development, the social aspect of sustainable development relates more closely to the focus of this chapter. Today, sustainable development is now seen as an issue that is confronting all humanity, and not half of humanity. The need for equal participation and equity in tackling and responding to global challenges and problems cannot be overlooked. As stated above, a socially sustainable society is meant to ensure distributional equity, adequate provision of social services including health and education, gender equity, political accountability and participation, not excluding respect for human rights and adequate protection of civilians in conflict and postconflict times. There is no gainsaying that a socially sustainable society reflects a democratic order, where principles of basic human rights are to be protected and secured. The term "democratic" is not just used to characterize a form of government formed in the people's interest but also used to define a type of society characterized by conditions of equality, a society of equals, with equal rights and equal status. Respect for human rights is perceived either to be a prerequisite for democracy or democracy is perceived as a prerequisite for the respect of human rights. It is believed that the greatest protection of human rights emanates from a sustainable democratic framework grounded in the rule of law. Thus, sustainable development must be geared toward a sustainable democratic order where not only the interests of the people are put forward but where adequate provisions are made to address the needs and challenges of the masses both in peace and conflict times.

WOMEN, CONFLICT CHALLENGES AND SUSTAINABLE DEVELOPMENT AGENDA: NIGERIA AS A REFERENCE POINT

Studies have shown that women are worst hit in situations of violent conflict and are affected differently from men during conflicts.[14] When men engage in war and are killed, disappear or take refuge outside their country's borders, women are left with the burden of ensuring family livelihood, which exposes them to danger and insecurity. Women struggle to protect their families' health and safety, a task, which rests on their ability to cope pragmatically with change and adversity.[15]

Conflicts have continued to have devastating effect on the lives and dignity of women. Women are often confronted with gender-based violence and specific threats that compound their cases. Women suffer in ways specific to women. Yet they should not be seen as a homogenous group as different women will have different needs, vulnerabilities and coping mechanisms.[16] While thousands and millions of people die, men and women often die different deaths and are tortured and abused in different ways, sometimes for biological reasons. It has been argued that violence against women in conflict is one of history's great silences.[17] Even though men and boys as well as women and girls are the victims during conflict, women, much more than men, suffer gender-based violence. Women are kidnapped or abducted, used as sexual slaves and also undergo emotional, psychological and physical/ health challenges. Women's experience of armed conflict is multifaceted: it means abduction, increased risk of sexual violence such as forced impregnation, forced termination of pregnancy, sexual slavery and others harsh experiences such as separation, loss of relatives, physical and economic insecurity, wounding, detention, deprivation and even death. Women's bodies, deliberately infected with HIV/AIDS or carrying a child conceived in rape, have been used as envelopes to send messages to the perceived "enemy."[18]

Certainly the picture of violence against women during conflict is not monochromatic. In the height of the conflict in Niger Delta (before the Nigerian government declaration of Amnesty in 2009), Niger Delta women bore the greater brunt of the conflict. The plights of women during the conflict were enormous. For instance, Niger Delta women suffered both physical and mental harms such as killing, torture and mutilation, and cruel, inhuman and degrading treatments in the hands of military personnel.[19] Eze et al. noted that during the Odi community onslaught for example, women and girls were brutally raped and killed by the military officers.[20] Also, over 238 Ijaw women were raped in four major crackdowns on Ijaw resistance in Kaiama, Yenagoa, Warri, and Odi,[21] and many remained unreported due to cultural alienation and stigmatization.[22]

In an interview with Emen Okon, a Niger Delta woman activist, she maintained that the major challenges women faced in Niger Delta was the military personnel and the Joint Task Force (JTF) that subjected women to indecent sexual assault. Also, according to Okonta and Douglas, the military occupation of oil communities marked out the Niger Delta as the only part of Nigeria where a special military occupation force took over the lives of the people, killing, maiming, and raping thousands of women.[23]

With such inhuman treatment such as rape and other forced sexual assault, Niger Delta women and girls faced the risks of sexually transmitted diseases such as HIV and AIDS, pregnancy, miscarriage, menstrual problems, psychological, mental and physical trauma, and even death.[24] Victims of rape or sexual violence sometimes face further problems such as ostracism (both from their family and community), or retribution (the perpetrators must have told them that if they report the violation they, or their families, will be subjected to further violence), when their cases are made public. It is well-known fact that when men go into fighting or hiding as the case may be, women are burdened with the task of providing and caring for their respective families, and in the process, their security is threatened. Increased insecurity and fear of attack caused many women to flee with their children to refugee camps and as a result women and children form the majority of the refugees and the displaced in the many refugee camps. According to Ekine when the Ijaw Community of Gbaramatu was invaded by JTF in 2009, women had to flee and over 2,000 women were eventually housed in a refugee camp for months before returning home.[25] Being forced by conflict to relocate to refugee camps becomes a great challenge for women to cater for themselves and children in a "typical refugee camps" that are hardly well equipped.

In a similar vein, the current Boko Haram insurgency in Northern part of Nigeria has subjected women to all forms of violence. Women have been kidnapped, abducted, detained, and sexually assaulted. The sexual assault had come either from the Boko Haram group or from the military forces. In 2013, the U.S. Bureau of Intelligence accused the Nigerian military of human rights violations and impunity, and these include forced sexual activities against women, which led to U.S. withdrawal of its military assistance to Nigerian government in fighting Boko Haram. The Boko Haram on its part has also targeted women. According to Amnesty International Report, Boko Haram has abducted at least 2,000 young women and girls and subjected them to forced marriage.[26] Abduction of girls is no longer a new story. In April 14, 2014, the Boko Haram group abducted more than 200 Chibok girls and they are all yet to be rescued. The girls were used as sex slaves and were forced into early motherhood, as some of the rescued Chibok girls came home with a baby.

The challenges women face during conflicts (as seen in Niger Delta and Boko Haram insurgency) sometimes (if not most times) hunt them through life. The violation of young girls and women in times of conflict is area that has not received adequate attention by the government. In reference to Boko Haram activities in the North, for instance, Walker noted that the tactics employed by the government security agencies against Boko Haram have been consistently brutal and counterproductive, and in their brutal acts, women often receive greater share.[27] Nigerian government rarely adopts a proactive measure to protect women during conflict, and in postconflict times, women are often sidelined in peace processes. Nigeria is not alone, in the neglect of the issues of women and conflict. The inadequate attention paid by government all over the world has been a major concern. In post conflict reconstruction and peace building, women are hardly consulted, and these major victims of conflict "forgotten." According to Sorensen, women tend to fade into the background when official peace negotiations begin and the consolidation of peace and rebuilding of the economy becomes a formal exercise.[28] UNIFEM estimated that women account for less than 10 percent of members in formal peace negotiations and less than 2 percent of signatories to peace agreements.[29]

It should be recalled that in year 2000 the international community through the umbrella of United Nations set up the Millennium Development Goals for countries to work toward achievement. The eight goals include eradicate extreme poverty and hunger; achieve universal primary education; promote gender equality and empower women; reduce child mortality; improve maternal health; combat HIV/AIDS, malaria, and other diseases; ensure environmental sustainability; and develop a global partnership for development. One of the goals pertaining to women was Goal 3, which is to promote gender equality and empower women. The same Goal is also included in the Sustainable Development Goals as Goal 5. The adoption of SDGs is follow-up for many countries to address those areas that are still posing great challenges to their respective nations and the world at large. The SDGs were put forward as a blueprint for countries to pursue for their overall economic, political, environmental, social, cultural development and for the achievement of a peaceful world.

Prior to the initiation of MDGs and the current SDGs that recognized the aspect of gender equality and empowerment of women, the international community had reached consensus for governments to include women in all aspects of decision-makings and recognize the differential impact of armed conflict on women. The United Nations, for instance, pointed to the importance of gender mainstreaming in all areas. Gender mainstreaming is defined as the process of assessing the implications for men and for women of any planned action, including legislation, policies or programmes, in all areas and at all levels. It is a strategy for making women's as well as men's concerns and experiences an integral dimension of the design, implementation, monitoring and evaluation of policies and programmes in all political, economic and societal spheres so that women and men benefit equally and inequality is not perpetuated.

As an important aspect of gender mainstreaming, the United Nations has focused on the importance of recognising women in conflict resolution and peace processes, especially as victims of conflicts. Starting with the UN Convention on the Elimination of All Forms of Discrimination against Women (CEDAW) in 1979, the full development and advancement of women for the purpose of guaranteeing the exercise and enjoyment of human rights and fundamental freedoms on a basis of equality with men were first canvaseed. The Beijing Platform for Action arising from the Fourth Women Conference in Beijing in 1995 identified twelve key areas of critical concern for women, including the effects of armed conflicts on women, and encouraged governments to translate commitments into actions to achieve gender equality in all dimensions of life.

As a follow-up in year 2000, the UN Security Council adopted Resolution 1325 on Women, Peace and Security, which focused on impact of war on women and need to recognize women's experiences in conflict. Subsequently in 2009, UN Security Council adopted Resolutions 1820, 1888, and 1889. Resolution 1820 calls for an end to widespread conflict-related sexual violence. The Resolution also noted that "women and girls are particularly targeted by the use of sexual violence, including as a tactic of war to humiliate, dominate, instill fear in, disperse and/or forcibly relocate civilian members of a community or ethnic group."[30] Ten years after the passage of resolution 1325 (2000), the UN Open days on Women, Peace and Security came up, in 2010. In many of the UN documents, the international community has recognized women as victims, survivors, and even wagers of armed conflict as major stakeholders in conflict and the course that would be set for future development of any nation. That is to say that, any government committed to achieving sustainable development cannot underestimate women's concerns, particularly in conflict times.

Just like many other countries of the world, Nigeria agreed to partake in the world sustainable development agenda. Nigeria has often tried to participate and cooperate in international initiatives and programmes (at least in theory and by being a signatory to international agreements). Nigeria was actively involved in the processes leading to the UN Conference on Sustainable Development (Rio+20). For instance, the economic, social, and environment pillars of sustainable development are embedded in the country's 1999 Constitution. In particular, the Nigerian Constitution states that the Federal Republic of Nigeria operates on the principles of democracy and social justice for all encompassing the social, economic, political, as well as equality of status of opportunity and the dignity of the individual, which in essence reflect an agenda toward a socially sustainable society.

Despite the efforts to partake and domesticate international agreements, little contributions are seen in practice. Women are still marginalized and their rights trampled upon. Women are still sidelined sometimes due culture, traditional norms and practices, as well as religion that exclude women in

seen. Women continue to bear greater brunt of the conflict in the current Boko Haram insurgency in the Northern parts of Nigeria. While the world's sustainable development agenda commits all signatory countries to work to promote sustained and inclusive economic growth and ensure that every person fulfills his or her potentials in dignity and equality in a healthy environment, women are still marginalized in all spheres. Although the SDGs came into existence just two years ago and it could be argued that it is too early to reach a conclusion on the road to SDGs in Nigeria, there seems to be no clear agenda for gender issues (especially with regards to the marginalized group: the women) at the moment and no policy dimensions. The country's economy in recent time nose-dived into recession with untold hardship on the citizens, and the government is struggling to revive the economy. In terms of priority, the SDGs or more specifically gender issues are not the major target of the government that is battling with economic meltdown.

However, if truly, achieving the SDGs depends on completing the unfinished business of the MDGs, then broadening the focus of the MDGs to new activities and sectors, and deepening the few successes made during MDGs pursuit will help ensure that the achievement of the SDGs is truly universal and no one is left behind.[33] The neglect of the vulnerable groups and great pillars of the family and society who are often tortured and traumatized in times of conflict would not only distort the meeting of the needs of the present generations but would compromise the ability of future Nigerian generations to meet their needs. Thus, the Nigerian government sustainable development agenda must look into the issue of women and specific challenges women face in conflict in its bid to achieve the sustainable development goals by 2030, bearing in mind that the new development agenda is expected to deliver democratic dividends and improve the lives of the people, men and women alike.

CONCLUSION

It is clear that conflicts have often taken a great toll on women. Whether it breaks out as full-scale war, ethnic or religious conflict, militancy or terrorism, the plights of women are enormous. In Nigeria for instance, during the Niger Delta militancy, Nigerian women were confronted with dehumanising treatments such as rape, forced impregnation, among others. In this time of Boko Haram insurgency, women are major targets for kidnap and abduction. While Nigerian government has often responded by deploying military forces to the conflict-engulfed communities/region, there have not been adequate attention and strategy for the protection of women during conflict. The responses of Nigerian government to conflict have been reactive instead of proactive; and even in such reactive responses, women still receive threat and sexual assault from security personnel. In postconflict reconstruction era, these particular victims of conflict (women) are often "forgotten" and are not involved in reintegration and peace building processes. While Nigeria government has keyed in, into the sustainable development agenda, the gender dimension of development rarely features. There is no comprehensive policy framework on gender dimension of development to make the country's sustainable development agenda an inclusive one.

Thus, as the Nigerian government works toward the achievement of the sustainable development goals, especially gender equality and women empowerment (Goal 5) by 2030, it becomes important for the government to address the challenges of women during armed conflict. It is essential that the issues women face in conflict are addressed (particularly how to reduce/eliminate sexual violence as well as the prosecution of the perpetrators of the act) for the country's sustainability. This is an important area to consider in sustainable development because if women are left to be dehumanised, degraded, and violated and displaced in times of conflict and later "forgotten" in postreconstruction times, it means gender dimension of sustainable development cannot be guaranteed, even beyond the year 2030. As long as violence against women during armed conflict continues and no strategy in place to address it, Nigeria (just like other countries in the world) cannot claim to be making progress toward gender equity, women's rights protection, equality and a socially sustainable society.

Hence, this chapter recommends that Nigerian government should look into experiences of women during armed conflict and include ways to address them as part of strategic plans for achieving gender equality and women empowerment in year 2030. Nigerian government should also pass laws that address violence (especially sexual violence) against women during armed conflict, and make sure that such law enforced with great penalties. Also, nongovernmental organisations (NGOs) such as Amnesty International should continue to raise awareness on the violence against women during armed conflict; the greater number of women refugees in order to put governments on their toes to ensuring women's human rights, and empowerment. NGOs should create awareness that would help victims of conflicts to know the services and legal actions available to them (if any) especially in times of rape. Nigerian government must accept its responsibility to eliminate violence against women during armed conflict, and give national action plans the clout they need to make the sustainable development goals agenda achievable. It is therefore important that governments (in this case Nigerian government) rise up and recognise the challenges of women in conflict in its sustainable development agenda, if the sustainable development goals must be achieved and sustainable in the future.

NOTES

1. Damilola T. Agbalajobi, "The Role of African Women in Peace Building and Conflict Resolution: The Case of Burundi," *African Journal for the Psychological Study of Social Issues* 12, nos. 1–2 (2009).

2. Ibid.

3. Maria Nzomo, "Gender, Governance and Conflict in Africa," Dakar, Senegal, 2002, accessed May 10, 2017, http://unpan1.un.org/intradoc/groups/public/documents/cafrad/unpan008250.pdf. Cited in Adaora Osondu-Oti, "Weaning Africa from Conflict: The Role of Women in Conflict Management and Peacebuilding," Abuja: Friedrich Ebert Stiftung, 2017.

4. Cited in Nzomo, "Gender, Governance and Conflict."

5. Cited in Agbalajobi, "The Role of African Women," 2.

6. Noninternational armed conflicts occur between governmental armed forces and the forces of one or more armed groups, or between such groups arising on the territory of a state. The armed confrontation must reach a minimum level of intensity and the parties involved in the conflict must show a minimum of organisation. In this case, the conflict occurred between the Nigerian armed forces and Niger Delta's militant groups.

7. Elisabeth Kvitashvili, "Women and Conflict: An Introductory Guide for Programming," Office of Conflict Management and Mitigation, USAID, 2007, accessed May 10, 2017, https://www.usaid.gov/sites/default/files/documents/1865/toolkit_women_and_conflict_an_introductory_guide_for_programming.pdf.

8. Ibid.

9. Frances Stewart, "Women in Conflict and Post-Conflict Situations," June 30, 2010, accessed May 10, 2017, http://www.un.org/en/ecosoc/julyhls/pdf10/frances_stewart.pdf.

10. Adaora Osondu, "Challenges to the Fundamental Rights of Women in Niger Delta," in *Natural Resources, Conflict, and Sustainable Development: Lessons from Niger Delta*, eds., Okechukwu Ukaga, Ukoha Ukiwo, and Ibaba S. Ibaba (New York: Routledge, 2012).

11. Sharachchandra Lele, "Sustainable Development: A Critical Review," *World Development*, 19, no. 6 (1991): 607–621.

12. David W. Pearce, and Jeremy J. Watford, *World without End: Economics, Environment, and Sustainable Development* (New York: Oxford University Press, 1993).

13. For a list of sustainable development goals and target, see United Nations, "Sustainable Development Goals: 17 Goals to Transform Our World," accessed May 10, 2017, http://www.un.org/sustainabledevelopment.

14. Agbalajobi, "The Role of African Women."

15. Brigitte Sorensen, "Women and Post-Conflict Reconstruction: Issues and Sources," UNRISD War-Torn Societies Project Occasional Paper, No. 3 (1998).

16. Charlotte Lindsey-Curtet, Florence Tercier Holst-Roness, and Letitia Anderson, "Addressing the Needs of Women Affected by Armed Conflict: An ICRC Guidance Document," (Geneva: ICRC, 2004), accessed May 12, 2017, https://www.icrc.org/eng/assets/files/other/icrc_002_0840_women_guidance.pdf.

17. Elizabeth Rehn and Ellen Johson Sirleaf, "Women, War and Peace: The Independent Experts' Assessment on the Impact of Armed Conflict on Women and Women's Role in Peace building" (New York: UNIFEM, 2002), accessed May 12, 2017, https://www.unfpa.org/sites/default/files/pub-pdf/3F71081FF391653DC1256C69003170E9-unicef-WomenWarPeace.pdf.

18. Ibid.

19. Osondu, "Challenges to the Fundamental Rights of Women in Niger Delta."

20. Chukwuemeka Eze, Bridget Osakwe, Bukola Akosile, and Evelyn Mere, "Ending the Niger Delta Crisis: Exploring Women's Participation Peace Processes," WARN Policy Brief, August 15, 2009, assessed May 24, 2017, http://www.wanep.org/wanep/attachments/article/83/pb_nigeria_aug09.pdf.

21. Sam Onwuemeodo, "2,626 Ijaws killed since 1997 Group," *The Vanguard*, December 10, 1999.

22. Osondu, "Challenges to the Fundamental Rights of Women in Niger Delta."

23. Ike Okonta and Oronata Douglas, W*here Vultures Feast: Shell Human Rights and Oil* (London: Verso, 2003).

24. Cited in Osondu, "Challenges to the Fundamental Rights of Women in Niger Delta."

25. Sokari Ekine, "Niger Delta: A Quiet Resistance," Red Paper, December 26, 2011, accessed May 10, 2017, https://www.redpepper.org.uk/niger-delta-a-quiet-resistance.

26. Amnesty International, "Stars on Their Shoulders, Blood on Their Hands: War Crimes Committed by the Nigerian Military" (United Kingdom: Amnesty International, 2015).

27. Andrew Walker, *What Is Boko Haram?* (Washington: United States Institute for Peace, 2012).

28. Sorensen, "Women and Post-Conflict Reconstruction."

29. Cited in Frances, "Women in Conflict and Post-Conflict Situations."

30. Kimberly Theidon, Kelly Phenici, and Elizabeth Murray, "Gender, Conflict and Peace Building," United States Institute of Peace, September 29, 2011, accessed May 15, 2017, https://www.usip.org/publications/2011/09/gender-conflict-and-peacebuilding.

31. UNDP, "Nigeria's Path to Sustainable Development through Green Economy: Country Report to the Rio +20 Summit," UNDP, June 2012, accessed, May 10, 2017, https://sustainabledevelopment.un.org/content/documents/1023nigerianationalreport.pdf.

32. UNDP, "Nigeria's Road to SDGs', Country Transition Strategy," UNDP, October 2015, accessed May 10, 2017,

33. Ibid.

Chapter 12

Gabon's Giant Step in Health Care

Biale Zua

INTRODUCTION

The importance of health to the fundamental growth and existence of any nation cannot be overemphasized. Health is a major indicator of human development. It is an element of the overall well-being of an individual and nation at large. As stated by Germano Mwabu, health is a component of human capital, which is a determining factor in the creation of wealth.[1] The close relationship between health and wealth was emphasized by Pritchett Lant and Lawrence Summer who concluded that healthier nations are wealthier nations.[2] Wealthier nations can provide better health to the population. Better health in turn increases labor productivity thereby enhancing wealth. The better the health of the work force, the more productive they are. Countries with poor health care and nutrition have less productive workers. Thus, such countries require more input for greater output per worker. They also use more capital per worker.

As suggested by Germano Mwabu, health is not just a constituent part of human welfare and a factor of production, but good health contributes directly to enjoyment of life such as housing and education.[3] Therefore, investment in health for the overall growth of the nation should be the priority of every government. However, more health expenditure is not a sufficient condition to improve health. There is no consensus regarding the effectiveness of monetary health inputs for health outcomes. Thus, Walker Ray and Tim Norbeck concluded that several variables should be considered to determine the outcome of health expenditure.[4] Such variables include whether the spending is for basic health care services, reducing mortality and morbidity, improving the quality of life, or increasing the longevity of the population.

Elusiveness of adequate health care has been one of the challenging problems facing African countries. The problem that African countries face in establishing good medical care can be explained by the flaws in health care prevention and health care management systems. By examining the current trend, preventive measures are still lacking. Most of the diseases are due to poor preventive measures. The examples of some poor preventive measures include poor sanitation, poor water supply, and the lack of basic hygienic necessities. Consequently, there is a prevalence of communicable diseases that are preventable. Noncommunicable diseases require technology. African countries are still behind in advancing modern medical technology despite several endeavors to purchase the essential medical equipment to provide effective services to patients. Modern medical technology involves the use of equipment in both diagnosis and treatment. The problem is not only in the cost of importation of these equipment but also in the cost of manufacturing and maintenance. This is compounded by a lack of adequately trained personnel and the lack of accountability of funds earmarked for these projects by the government.

In terms of management, proper treatment and follow-up is lacking in most African countries. Follow-up care is important because it helps to identify changes in health, aids in prevention, and provides early detection of sicknesses and diseases. Follow-up care may involve regular medical checkups that include a review of medical history and a physical examination. It may also include imaging procedures, endoscopy, blood work, and other lab tests. Therefore, management and the overall care of patients are lacking in these areas within several countries.

Unfortunately, the cost of affording adequate health care turns out to be too exorbitant for the average citizen. Thus, most Africans cannot get proper treatment in their country. The rich are forced to seek medical attention in developed countries, while the poor do not receive any health care due to the high cost of such care. Few people can pay for medical care due to subsistence living. Apparently, African countries have a large population of uninsured citizens who are unable to pay for healthcare due to poverty. Therefore, some people resort to nontraditional medicines. Most of these problems have been achieved in the Western world through the insurance of its citizens.

GABON'S STEPS TOWARD GOOD HEALTH

Several African countries at different times have attempted health-improvement measures, especially managed by trained and qualified licensed professionals. Some countries have made remarkable strides in achieving better health care systems designed to provide its teeming population better health and meaningful future. One of such countries that have achieved significant strides in providing adequate health care for its citizenry is the Republic of Gabon, a Francophone country in Central African. With a population of 1,725,000 million people in 2015, a high rate of urbanization (86.2 percent),[5] and 50 percent of its population made up of young people and 60 percent living on $1.25 per day,[6] Gabon has, nevertheless, been able to cover its citizens under one social health insurance scheme in a bid to achieve health improvement for all.[7] Indeed, in 2007, Gabon provided adequate health care for its teeming population in terms of availability, accessibility, affordability, efficiency, and good quality.

This was a giant stride in health care for a country like Gabon because it is a country of paradoxes. It has low social indicators, but the per capita income was estimated to be $12,460 in 2009.[8] This placed Gabon as one of the richest countries in Sub-Saharan Africa. With the literacy rate of about 83.2 percent in 2015,[9] the per capita income is unequally distributed within the country. Fifty percent of the national income is controlled by the rich, while 33 percent of the population live below the national poverty line.[10] An examination of the dichotomy between the rich and the poor in Gabon shows that the most disadvantaged children come from the poorest group followed by those living in the rural areas. However, with the high rate of urbanization, majority of those in poverty live in the city.[11]

Therefore, when Gabon's government created the National Health Insurance and Social Welfare Fund (Caisse Nationale d'Assurance Maladie et de Garantie Sociale (CNMGS)) by law in August 2007, the priority was clearly spelled out. The purpose was to provide health insurance to Gabonais Economiquement Faibles (Gabonese with Low Income, GEF) in the first instance, yet extending it to other members of the population thereafter. It is a comprehensive health insurance scheme that attracted almost every member of the population despite the structural poverty that is prevalent in Gabon. The insurance scheme cuts across different socioeconomic groups by providing coverage to the poorest Gabonese, which includes students and the elderly. It later extended coverage to public and private sector workers. Virtually all groups covered by the CNAMGS receive the same package of benefits. These benefits include the following:

- Outpatient care, which includes medical consultation, nursing, and diagnostic services;
- Comprehensive basic maternal health care services and hospital care; and
- General health care coverage for a broad range of procedures with the reduction in copayments.

With all these benefits to everyone under CNAMGS coverage, Gabon moved toward universal health coverage for its citizenry thereby making the poor healthier. This certainly impacted the nation for, according to the popular adage, "a healthy nation is a wealthy nation."

GABON'S HEALTH INSURANCE SCHEME

The legal framework of the Gabonese National Health Insurance and Social Welfare Fund (CNMGS) was implemented in 2007 with application decrees and launched in 2008. The headquarters is located at Libreville, which is the country's capital. The status of the GEF was expanded to include the unemployed, peasant farmers, self-employed, the poor, and all those excluded from existing structures. The health care package was clarified to include a care package that comprised accessible services and a conventional procedure for practitioners. Hence, the pilot phase began in December 2008 to March 2009. The initial registration of the GEF was followed by a roll out in 2011 when other socioeconomic groups were registered.[12] This was done basically to extend health coverage to the poor because several attempts to cover the poor had failed in the past. There were pre-existing programs that provided health services to different population subgroups in Gabon before the inauguration of CNMGS in 2007. For example, in the 1970s when the social security system Caisse Nationale de Securite Sociale (CNSS) started, workers in the private sector had access to health services in CNSS-contracted facilities. This was followed by the Caisse Nationale de Garantie Sociale (CNGS) in 1983. Under the CNGS, civil servants had access to subsidized health services in public facilities. CNGS covered informal and self-employed workers including the poor. Although both the state budget fully subsidized programs, it was minimal and faced recurring deficits. This led to the deterioration of the quality of health services that were provided. Dissatisfied beneficiaries, who could afford payments, therefore enrolled in private for-profit insurance systems that only offered access to services in private facilities.

Consequently, through a law in 1991, the government committed to provide free health care services. The health care services that were provided at public facilities became subsidized for many population subgroups. The recession that occurred between 1999 and 2002 resulted in a huge financial burden on the government. As a result, this caused the government to introduce copayments. According to Musango Laurent and Aboubacar Inoura, this system failed to recover from deficits and deficiencies.[13] Therefore, major reforms in the health system were carried out with the goal of establishing a national health insurance program under the CNAMGS. After the law was enacted in 2007, the whole health system was reorganized under the National Health Insurance Scheme. The purchaser and provider functions were separated from each other. The CNAMGS, which purchased the services, came under the Ministry of Economy, while the health care providers came under the Ministry of Health and Public Hygiene (MOHPH). The CNAMGS took over all health insurance structures that were previously under CNSS and CNGS and held the funds for multiple independent plans. Therefore, all the health care plans came under one umbrella institution known as the CNAMGS. The CNAMGS is a public institution that enjoys autonomy in administrative and financial management. However, it is under the supervision of the Ministry of Social Welfare. It comprises a director general and a sixteen-member board of directors that represent the state employers in both the private and public sectors.

GABON'S HEALTH CARE REFORMS

The government of Gabon recognized the need to improve the average health status of its citizenry. This was following the UN declaration in 1978.[14] The need for improved health care was recognized by the World Health Organization (WHO) and UN International Children's Emergency Fund (UNICEF) in 1978 when a strategy of "Health for All by the year 2000" was adopted. The strategy of WHO/UNICEF was to address the inequality in the health status of people not only within a country, but among countries. Health was then declared a fundamental human right.

In conformity to this declaration, President Obama, in 2009, indicated in his address on health reforms in the United States that health reforms were a moral obligation.[15] Thus, on March 23, 2010, he signed into law the Patient Protection and Affordable Care Act (PPACA), or Affordable Care Act (ACA) for short, and popularly referred to as "Obamacare." In a pool of the American people, it was claimed that the liberals believed that health care provision to all Americans was the government moral responsibility.[16] The goal of Obamacare was to give more Americans access to affordable, quality health insurance and reduce growth in the United States health care spending.[17] Obamacare expands the affordability, quality, and availability of private and public health insurance. This is done through consumer protection, regulations, subsidies, taxes, insurance exchanges, and other reforms.

Therefore, Gabon's health care reform was a right step in the right direction since the insurance scheme initially was focused on the country's most vulnerable citizens. These people were the poor, later to government workers in 2010, and subsequently to the private sector employees in 2013. Different socioeconomic groups were brought under one umbrella. Thus, the health reforms moved Gabon toward universal coverage.

The tenet of Universal Health Coverage (UHC) is that all people receive the health services they need without suffering financial hardship while paying for them. Therefore, Gabon instituted a National Health Strategic Plan in 2011–2015 called Plan National de Development Sanitaire (PNDS). Following the establishment of the health plan, the health sector was given a priority and the government spending on the health sector increased. Through increasing spending on this sector, an order was instituted to equate Gabon's health system with international standards by the year 2025 as well as to increase the country's efforts to strive toward meeting the 2015 Millennium Goals.

Embedded in the National Development Plan were ways of speeding up reforms that would reduce infant and maternal mortality as well as include free maternal care. Invariably, the governance of the health sector was greatly improved upon so that users of the health services would not be exposed to financial hardship. This granted the poor access to health care. This conformed to the UHC principle that the promotive, preventive, curative, rehabilitative, and palliative health services needed by patients should be of sufficient quality to be effective.[18] If people should pay for most of the cost out of their own pockets, the poor will not be able to obtain many of the services they need. The rich will be exposed to financial hardship in the event of severe or long-term illness. Therefore, the National Health Plan incorporated the financial burden of users.

As asserted by Swinnerton Sally, poverty has been identified as the greatest threat to health.[19] The poor, who use public facilities, have less access to health care than the more affluent who are often covered by medical aid insurance. Therefore, taking into consideration the pervasive link between poverty and health, Gabon's improvement in health care was committed to reducing poverty.[20]

According to Michael Carney, in 2010, the government moved toward economic diversity.[21] Other sectors of the economy such as mining, tourism, energy, and foresting were developed to shift the country's total dependence on oil. The oil industry accounted for about 50 percent of the Gross Domestic Product. The government raised the monthly minimum wage and created a solidarity allowance for the benefit of low-income workers.[22] Efforts were made to attract investors to create employment for the teeming unemployed youths.

Sustainability

Efforts were geared toward making the health care program a huge success. Consequently, Gabon operated with different developmental partners that were international and local. Additionally, they joined with Non-Governmental Organizations (NGOs) to further this cause. Some partners provided financial assistance, while others provided technical support. Almost the government financed all the health care budget. To adequately manage the health care delivery, the budget was increased from 6.83 percent of the national budget in 2009 to 7 percent in 2011. Development partners such as the World Health Organization (WHO), UNICEF, the UN Population Fund

(UNFPA), the African Development Bank, and the Global Funds to fight AIDS only attempted to provide technical support rather than financial assistance. Any financial assistance received from foreign partners were loans. The French Development Agency (Agence Francaise de Development, AFD) provided a loan of €50 million for the 2015–2019 period. This was sequel to a previous loan of €10.5 million given to Gabon between 2007 and 2014 for the refurbishment of seven maternity centers in Estuaire and Woleu-Ntem provinces.[23] The new loan was to be used to refurbish thirty health centers in four provinces namely, Woleu-Ntem, Haut-Ogooue, Ogooue Ivindo, and Ngouine. Also, the loan was to be used for the provision of medical equipment and staff training.[24]

Funding

Taxes fund the health insurance scheme. The funds are allocated into two categories, namely, the general tax, which accounted for 12 percent and indirect taxes, which were 88 percent.[25] The indirect taxes came from a 10 percent levy on the mobile phone company revenue and a 1.5 percent levy on money transferred outside the economic community of Central African states (CEMAC). Thus, Gabon raised $30 million under the solidarity levies for health in 2009 by imposing a 1.5 percent levy on companies handling remittance from abroad.

Health System

Gabon's health system comprises primary health care, public health, and other institutions that are structured in such a way that most health facilities belonged to the public sector. Only about the private sector shoulders 17.5 percent outlay.[26] The organization of the health system is three tiered with the central coordination located in Libreville, which is the country's capital. It is implemented through the Ministry of Health. The country is divided into ten health regions that constitute the second tier. Each region comprises a public central hospital excluding Libreville and Owendo. The regions are subdivided into fifty-one departments with several smaller health facilities like medical centers and dispensaries. The third tier is made up of the local levels that run about 700 medical centers and dispensaries of which 9 are considered very important.

In addition to the regional hospitals, there are three main hospitals and one major military hospital. The main hospitals are Jeanne Ebori Foundation Hospital (Libreville), Paul Igamba Hospital (Port-Gentil), and Pediatric Hospital (Owendo). These three main hospitals are complemented by several medical centers across the country, and they are operated by the public sector. As part of the reorganization, the Ebori Hospital was transformed into a facility for mothers and infants.

The private sector is divided into two institutions, which are the private for-profit and the private not-for-profit (nongovernmental organizations). There are two main private hospitals named Bongolo Evangelical Hospital in Ngounie and Albert Schweitzer Hospital in Lambarene. Both hospitals offer nonprofit services. There are also nonprofit dispensaries run by nongovernmental organizations beside a network of for-profit pharmacies, medical clinics, and dental centers.

Health Service Infrastructure

According to Karima Saleh, Bernard Couttolene and Helene Barroy, Gabon has a comprehensive health service delivery network.[27] Gabonese health sector is made up of three subsectors. The public sector is managed by the Ministry of Health and Public Hygiene (MOHPH). The para-public sector made up of National Health Insurance Program (NHIP) and the private sector. The national development plan under the health care system led to a significant expansion of the network of health centers and primary care services as shown in Table 12.1. This offered a significant opportunity for coverage and better control of disease through public health interventions. It reduced maternal death and childhood mortality and morbidity.[28] As a result, the health system infrastructures were strengthened in line with the Primary Health Care (PHC) approach. Various attempts were made to integrate clinical medicine into public health while incorporating health into other sectors at the same time.[29]

To match the health system infrastructure with international standard, Gabon embarked on a massive building project of constructing new hospitals while old hospitals were refurbished. Gabon collaborated with VAMED, an Austrian health consulting and development firm, to build most of its infrastructure. The building of its infrastructure was not only geared toward upgrading the service quality but also to expand hospital capacity and access. According to the World Bank, hospital capacity rose from 1.3 beds per 1,000 people in 2008 to 6.3 beds in 2010.[30] One of the facilities that were built under the health care reform is the Angondje University Hospital, which was the Cancer Treatment Institute in Libreville. The building of the Angondje Cancer Institute was completed in 2011. The Owendo Children's Hospital was transformed and upgraded to the status of a University Teaching Hospital in 2013.[31] The International Medical Research Center (CIRMF), located in Franceville, which is southeast of Gabon, was established in 1979. Its infrastructure was enhanced tremendously under the new health care reforms. Other infrastructures included a biosafety level and four laboratories

Table 12.1 Gabon Health Facilities by Types and Ownership

Types of Health Facilities	*Public*	*Para-public*	*Private For-profit*	*Private Not-for-profit*	*NGO/ Humanitarian*	*Total*
General hospitals	12	2		2		16
Specialist hospitals	12	1				13
Clinics			19			19
Polyclinics			1	1		2
Medical centers	41	9				50
Mother and baby centers	51					51
Dispensaries	413			4		417
Health posts	157					157
Health centers	37				8	45
Private practice			79			79
Testing laboratories			4			4
Pharmacies			33			33
Total	*729*	*13*	*136*	6	*8*	*884*
Percentage	82%	1%	15%	1%	1%	100%

Source: Gabon, National Health Development Plan, 2011–2015.

for working with dangerous pathogens. There were installations of new laboratory equipment that allowed for rapid discovery and characterization of pathogens.[32] To further enhance the health care delivery system, four University Teaching Hospitals were established in Libreville while the fifth one was established in Lambarene.

Public hospitals were restructured while the University Hospitals that specialized in surgery, maternal and child health, orthopedics, and trauma treatment were being established. Easy access, lesser cost of certain treatment, and prevention methods were giant steps taken by the Gabonese government to maintain health care for its citizens. Although both communicable and non-communicable diseases (NCDs) were prevalent, Gabon continued to improve upon exiting medical structures.

Primary and Preventive Care

Majority of diseases in Gabon are due to poor primary and preventive care. Examples of preventive measures are poor sanitation, poor water supply, and basic hygiene. Gabon took several measures to overhaul its health facilities and treatment pathways. This was enacted to emphasize primary care services that educate people about healthy lifestyles, keep them in good health, and help them to manage chronic conditions. The focus was shifted to preventive care as a way of managing chronic conditions, promoting wellness, and reducing expensive hospital stays. There were massive immunization and health education-awareness campaigns in the fight against HIV/AIDS, malaria, and tuberculosis.[33] Gabon's Expanded Vaccination Program (Programme Elargi de Vaccination, PEV) was implemented to improve upon the immunization coverage. According to Simon Adegbo et al, this strategy was deemed effective as the Expanded Program on Immunization (EPI).[34] The immunization program was integrated not only in the primary health care centers but also in other peripheral health centers outside of EPI where awareness and catch up campaigns were undertaken. The vaccines were monitored in the Maternal and Child Health Centers (MCH) that were staffed with skilled nurse practitioners and other medical personnel. EPI vaccines administered to children aged zero to eleven months included BCG (Calmette-Guérin bacillus), DPT3 (third combination dose for diphtheria-tetanus-pertussis), Hib3 (third dose of Haemophilus influenzae type b), OPV3 (third dose of oral polio vaccine), IPV3 (third dose of injectable polio vaccine, often in combination), HEB3 (third dose of hepatitis B), yellow fever vaccine, and measles vaccine. The non-EPV vaccines for children aged twelve to fifty-nine months included HiB4, DPT4, HEB4, IPV4, MMR (combined measles-mumps-rubella), meningococcal vaccine A and C, Typhim Vi (typhoid polysaccharide vaccine), and Pneumo 23 (pneumococcal vaccine). Clinics were staffed with skilled nurse practitioners who helped in monitoring conditions such as diabetes, hypertension, and chronic obstructive pulmonary disease (COPD). These changes resulted in a revolution in the health care delivery of Gabon.

Disease Burden before and after the Health Insurance Scheme

The introduction of the insurance scheme led to significant changes in the disease burden of Gabon. However, communicable diseases were prevalent before and after the introduction of the health insurance scheme. Malaria remained the most prevalent cause of morbidity among all age groups and the highest cause of death among children under five years despite the existence of cost-effective intervention.[35] In 2005, before the introduction of the scheme, the incidence of tuberculosis per 100,000 people was 586 but by 2010 after the insurance scheme was introduced, the incidence of tuberculosis per 100,000 people was 475.[36] HIV/AIDs death was 2,700 in 2005 but 2,600 in 2010.[37]

Fifty-six percent of communicable, maternal, perinatal, and nutritional conditions are factors that contribute to the proportional mortality rate. Eleven percent of other NCDs, 2 percent related to diabetes, 3 percent connected to chronic respiratory disease, 4 percent linked to cancers, 16 percent associated with cardiovascular diseases, and 8 percent concurrent with injuries speak to the rates that directly affect the population of Gabon as shown in figure 12.1. Communicable disease remains at the forefront of major health concerns

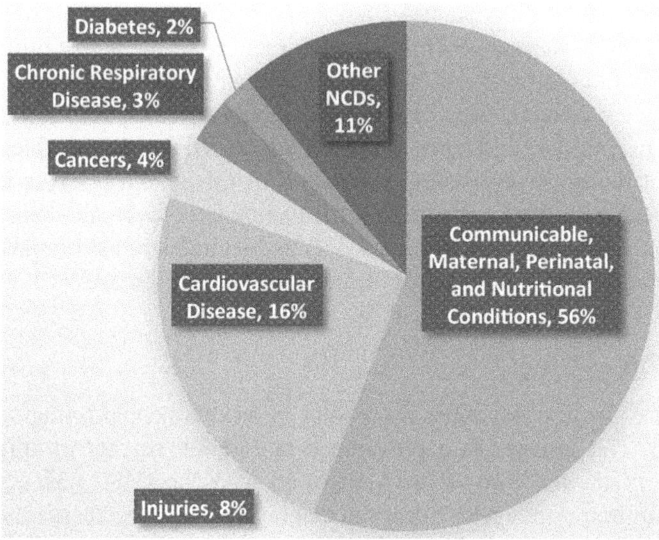

Figure 12.1 Proportional Mortality, Percentage of Total Deaths, All Ages, Both Sexes. *Source*: World Health Organization-Noncommunicable Diseases (NCD) Country Profiles, 2014.

according to the chart. This is the primary contribution to loss of life, which totals 56 percent. It is followed by 36 percent of noncommunicable diseases and 8 percent of injuries.

Due largely to the changing lifestyle in urbanization, there is a rise in noncommunicable diseases such as hypertension, stroke, chronic respiratory disease cancer, diabetes, and other cardiovascular diseases. According to Edgar Ngoungou et al., there is an epidemiological transition from infectious diseases to chronic diseases.[38] There is also an increasing burden of hypertension.[39] According to the World Health Ranking, the top ten causes of death in Gabon are HIV/AIDS, influenza and pneumonia, stroke, coronary heart disease, malaria, tuberculosis, diarrheal disease, malnutrition, lung disease, and diabetes mellitus.[40] The body mass index (BMI) views Gabon as one of the Sub-Saharan countries where the burden of noncommunicable disease will exceed that of communicable disease.[41] Essentially, these are some of the disease burden in Gabon.

Communicable Diseases

Gabon has a high burden of communicable diseases. Communicable diseases remain the main health concern in Gabon. HIV/AIDS constituted 15–49 percent and malaria 5–14 percent continued to be the main causes of death in citizens of this country. Communicable diseases are preventable by using preventive measures. This has been reduced to the barest minimum in countries with high levels of income. The prevalent communicable diseases are contracted through food or they are waterborne. Diseases like bacterial diarrhea, hepatitis A, and typhoid fever are high-risk communicable diseases that affect the poverty-stricken population of this country. Other high-risk communicable diseases are vector-borne like malaria fever and dengue fever. Water-contact diseases are at high levels and includes schistosomiasis while rabies remains the prevalent high-risk animal contact disease.

HIV/AIDS

UNAIDS estimates that there are a total of 41,000 people living with HIV in Gabon. This equates to a prevalence rate of 3.9 percent of adults aged between fifteen and forty-nine. A reported XAF2bn (USD3.37 million) is spent on antiretroviral (ARV) drugs in Gabon annually, and there is no charge for HIV testing or for ARVs in the country. National coverage by services for the prevention of mother-to-child transmission (PMTCT) remains low at 48.5 percent. Gabon was able to reduce the rate of new HIV infections by 54 percent between 2001 and 2011, with coverage of ARV therapy among adults increasing to 67 percent from 23 percent in 2006; however, coverage among children remains low at 24 percent.

Malaria

According to the World Health Organization (WHO)'s World Health Statistics 2014, the incidence rate of malaria in Gabon was 24,892 per 100,000 of the population in 2012. Malaria remains the most prevalent cause of morbidity among all age groups and the highest cause of death among children under five. Only a quarter of all children under five with malaria are taking antimalarial drugs, and only half sleep under a mosquito net.

Tuberculosis

According to World Health Organization (WHO) report in 2014, tuberculosis death in Gabon reached 666 (4.78 person) of total death. This is against 1,462 in 2007 before the introduction of the insurance scheme. The age adjusted death rate ranked Gabon as the twentieth country in the world with the highest death rate from tuberculosis. Nevertheless, the incidence of tuberculosis (per 100,000 people) was 425 in 2013 but increased to 465 in 2015. For men, the deadlines of tuberculosis in Gabon peaks at age eighty and above. It kills men at the lowest rate at age five to nine. At 593 deaths per 100,000 men in

2013, the peak mortality rate for men was higher than that of women, which was 168 per 100,000 women. Women are killed at the highest rate from tuberculosis in Gabon at age eighty and above. It was least deadly to women at age ten to fourteen.[42] The incidence of tuberculosis decreased over time since the commencement of the insurance scheme.

Noncommunicable Diseases

Due largely to the changing lifestyle in urbanization, there is a rise in noncommunicable diseases such as hypertension, cancer, diabetes, and other cardiovascular diseases. According to Ngoungou et al., there is an epidemiological transition from infectious diseases to chronic diseases.[43] There is also an increasing burden of hypertension.[44] According to the World Health Ranking, the top ten causes of death in Gabon are HIV/AIDS, influenza and pneumonia, stroke, coronary heart disease, malaria, tuberculosis, diarrheal disease, malnutrition, lung disease, and diabetes mellitus.[45] This is in confirmation of the assertion of global-health.healthgrove.com that in Gabon, cardiovascular diseases, cancer, and diabetes, urogenital, blood, and endocrine diseases are the deadliest noncommunicable diseases.[46] The body mass index (BMI) views Gabon as one of the Sub-Saharan countries where the burden of noncommunicable disease will exceed that of communicable disease soon.[47]

Diabetes

According to the International Diabetes Federation (IDF), Gabon has the third highest prevalence of diabetes in Africa at 10.7 percent.[48] In 2013, an estimated 76,590 of the adult population (aged twenty to seventy-nine) were diagnosed with diabetes with 1,594 estimated deaths in 2013. By 2013, diabetes mellitus killed 31 out of every 100,000. Male and female were affected differently. While there was a continuous growth in the incidence of diabetes in females from ages sixty-five to eighty years, there was a decrease in the male population between seventy-five and seventy-nine years.

Cancer

According to Globocan data, the top five most common cancers in both sexes by incidence are cervical, breast, prostate, uterine, and lung cancers.[49] The leading five by mortality are prostate, cervical, breast, lung, and colorectal. The number of new cancer cases a year in males is estimated at 4,000, with 6,000 new cases a year in females. The risk of developing cancer before the age of seventy-five is 8.9 percent in men and 10.5 percent in women.

Injuries

In Gabon, transport injuries, unintentional injuries, and self-harm and interpersonal violence are the deadliest injuries.[50] Road Injuries killed 41.0 people out of every 100,000. Furthermore, its mortality ratc increased by 24 percent since 1990. Women between the ages twenty and twenty-four years were more affected by transport injury with a 19.3 percent while men between ages twenty-five and twenty-nine were more affected than any other age group with 82.1 percent. The mortality rate of other transport injuries had increased by 13 percent since 1990, claiming the lives of 2.3 persons per 100,000.[51]

OUTCOME OF THE SOCIAL HEALTH INSURANCE COVERAGE

Although Gabon did not meet the millennium development goal (MDG) targets for maternal and child health by the year 2015 as illustrated in figure 12.2, it did get its citizens covered under one social health insurance scheme. Before the introduction of the social health insurance scheme, access to health facility in the rural areas was limited. But to create access to health facilities, the scheme was mandated to use public monies to purchase services

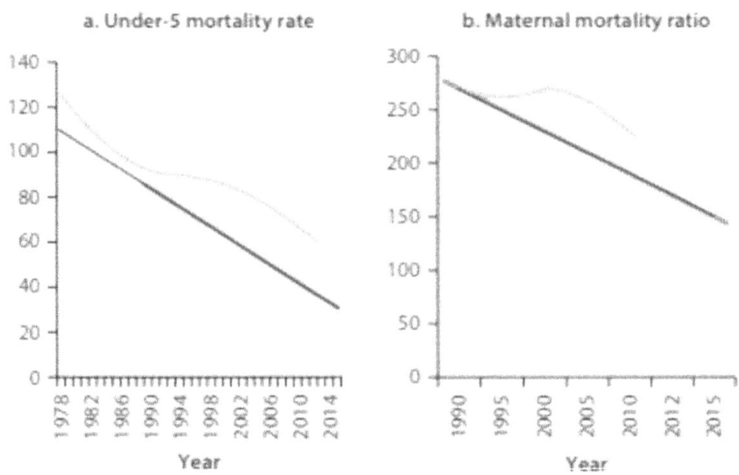

Figure 12.2 Trends in Under-Five Mortality Rate and Maternal Mortality Ratio as Compared to Millennium Development Goal Targets. *Source*: World Bank Study on Health Financing in the Republic of Gabon by Karima Saleh, Bernard F. Couttolenc, and Helene Barroy. Washington, DC: World Bank, 2014.

decision-makings and ultimately have their concerns, and needs neglected. Although Nigerian government has made progress in greater (more than 70 percent at primary level) enrollment of girls in schools (especially girls from the Southeastern region) due to adoption of Universal Basic Education in public schools, gender mainstreaming remains a distant dream in many spheres of political life in Nigeria. Ensuring that women are not sidelined in development plans and programmes and the recognition of specific needs, especially in conflict are yet to be considered by the government.

Like any other developing nation, Nigeria faces challenges in its development strides, which include poverty reduction, corruption, external debt, poor and bad governance, inadequate and inefficient infrastructure, inadequate development of human resources and capital[31] that would help meet the needs of the citizens. These challenges have hindered development efforts in the country and have even pushed the gender empowerment and equality agenda to the back seat. It should be recalled that the first Gender and Equal Opportunity Bill presented to the Senate in April 2014 was rejected. The argument for rejection was that women equality with men is against Nigerian culture and religion. Although the modified version of the Bill (where the language of equality has been removed) passed second reading in the Senate, the Nigerian society is not encouraging for women. While other African countries such as Rwanda (now a global leader in women representation in parliament) and South Africa have made significant progress toward gender parity and are working assiduously to give women a voice and address their concerns, Nigeria remains at the bottom ladder. Although Nigerian government adopted the National Gender Policy in 2006, and the past governments under the leadership of Olusegun Obasanjo and Goodluck Jonathan as well as current government of Muhammadu Buhari have appointed women into key positions, women still account for less than 15 percent representation in political offices.

Just as evidence on ground cannot suggest that Nigeria is on path to gender equality and cannot suggest that achievement is soon, addressing the specific area of women and conflict becomes another issue altogether, which rarely features. There is still no comprehensive policy framework to guide the gender dimension of the country's sustainable development agenda or other sustainable development goals as the case may be. It has been argued that the MDGs were pursued in Nigeria without any comprehensive legal or policy framework,[32] and that is one major reason the country falls short of meeting the 2015 target. In the sustainable development agenda pursuit, the situation remains the same.

One would think that the militancy in Niger Delta and its adverse impact on women could serve as a wake-up call to the government to address the challenges of women in conflict and post conflict times but this is yet to be from the public and nonpublic sectors.[52] There was low utilization of health services, poor performance, and poor-quality care prior to the introduction of the insurance scheme. Nevertheless, a provider payment mechanism was used to create incentives that attracted the use of health services.[53] Consequently, access to services improved because the provider payment mechanism was based on output. There was more reliable funding following the introduction of the scheme. This resulted in the decline of the out-of-pocket total health spending. In 2012, the out-of-pocket spending declined from 50 percent and more between 1995 and 2008 to 41 percent in 2012.[54]

Gabon attained universal coverage in antenatal care with the introduction of the national insurance health program. Life expectancy was 59.84 years in 2005 before the insurance coverage. But with the insurance coverage, life expectancy increased to 62.21 in 2009. Life expectancy has consistently increased since the introduction of the insurance scheme as shown in figure 12.3.

Improvements were seen in the incidence of human immunodeficiency virus/acquired immune deficiency syndrome (HIV/AIDS) and its transference from mother to child.[55] According to Inge Valerie Track, the risk of transmitting HIV within couples was reduced by 96 percent.[56] By 2011, after the introduction of the social health insurance scheme, Gabon was able to

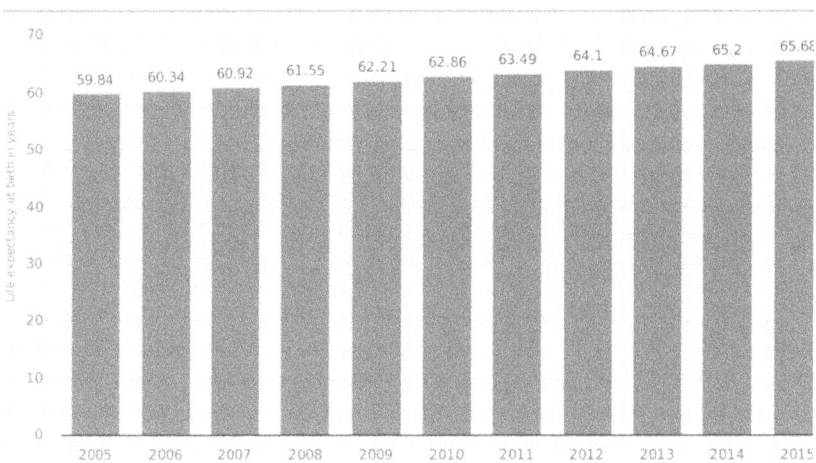

Figure 12.3 Gabon Life Expectancy at Birth, 2005–2015. *Source*: World Bank. Data compiled by the World Bank from the following sources: United Nations Population Division. World Population Prospects: 2017 Revision, or derived from male and female life expectancy at birth from sources such as: Census reports and other statistical publications from national statistical offices, Eurostat: Demographic Statistics, United Nations Statistical Division Population and Vital Statistics Report (various years), U.S. Census Bureau: International Database, and Secretariat of the Pacific Community: Statistics and Demography Programme.

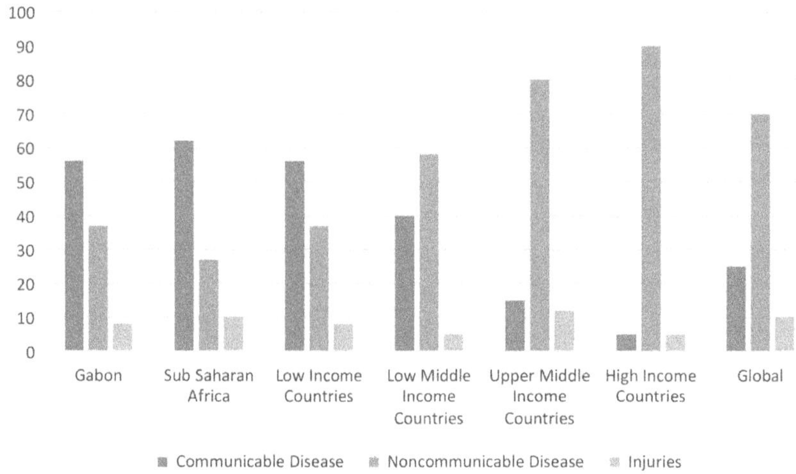

Figure 12.4 Causes of Mortality, in Percent, 2010. *Source*: World Health Organization, World Health Statistics, 2014.

reduce the rate of new HIV infections by 54 percent. This is an outstanding achievement. Positive development was seen in the incidence of tuberculosis. Improvements were seen in child health service use such as immunization coverage and improved use of acute respiratory infection (ARI) treatments.[57] Efforts were made to improve access to health services. More community health care centers were built.

Gabon's health insurance scheme greatly reduced child and maternal mortality rate as shown in figure 12.2. Several preventive measures were put in place. There were awareness campaigns in the fight against HIV/AIDS, malaria, and tuberculosis, which yielded positive results. The building of the cancer institute was a good preventive measure because in the past, patients were evacuated abroad to France, Morocco, and South Africa, thereby resulting in huge financial burden on both the individual and government. The United Nations recognized Albert Schweitzer Hospital as one of the five leading malaria research centers in Africa. This was a great achievement for Gabon.

Nevertheless, according to Karima Saleh et al., Gabon is an upper-middle level income country with sufficient spending on health, but the health outcome is like that of a country with a low-middle level of income, depicting underdevelopment.[58] Upper middle and high-income countries are developed countries. Developed countries typically have significantly older populations than do developing countries. The quality of life is substantially higher in developed countries than developing countries. Hence, they have more accessible medical care. Thus, if a disease or injury has a disproportionately larger impact upon elderly people, for example, it can have a higher population-level impact on developed countries despite impacting people at a lower rate across most or all age group.[59] Hence the disparity in health outcomes for Gabon when compared to developed countries.

Despite Gabon's substantial healthcare expenditures, the leading causes of death are communicable deaths (56 percent of deaths), followed by 36% of deaths by non-communicable diseases and 8% from injuries. This is in contrast to upper middle-class countries where 80% of deaths are a result of non-communicable diseases, with only 15% caused by communicable diseases, and 12% from injuries as illustrated in figure 12.4. Although there was improvement in life expectancy in Gabon, it is below average compared to countries with similar income. Gabon has a hospital-centric health delivery system where hospital care is largely funded at the detriment of community care.

CONCLUSION

Gabon made a giant stride in health care under the social health insurance scheme, which provided health coverage for its teeming population. The poor had access to health care because of the insurance coverage. This led to remarkable changes in the infrastructure, health delivery system, and subsequent health improvement of the Gabonese. Some diseases and illness were brought under control. However, communicable diseases remained the primary cause of morbidity and mortality. Financing and sustaining the scheme presented a huge problem. Thus, Gabon still presents a pattern of disease burden faced by low-income countries. Nevertheless, the national health insurance scheme was a remarkable achievement.

NOTES

1. Germano Mwabu, "Health Development in Africa," African Development Bank, Economic, Research Papers No. 38, accessed March 20, 2018, https://www.afdb.org/fileadmin/uploads/afdb/Documents/Publications/00157610-EN-ERP-38.PDF.
2. Pritchett Lant and Lawrence, "Wealthier is Healthier," *Journal of Human Resources* 30, no.4 (1996): 841–868.
3. Ibid.
4. Walker Ray and Tim Norbeck, "Does More Health Spending Mean Better Health?" accessed March 21, 2018, https://www.forbes.com/sites/physiciansfoundation/2014/08/01/does-more-health-spending-mean-better-health/#665f469c26b9.
5. World Health Organization Report on Non-Communicable Diseases, Country Profile, 2014, accessed July 5, 2016, http://www.who.int/nmh/publications/ncd-profiles-2014/en.

6. World Data Atlas, "Poverty Gap at $1.25 per day (PPP) %," accessed June 6, 2016, https://knoema.com/atlas/topics/Poverty/Poverty-Gap/Poverty-gap-at-dollar125-a-day.

7. "Gabon: A Decade of Tracking Progress for Maternal, Newborn and Child Survival," The 2015 Report, accessed June 6, 2016, http://www.countdown2015mnch.org/country-profiles/gabon.

8. United Nations Development Programme, "Human Development Reports: General Human Development Report Gabon 1998," accessed June13, 2016, http://hdr.undp.org/en/content/general-human-development-report-gabon-1998.

9. World Data Atlas; Gabon: Adult (15+) Literacy Test, 2015, accessed June 15, 2018, https://knoema.com/atlas/Gabon/topics/Education/Literacy/Adult-literacy-rate

10. Gabonese Poverty Assessment Survey, 2005, accessed June 10, 2016, https://knoema.com/atlas/topics/Poverty/Poverty-Headcount-Ratio/Poverty-ratio-at-rural-poverty-line.

11. Ibid.

12. News, "Gabon Gets Everyone Under One Social Health Insurance Roof," *Bulletin of the World Health Organization*, 91 (2013): 318–319, accessed March 13, 2016, http://www.who.int/bulletin/volumes/91/5/13-020513/en.

13. Musango Laurent, and Aboubacar Inoua, "Assurance Maladie Obligatoire au Gabon: Un Atout Pour le Bien Etre de la Populaion," World Health Report, Background Paper, 16, 2010, accessed January 16, 2016, http://www.who.int/healthsystems/topics/financing/healthreport/GabonNo16FINAL.pdf?

14. Declaration of Alma-Ata International Conference on Primary Health Care, Alma-Ata, USSR, September 6–12, 1978, accessed May 25, 2016, http://www.who.int/publications/almaata_declaration_en.pdf.

15. Ethelwynn Stellenberg, "Accessibility, Affordability and use of Health Services in an Urban Area in South Africa." 2015, accessed April16, 2016, http://www.curationis.org.za.

16. Jennifer De Pinto, "Americans Split on Healthcare as Moral Responsibility," *CBS News*, 2009 accessed May 10, 2016, http://www.cbsnews.com/8301-503544_162-5356023-503544.html.

17. "Health Care Facts: Why We Need Health Care Reforms," Obamacare Facts, 2012. accessed May 20, 2016, http://obamacarefacts.com/healthcare-facts/.

18. World Health Organization, "Health Financing for Universal Coverage," *WHO Report*, 2017, accessed May 24, 2018, www.who.int/health_financing/universal_coverage_definition/en.

19. Swinnerton Sally, "Living in Poverty and its Effects on Health," *Contemporary Nurse*, 22, no. 1 (2006): 75–80.

20. Paula Braveman and Sofia Gruskin, "Poverty, Equity, Human Rights and Health," *Bulletin of the World Health Organization*, 81 (2003): 539–545.

21. Michael Carney, "Oil, Inequality, and Youth: Poverty in Gabon," 2013, accessed Jan 14, 2016, http://borgenproject.org/oil-inequality-and-youth-poverty-in-gabon.

22. Ibid.

23. "Loan Injection to Boost Gabon's Healthcare Services," 2015, accessed June 4, 2016, http://www.en.legabon.org/news/1890/loan-injection-boost-gabon%E2%80%90s-health-care-services.

24. Ibid.

25. Karima Saleh, Bernard Couttolene, and Helene Barroy, "Health Financing in the Republic of Gabon," *World Bank Group*, 2014.

26. "Gabon Health Insurance," Pacific Prime, 2006, accessed June 28, 2016, https://www.pacificprime.com/country/africa/gabon-health-insurance.

27. Saleh et al., "Health Financing in the Republic of Gabon."

28. Dan Kaseje, "Health Care in Africa: Challenges, Opportunities and an Emerging Model for Improvement," 2006, accessed June 18, 2016, https://www.wilsoncenter.org.

29. Ibid.

30. "Health Outcomes," 2014, accessed June 14, 2016, at www.oxfordbusinessgroup.com/country/gabon/

31. World Health Organization, "Gabon Health Reforms," 2014, accessed June 5, 2016, www.who.int/countries/gab/en.

32. Encyclopedia Britannica, "Gabon" (Chicago: Encyclopedia Britannica, Inc., 2014), accessed June 12, 2016, http://www. britannica.com/EBchecked/topic/223148/Gabon.

33. "Health Outcomes."

34. Simon Adegbo, Edgard Brice Ngoungou, Jean Koko, Yolande Vierin, Carine Eyi Zang Ndong, and Andre´ Moussavou Mouyama, "Immunization Coverage of Children aged 0 to 5 years in Libreville (Gabon)," *Santé* 20, no. 4 (2010): 215–219.

35. Karima Saleh, Karima Saleh, Bernard Couttolene, and Helene Barroy, "Health Financing in the Republic of Gabon," *World Bank Group*, 2014.

36. "Gabon Diseases Stats," NationMaster. 2003, accessed July 23, 2017, http://www.nationmaster.com/country-info/profiles/Gabon/Health.

37. Ibid.

38. Edgar Ngoungou, et al., "Prevalence of Cardiovascular Disease in Gabon: A Population Study," *Archives of Cardiovascular Disease* 105 (2012): 77–83.

39. Ibid.

40. World Health Rankings, "Health Profile: Gabon," 2017, accessed July 12, 2017, http://www.worldlifeexpectancy.com/country-health-profile/gabon.

41. "Non-Communicable Disease to Dominate in the Near Future." 2015, accessed July12, 2017, bmiresearch.com/articles/non-communicable-disease-to-dominate-in-near-future.

42. "Tuberculosis in Gabon by Sex over Lifetime, 2017, accessed July14, 2017, http://global-disease-burden.healthgrove.com/l/1149/Tuberculosis-in-Gabon.

43. Ngoungou et al., "Prevalence of Cardiovascular Disease."

44. Ibid.

45. World Health Rankings, "Health Profile: Gabon."

46. "Non-Communicable Diseases," 2017 accessed July 21, 2017, http://global-health.healthgrove.com/l/120/Gabon.

47. "Non-Communicable Disease to Dominate in the Near Future," 2015, accessed July12, 2017, bmiresearch.com/articles/non-communicable-disease-to-dominate-in-near-future.

48. Ibid.

49. JFerlay, et al., "Globocan 2012: Estimated Cancer Incidence, Mortality and Prevalence Worldwide in 2012," World Health Organization, 2012, accessed July 24, 2017, http://globocan.iarc.fr/Default.aspx.

50. "Injuries." 2017, accessed July 21, 2017, http://global-health.healthgrove.com/l/120/Gabon.

51. Ibid.

52. Karima Saleh, Karima Saleh, Bernard Couttolene, and Helene Barroy, "Health Financing in the Republic of Gabon," *World Bank Group*, 2014.

53. Ibid.

54. Ibid.

55. United Nations Joint Program on AIDS (UNAIDS). 2013. Global Report 2013. UNAIDS, Geneva. 2013 accessed March 23, 2018, http://files.unaids.org/en/media/unaids/contentassets/documents/epidemiology/2013/gr2013/UNAIDS_Global_Report_2013_en.pdf.

56. Inge Valerie Track, "Universal Health Insurance is Being Rolled Out," Oxford Business Group, 2014 accessed March 23, 2018, http//www.oxfordbusinessgroup.com/overview/universal-health-insurance-being-rolled-out.

57. United Nations Development Program (UNDP), "Human Development Report 2013," New York, 2013, accessed March 23, 2018, http://hdr.undp.org/en/2013-report.

58. Karima Saleh, Helene Barroy, and Bernard F. Couttolenc, *Health Financing in the Republic of Gabon* (Washington, DC: World Bank Group, 2014), http://documents.worldbank.org/curated/en/875521468252026617/Health-financing-in-the-Republic-of-Gabon.

59. "Breast Cancer: International Statistics on Mortality and Affected Populations," 2017 accessed July 24, 2017, http://global-diseases.healthgrove.com/l/97/Breast-Cancer.

Bibliography

Abegunrin, Olayiwola, ed. *Africa in the New World Order: Peace and Security Challenges in the Twenty-First Century*. Lanham: Lexington Books, 2014.

———. *Economic Dependence and Regional Cooperation in Southern Africa: SADCC and South Africa in Confrontation*. Lewiston, NY: E. Mellen Press, 1990.

———. *Nigeria, Africa, and the United States: Challenges of Governance, Development, and Security*. Lanham: Lexington Books, 2017.

———. *Nigeria, the United States, and Foreign Policy in Africa: Security, Governance, and Resources*. New York City: Palgrave Macmillan, 2015.

Abique, M. *The Development of African Economic Underdevelopment*. Ikeja, Nigeria: Afrografika Publishers, 1977.

Aboyade, Ojetunji. *Issues in the Development of Tropical Africa*. Ibadan: Ibadan University Press, 1976.

Achebe, Chinua. *A Man of the People*. New York: Penguin Books, 1996.

———. *There Was a Country: A Personal History of Biafra*. London: Penguin Books, 2012.

———. *Trouble with Nigeria*. Portsmouth, NH: Heinemann Educational Books, 1983.

Ackah, William. *Pan-Africanism, Exploring the Contradictions: Politics, Identity, and Development in Africa and the African Diaspora*. Brookfield, VT: Ashgate, 1999.

Adams, W. M. *Green Development: Environment and Sustainability in the Third World*. New York: Routledge, 1990.

Adebanwi, Wale and Ebenezer Obadare, eds. *Democracy and Prebendalism in Nigeria: Critical Interpretations*. New York, NY: Palgrave Macmillan, 2013.

Adedeji, Adebayo, ed. *Africa within the World: Beyond Dispossession and Dependence*. London: Zed Books, 1993.

Adejumobi, S., and A. Momoh, eds. *The Political Economy of Nigeria under Military Rule: 1984–1993*. Harare: SAPES Books, 1995.

Adekunle, Julius O., ed. *Religion in Politics: Secularism and National Integration in Modern Nigeria*. Trenton, NJ: Africa World Press, 2009.

Adepoju, Aderanti. *The Impact of Structural Adjustment on the Population of Africa: The Implications for Education, Health, & Employment.* London: James Curry, 1993.

Agbaje, Adigun A. B., Larry Diamond, and Ebere Onwudiwe, eds., *Nigeria's Struggle for Democracy and Good Governance: A Festschrift for Oyeleye Oyediran.* Ibadan: Ibadan University Press, 2004.

Ajaegbu, Hyacinth. *Urban and Rural Development in Nigeria.* London: Heinemann, 1976.

Ake, Claude, ed. *Political Economy of Nigeria.* London; Longman, 1985.

———. *A Political Economy of Africa.* Harlow, Essex: Longman Group Ltd., 1981.

———. *Democracy and Development in Africa.* Washington, DC: Brookings Institution, 1996.

———. *Democratization of Disempowerment in Africa.* Lagos, Nigeria: Malthouse Press, 1994.

———. *Development Strategy for Nigeria after the Structural Adjustment Programme.* Ibadan: Development Policy Centre, 1996.

———. *Marginalization of Africa: Notes on a Productive Confusion.* Ikeja, Nigeria: Malthouse Press Limited, 1996.

———. *Social Science as Imperialism: A Theory of Political Development.* Ibadan: Ibadan University Press, 1979.

Akeredolu-Ale, E. O. *The Underdevelopment of Indigenous Entrepreneurship in Nigeria* Ibadan: Ibadan University Press, 1975.

Akinyele, Rufus T. *Isaac Adaka Boro: Patriarch of Minority Activism in the Niger Delta. Lagos.* University of Lagos, 2006.

Akinyoade, Akinyinka, Jos Damen, Ton Dietz, Blandina Kilama, and Gerrit van Omme. *Africa Population Dynamics.* Leiden University, the Netherlands: African Studies Centre, 2014.

Alao, Abiodun, *Natural Resources and Conflict in Africa: The Tragedy of Endowment.* Rochester, NY: Rochester Press, 2007.

Albert, Isaac Olawale, et al. *Urban Management and Urban Violence in Africa.* Ibadan: Institute for French Research in Africa, 1994.

Amin, Samir. *Accumulation on a World Scale: A Critique of the Theory of Underdevelopment.* New York: Monthly Review Press, 1974.

———. *Eurocentrism.* New York: Monthly Review Press, 1989.

———. *Imperialism and Unequal Development.* New York: Monthly Review Press, 1977.

———. *Neo-Colonialism in West Africa.* New York: Monthly Review Press, 1974.

———. *Unequal Development: An Essay on the Social Formations of Peripheral Capitalism.* New York: Monthly Review Press, 1976.

Amoah, Michael. *Nationalism, Globalization, and Africa.* New York: Palgrave Macmillan, 2011.

Amtaika, Alexius, ed. *Socio-Economic Development in Africa: Challenges and Dimensions.* Austin, TX: Pan-African University Press, 2017.

Amutabi, Maurice N., ed. *Beyond Agency, Voice and Space in Africa's Development.* Nairobi, Kenya: The Centre for Democracy, Research and Development, 2017.

Amutabi, Maurice N., and Linnet Hamasi, eds. *Africa: A Continent in Transition*. Nairobi, Kenya: The Centre for Democracy, Research and Development, 2017.

Andræ, G. and B. Beckman. *The Wheat Trap: Bread and Underdevelopment in Nigeria*. London: Zed, 1986.

Apter, David E. *The Politics of Modernization*. Chicago: University of Chicago Press, 1965.

Arikpo, O. *The Development of Modern Nigeria*. Baltimore: Penguin, 1967.

Arlinghaus, Bruce E. *Military Development in Africa: The Political and Economic Risks of Arms Transfers*. Boulder, CO: Westview Press, 1984.

Arnold Stephen H. and Andre Nitecki, eds. *Culture and Development in Africa*. Trenton, NJ: Africa World Press, 1990.

Arnold, Guy. *A Guide to African Political and Economic Development*. London and Chicago: Fitzroy Dearborn Publishers, 2001.

Asefa, Sisay and Wei-Chiao Huang, eds. *Political Economy of Good Governance*. Kalamazoo, Michigan: W.E. Upjohn Institute for Employment Research, 2015.

Asiwaju, A. I., ed. *Partitioned Africans: Ethnic Relations across Africa's International Boundaries, 1884–1984*. London: C. Hurst and Coy, & University of Lagos Press, 1984.

Assefa, Taye, Severine M. Rugumamu, and Abdel Ghaffar M. Ahmed, eds. *Globalization, Democracy, and Development in Africa: Challenges and Prospects*. Addis Ababa: Organization for Social Science Research in Eastern and Southern Africa, 2001.

Aturu, Bamidele. *A Handbook of Nigerian Labour Laws*. Lagos: Friedrich Ebert Stiftung, 2001.

Ballington, Julie et al., eds. *Empowering Women for Stronger Political Parties—A Guide Book to promote Women's Political Participation*. New York: United Nations Development Programmes and National Democratic Institute, 2012.

Bangura, Yusuf and George A. Larbi, eds. *Public Sector Reform in Developing Countries: Capacity Challenges to Improve Services*. New York: Palgrave Macmillan/UNRISD, 2006.

Bangura, Yusuf, ed. *Ethnic Inequalities and Public Sector Governance*. New York: Palgrave Macmillan, 2006.

———. *Britain and Commonwealth Africa: The Politics of Economic Relations, 1951–75*. Dover, NH: Manchester University Press, 1983.

———. *Development, Democracy and Cohesion: Critical Essays with Insights on Sierra Leone and Wider Africa Contexts*. Freetown, Sierra Leone: Osman Sankoh, 2015.

———. et al. *Combating Poverty and Inequality: Structural Change, Social Policy and Politics*. Geneva: United Nations Research Institute for Social Development, 2010.

———. *Search for Identity: Ethnicity, Religion and Political Violence*. Geneva: UNRISD, 1994.

Barber, Benjamin R. *Place for Us: How to Make Society Civil and Democracy Strong*. New York: Hill and Wang, 1998.

Barkan, Joel D., ed. *Legislative Power in Emerging African Democracies*. London: Lynne Rienner Publishers, 2009.

Beckerman, Wilfred. *Poverty of Reason: Sustainable Development and Economic Growth*. Oakland, CA: Independent Institute, 2003.

Beckett, Paul A. and Crawford Young, eds. *Dilemmas of Democracy in Nigeria*, Rochester, NY: University of Rochester Press, 1997.

Bende-Nabende, Anthony. *Globalisation, FDI, Regional Integration and Sustainable Development: Theory, Evidence, and Policy*. Burlington, USA: Ashgate, 2002.

Benneh, George, Juha I. Uitto, and William B. Morgan, eds. *Sustaining the Future: Economic. Social, and Environmental Change in Sub-Saharan Africa*. Tokyo: United Nations University Press, 1996.

Bermeo, Nancy and Deborah J. Yashar, eds. *Parties, Movements and Democracy in the Developing World*. New York, NY: Cambridge University Press, 2016.

Berthélemy, Jean-Claude and Carlos Quenan, eds. *New Approaches to Financing Development in Africa*. Paris: Development Centre of the Organisation for Economic Co-operation and Development, 1996.

Bewaji, John Ayotunde Isola. *Narratives of Struggle: The Philosophy and Politics of Development*. Durham, NC: Carolina Academic Press, 2012.

Blewitt, John. *Understanding Sustainable Development*. New York, NY: Routledge, 2015.

Booth, David and Diana Cammack. *Governance for Development in Africa: Solving Collective Action Problems*. New York: Zed Books, 2013.

Boyer, David. *Role of Northern NGOs in the Promotion of Sustainable Development in Africa*. Edinburgh, Scotland: Centre of African Studies, University of Edinburgh, 1990.

Cervigni, Raffaello and Michael Morris, eds. *Confronting Drought in Africa's Drylands: Opportunities for Enhancing Resilience*. Washington, DC: World Bank, 2016.

Chandra, Kanchan. *Why Ethnic Parties Succeed Patronage and Ethnic head Counts in India*. New York, NY: Cambridge University Press, 2004.

Cheeseman, Nic, David Anderson, and Andrea Scheibler, eds. *Routeledge Handbook of African Politics*. London: Routeledge, 2013.

Chilivumbo, Alifeyo. *Migration and Uneven Rural Development in Africa: The Case of Zambia*. Lanham, MD: University Press of America, 1985.

Chirambo, Kondwani, ed. *Political Cost of AIDS in Africa: Evidence from Six Countries*. Pretoria, South Africa: IDASA, 2008.

Cilliers, Jakkie. *Africa in the New World: How Global and Domestic Developments Will Impact by 2025*. Tshwane, South Africa: Institute for Security Studies, 2008.

Cohen, D. L. and J. Daniel, eds. *Political Economy of Africa*, London: Longman Group, 1981.

Collier, Paul. *Women in Development: Defining the Issues*. Washington, DC: Population and Human Resources Department, the World Bank, 1988.

Coltart, David. *Struggle Continues: 50 Years of Tyranny in Zimbabwe*. Auckland Park, South Africa: Jacana, 2016.

Connor, A. M. O. *The Geography of Tropical African Development*. Oxford: Pergamon Press, 1978.

Conteh-Morgan, Earl. *Democratization in Africa: The Theory and Dynamics of Political Transitions*. Westport, CT: Paeger, 2007

Cooper, Frederick. *Africa in the World: Capitalism, Empire, Nation-State*. Cambridge, MA: Harvard University Press, 2014.

Dambisa, Moyo. *Dead Aid: Why Aid Is Not Working and How There Is a Better Way for Africa*. New York, NY: Furrar, Straus and Giroux, 2009.

Darkoh, Michael and Apollo Rwomire, eds. *Human Impact on Environment and Sustainable Development in Africa*. Burlington, VT: Ashgate, 2003.

Dauda, Bola, and Toyin Falola. *Nigerian Bureaucracy in an African Democracy*. Amherst: Cambria Press, 2017.

Davidson, Basil. *The Black Man's Burden: Africa and the Curse of the Nation-State*. London: James Currey, 1992.

Davis, John, ed. *Terrorism in Africa: The Evolving Front in the War on Terror*. Lanham, MD: Lexington Books, 2010.

Diamond, Larry. *Prospects for Democratic Development in Africa*. Stanford, CA: Hoover Institution, Stanford University, 1997.

———. *Class, Ethnicity, and Democracy in Nigeria: The Failure of the First Republic*. Syracuse, NY: Syracuse University Press, 1988.

Diamond, Larry, A. Kirk-Greene, and Oyeleya Oyediran, eds. *Transition without End, Nigerian Politics and Civil Society under Babangida*. Ibadan: Varitage Publications, 1997.

Diamond, Larry and Marc F. Platter, eds. *Nationalism, Ethnic Conflict, and Democracy*. Baltimore: Johns Hopkins University Press, 1994.

Diamond, Larry, J. L. Linz, and S. M. Lipset, eds. *Democracy in Developing Countries: Africa*. Boulder, CO: Lynne Rienner, 1988.

Dibua, Jeremiah I. *Modernization and the Crisis of Development in Africa: The Nigerian Experience*. Burlington, VT: Ashgate, 2006.

Doorenspleet, Renske and Lia Nijzink, eds. *Party Systems and Democracy in Africa*. New York, NY: Palgrave Macmillan, 2014.

Dudley, Billy J. *Instability and Political Order: Politics and Crisis in Nigeria*. Ibadan, Nigeria: Ibadan University Press, 1973.

Duncan, G., ed. *Democratic Theory and Practice*. London: Cambridge University Press, 1983.

Elliott, Jennifer A. *Introduction to Sustainable Development*. New York, NY: Routledge, Taylor & Francis Group, 2006.

Englebert, Pierre and Kevin C. Dunn. *Inside African Politics*. Boulder, CO: Lynne Rienner Publishers, 2013.

Ezeani, Emefiena. *Cooperative Collegial Democracy for Africa and Multi-Ethnic Societies: Democracy without Tears*. New York, NY: Peter Lang, 2013.

Ezrow, Natasha M. and Erica Frantz. *Dictators and Dictatorships: Understanding Authoritarian Regimes and Their Leaders*. New York, NY: Continuum, 2011.

Falola, Toyin. *Development Planning and Decolonization in Nigeria*. Gainesville, FL: University Press of Florida, 1996.

———. *Nigerian Political Modernity and Postcolonial Predicaments*. Austin, TX: Pan-African University Press, 2016.

———., ed. *Britain and Nigeria: Exploitation or Development*? Atlantic Highlands, NJ: Zed Books, 1987.

Falola, Toyin and Adebayo O. Oyebade. *Hot Spot: Sub-Saharan Africa*. Santa Barbara, CA: Greenwood, 2010.

Falola, Toyin and Emmanuel M. Mbah, eds. *Contemporary Africa: Challenges and Opportunities*. New York, NY: Palgrave Macmillan, 2014.

Falola, Toyin and Jessica Achberger. *Political Economy of Development and Underdevelopment in Africa*. New York, NY: Routledge, 2013.

Falola, Toyin and Julius O. Ihonvbere, eds. *Nigeria and the International Capitalist System*. Boulder, CO: L. Rienner Publishers, 1988.

Falola, Toyin and Mike Odugbo Odey, eds. *Poverty Reduction Strategies in Africa: The Ideology of the Family-State*. New York, NY: Routledge, Taylor & Francis Group, 2018.

Falola, Toyin and Jamaine Abidogun. *Issues in African Political Economies*. Durham, NC: Carolina Academic Press, 2017.

Fosu, Augustin Kwasi and Paul Collier, eds. *Post-Conflict Economies in Africa*. New York, NY: Palgrave Macmillan, 2004.

Frank, Andre. *Underdevelopment of Development*. Stockholm, Sweden: Bethany Books, 1991.

Fredland, Richard A. *Understanding Africa: A Political Economy Perspective*. Chicago: Burnham Inc., Publishers, 2001.

Freer, Gordon. *Southern Africa, Sustainable Development and South-South Co-Operation*. Bellville: University of the Western Cape, 1966.

Gana, Aaron and Y. B. Omelle, eds. *Democratic Rebirth in Nigeria, Vol. 1*. Abuja: AFRIGOV, 2003.

Gana, Aaron Tsado. *Promise of Liberal Democracy in Africa: The Nigerian Betrayal*. Jos, Nigeria: African Centre for Democratic Governance, 1996.

Ghartey, J. B. *Consolidating Accountability for Development in Africa*. Boston, MA: African Studies Center, Boston University, 1986.

Ghosh, Pradip K., ed. *Developing Africa: A Modern Perspective*. Westport, CT: Greenwood Press, 1984.

Gibbon, Peter, Yusuf Bangura, and Arve Ofstad, eds. *Authoritarianism, Democracy, and Adjustment: The Politics of Economic Reform in Africa*. Uppsala: Scandinavian Institute of African Studies, 1992.

Gordon, April A. *Transforming Capitalism and Patriarchy: Gender and Development in Africa*. Boulder, CO: Lynne Rienner, 1996.

Gordon, April A. and Donald L. Gordon. *Understanding Contemporary Africa*. London: Lynne Rienner Publishers, 2007.

Graybill, Lyn and Kenneth W. Thompson, eds. *Africa's Second Wave of Freedom: Development, Democracy, and Rights*. Lanham, MD: University Press of America, 1998.

Gurib-Fakim, Ameenah and Jacobus Nicolaas Eloff, eds. *Chemistry for Sustainable Development in Africa*. New York, NY: Springer, 2013.

Gurr, Ted. *Minorities at Risk: A Global View of Ethnoplitcal Conflicts*. Washington, DC: United State Institute of Peace Press, 1998.

Gyimah-Boadi, E., ed. *Democratic Reform in Africa: The Quality of Progress*. Boulder, CO: Lynne Rienner Publishers, 2004.

Hafkin, Nancy J. *Women and Development in Africa: An Annotated Bibliography*. Addis Ababa: United Nations, Economic Commission for Africa, 1977.

Hale, William and Eberhard Kienle, eds. *After the Cold War: Security and Democracy in Africa and Asia*. London: Tauris Academic Studies, 1996.

Haque, Shamsul, Anastase Shyaka, and Gedeon M. Mudacumura, eds. *Democratizing Public Governance in Developing Nations with Special Reference to Africa*. New York, NY: Routledge, 2017.

Harcourt, Mark and Geoffrey Wood, eds. *Trade Unions and Democracy: Strategies and Perspectives*. Manchester and New York: Manchester University Press, 2004.

Harrison, Graham. *Neoliberal Africa: The Impact of Global Social Engineering*. London: Zed Books, 2010.

Hassim, Shireen. *Women's Organizations and Democracy in South Africa: Contesting Authority*. Madison: University of Wisconsin Press, 2006.

Herman, Wasserman, ed. *Popular Media, Democracy and Development in Africa*. New York, NY: Routledge, 2011.

Herskovits, Jean. *Nigeria, Power and Democracy in Africa*. New York, NY: Foreign Policy Association, 1982.

Hess, Peter N. *Economic Growth and Sustainable Development*. New York, NY: Routledge, 2013.

House-Soremekun, Bessie and Toyin Falola, eds. *Globalization and Sustainable Development in Africa*. Rochester, NY: University of Rochester Press, 2011.

Hyden, Goran, Michael Leslie, and Folu F. Ogundimu, eds. *Media and Democracy in Africa*. New Brunswick, NJ: Transaction Publishers, 2002.

Igbafen, M. L. *Core Issues and Theories in Philosophy of Development*. Ekpoma: A. Inno Printing Press, 2014.

Iheduru, Obioma M. *Politics of Economic Restructuring and Democracy in Africa*. Westport, CT: Greenwood Press, 1999.

Ihonvbere, Julius. *Africa and the New World Order*. New York, NY: Peter Lang, 2000.

———. *Nigeria: The Politics of Adjustment and Democracy*. New Brunswick, NJ: Transaction Publishers, 1994.

———. *Reinventing Africa for the Challenges of the Twenty-First Century*. Lagos, Nigeria: Malthouse Press Ltd., 2011.

———. *Economic Crisis, Civil Society and Democratisation: The Case of Zambia*. Trenton, NJ: Africa World Press, 1995.

Ihonvbere, Julius Omozuanvbo and John Mukum Mbaku, eds. *Political Liberalization and Democratization in Africa: Lessons from Country Experiences*. Westport, CT: Praeger, 2003.

Ityavyar, D. and Z Gundu, eds. *NEPAD and the Challenges of Development in Nigeria*. Jos: Inter-GENDER Monograph Series, 2006.

James, Valentine Udoh, ed. *Sustainable Development in Africa: Prospects for the 21st Century*. San Francisco: International Scholars, 1999.

———, ed. *Women and Sustainable Development in Africa*. Westport, CT: Praeger, 1995.

Joseph, Richard. *State, Conflict, and Democracy in Africa*. Boulder, CO: L. Rienner, 1999.

Kalu, Kenneth, Olajumoke Yacob-Haliso, and Toyin Falola, eds. *Africa's Big Men: Predatory State-Society Relations in Africa.* New York, NY: Routledge, 2018.

Kasfir, Nelson, ed. *Civil Society and Democracy in Africa.* Portland, OR: Frank Cass, 1998.

Khor, Martin. *Globalisation and the South: Some Critical Issues.* Ibadan, Nigeria: Spectrum Books, 2000.

Lewellen, Ted C. *Dependency and Development: An Introduction to the Third World.* Westport, CT: Bergin & Garvey, 1995.

Leys, Colin. *The Rise and Fall of Development Theory.* Oxford: James Currey, 1996.

Lindberg, Staffan I. *Democracy and Elections in Africa.* Baltimore: Johns Hopkins University Press, 2006.

MacLean, Sandra J., H. John Harker, and Timothy M. Shaw, eds. *Advancing Human Security and Development in Africa: Reflections on NEPAD.* Halifax, NS: Centre for Foreign Policy Studies, Dalhousie University, 2002.

Mangala, Jack, ed. *New Security Threats and Crises in Africa: Regional and International Perspectives.* New York, NY: Palgrave Macmillan, 2010.

Marshall, Monty G., Ted R. Gurr, and Keith Jaggers. "Polity IV Project: Political Regime Characteristics and Transitions, 1800–2016." Vienna, VA: Center for Systematic Peace, 2017. http://www.systemicpeace.org/inscrdata.html.

Marston, Sallie, Paul Knox, and Diana Liverman. *World Regions in Global Contexts: People, Places and Environments.* Upper Saddle River, NJ: Prentice Hall, 2002.

Mbah, Emmanuel M. and Steven J. Salm. *Globalization and the African Experience.* Durham, NC: Carolina Academic Press, 2012.

Mbaku, John Mukum and Julius Omozuanvbo Ihonvbere, eds. *Transition to Democratic Governance in Africa: The Continuing Struggle.* Westport, CT: Praeger, 2003.

Mbanaso, Michael U. and Chima Korieh, eds. *Minorities and the State in Africa.* New York, NY: Cambria Press, 2010.

Mbondenyi, Morris Kiwinda et al., eds. *Human Rights and Democratic Governance in Kenya: A Post-2007 Appraisal.* Pretoria, South Africa: Pretoria University Law Press, 2015.

McNamara, Robert. *Africa's Development Crisis. Agricultural Stagnation, Population Explosion and Environmental Degradation.* Washington, DC: World Bank, 1991.

Meredith, Martins. *The State of Africa: A History of Fifty Years of Independence.* London: Free Press, 2006.

Mkandawire, Thandika, ed. *African Intellectuals: Rethinking Politics, Language, Gender and Development.* Dakar and London: CODESRIA Books & Zed Books, 2005.

Monga, Célestin. *Anthropology of Anger: Civil Society and Democracy in Africa.* Boulder, CO: Lynne Rienner Publishers, 1996.

Mudavadi, Musalia. *Rethinking Development in Africa in the 21st Century: The Case of Kenya.* Nairobi: East African Educational Publishers, 2002.

Mukherjee, Bumba. *Democracy and Trade Policy in Developing Countries.* Chicago: University of Chicago Press, 2016.

Munier, Nolberto. *Introduction to Sustainability: Road to a Better Future*. New York, NY: Springer, 2005.

Mustapha, Abdul and Lindsay Whitfield, eds. *Turning Points in African Democracy*. Woodbridge, Suffolk, and Great Britain: Boydell and Brewer, 2009.

Mustapha, Marda and Joseph J. Bangura. *Democratization and Human Security in Postwar Sierra Leone*. New York, NY: Palgrave Macmillan, 2015.

Mwereria, G. K. *African Global Initiative on the New Environmental Economic Order: An Action Programme for the Post Development Africa*. Nairobi, Kenya: Southern Networks for Environment and Development, Africa Region, 1993.

Ndegwa, Stephen N., ed. *Decade of Democracy in Africa*. Boston: Brill, 2001.

Niang, Abdoulaye. *Towards a Viable and Credible Development in Africa: The Push Factors*. Raleigh, NC: Ivy House Publishing Group, 2006.

Nyuirenda, Juma E., ed. *Women, Peace, and Development in Africa*. Lusaka, Zambia: Adult Education Association of Zambia, 1991.

Nzongola-Ntalaja, Georges and Margaret C. Lee, eds. *State and Democracy in Africa*. Trenton, NJ: Africa World Press, 1998.

Ohadike, Patrick O. *Development in Africa*. Legon: Regional Institute for Population Studies, University of Ghana, 1988.

Ojeleye, Olukunle. *The Politics of Post-War Demobilsation and Reintegration in Nigeria*. United Kingdom: Ashgate Surrey, 2010.

Okafor, Victor Oguejiofor. *Nigeria's Stumbling Democracy and its Implications for Africa's Democratic Movement*. Westport, CT: Praeger Security International, 2008.

Okome, Mojúbàolú Olúfúnké and Olufemi Vaughan, eds. *Transnational Africa and Globalization*. New York, NY: Palgrave Macmillan, 2012.

Oloruntoba, Samuel Ojo and Toyin Falola, eds. *Palgrave Handbook of African Politics, Governance and Developmen*t. New York, NY: Palgrave Macmillan, 2018.

Olukoju, Ayodeji and Muyiwa Falaiye, eds. *Global Understanding in the Age of Terrorism*. Lagos: University of Lagos Press, 2008.

Omoruyi, Omo. *Trial of Chief M.K.O. Abiola and the Criminalization of Democracy in Nigeria, 1994: Lessons for Us*. Somerville, MA: Advancing Democracy in Africa, 2001.

Oni, Ola and Bade Onimode. *Economic Development of Nigeria: The Socialist Alternative*. Ibadan: Nigerian Academy of Arts, Sciences, and Technology, 1975.

Onimode, Bade. *Africa in the World of the 21st Century*. Ibadan: Ibadan University Press, 2000.

———. *Imperialism and Underdevelopment in Nigeria: The Dialectics of Mass Poverty*. London: Zed Press, 1982.

———. *Political Economy of the African Crisis*. Atlantic Highlands, NJ: Zed Books, 1988.

Onwumechili, Chuka, and Ikechukwu Ndolo, eds. *Re-imagining Development Communication in Africa*. Lanham, MD: Lexington Books, 2013.

Osuji, E. E., ed. *Challenges Facing Industrial Relations in Nigeria in the Context of Emerging New World Economic and Political Order*. Ibadan: University of Ibadan Press, 1992.

Ottaway, Marina, ed. *Democracy in Africa: The Hard Road Ahead*. Boulder, CO: L. Rienner Publishers, 1997.

Oyebade, Adebayo, ed. *United States' Foreign Policy in Africa in the 21st Century: Issues and Perspectives*. Durham, NC: Carolina Academic Press, 2014.

Oyebade, Adebayo and Gashawbeza W. Bekele, eds. *Long Struggle: Discourses on Human and Civil Rights in Africa and the African Diaspora*. Austin, TX: Pan-African University Press, 2017.

Picard, Louis A. and Michele Garrity, eds. *Policy Reform for Sustainable Development in Africa: The Institutional Imperative*. Boulder: CO: L. Rienner Publishers, 1994.

Ranger, Terence O. *Evangelical Christianity and Democracy in Africa*. New York, NY: Oxford University Press, 2008.

Rasheed, Sadiq. *Development, Participation and Democracy in Africa. Four Essays.* Johannesburg and Pretoria: Foundation for Global Dialogue & Africa Institute of South Africa, 1996.

Republic of Gabon, Ministry of Health and Public Hygiene. "National Health Development Plan 2011-2015," December 2010. [Republique Gabonaise Union—Travail—Justice. Ministere de la Sante, des Affaires Sociales, de la Solidarite et de la Famille. "Plan Natiional De Developpement Saniitaiire 2011–2015," December 2010.]

Rodney, Walter. *How Europe Underdeveloped Africa*. London: Bogle-Louverture, 1972.

Sachs, Jeffery. *The Age of Sustainable Development*. New York, NY: Columbia University Press, 2015.

Saha, Santosh C., ed. *Perspectives on Contemporary Ethnic Conflict: Primal Violence or the Politics of Conviction*. Lanham, MD: Lexington Books, 2006.

Saleh, Karima, Bernard F. Couttolenc, and Helene Barroy. *Health Financing in the Republic of Gabon. A World Bank Study*. Washington, DC: World Bank, 2014. doi: 10.1596/978-1-4648-0289-8. License: Creative Commons Attribution CC BY 3.0 IGO.

Saliu, Hassan A. *Democracy, Governance and International Relations*. Ibadan: College Press and Publishers, 2010.

Schuurman, Frans J., ed. *Globalization and Development Studies: Challenges for the 21st Century*. London, Thousand Oaks, CA: SAGE, 2001.

Seeley, J. A. and W. M. Adams, eds. *Environmental Issues in African Development Planning*, Cambridge: African Studies Centre, 1988.

Sender, John and Sheila Smith. *The Development of Capitalism in Africa*. New York, NY: Methuen & Co. Ltd, 1977.

Simon, David. *Transport and Development in the Third World*. London: Routledge, 1996.

Siollun, Max. *Soldiers for Fortune, Nigerian Politics from Buhari to Babangida*. Abuja: Cassava Republic Press, 2013.

Smith, Robert S. *The Lagos Constipate 1851–1861*. London: The Macmillan Press Ltd, 1978.

Soubbotina, Tatyana P. *Beyond Economic Growth: An Introduction to Sustainable Development*. Washington, DC: World Bank, 2004.

Steele, Philip. *Uprisings in the Middle East and North Africa*. New York, NY: Crabtree Publishing Company, 2017.

Stock, Robert. *Africa South of the Sahara: A Geographical Interpretation*. New York, NY: The Guilford Press, 2013.

Thompson, Alex. *An Introduction to African Politics*. New York, NY: Routledge, 2007.

Thompson, L. A., ed. *Democracy, Democratization, and Africa: Essays in Commemoration of the 2,500th Anniversary of the Ancient Greek Discovery of Democracy*. Ibadan: Africa-Link Books, 1994.

Turnham, David, ed. *African Perspectives: Practices and Policies Supporting Sustainable Development*. Söbredden, Gentofte, Denmark: Scandinavian Seminar College; Avondale, Harare, Zimbabwe: Weaver Press, 2000.

Ukaga, Okechukwu and Osita G. Afoaku, eds. *Sustainable Development in Africa: A Multifaceted Challenge*. Trenton, NJ: Africa World Press, 2005.

Vaughan, Olufemi. *Nigerian Chiefs: Traditional Power in Modern Politics, 1890s–1990s*. Rochester, NY: University of Rochester Press, 2000.

———. *Religion and the Making of Nigeria*. Durham: Duke University Press, 2016.

———., ed. *Indigenous Political Structures and Governance in Nigeria*. Ibadan, Nigeria: Bookcraft Ltd., 2004.

Vivekananda, Franklin and Olayiwola Abegunrin, eds. *Political Economy of South South Cooperation: Towards a New International Economic Order*. Stockholm: Bethany Books, 1997.

Were, Gigeon S., ed. *Women and Development in Africa*. Nairobi, Kenya: Gideon S. Were Press, 1985.

Wilson, J. Zoë. *United Nations and Democracy in Africa: Labyrinths of Legitimacy*. New York, NY: Routledge, 2006.

Wiseman, John A. *New Struggle for Democracy in Africa*. Brookfield, VT: Avebury, 1996.

Wonkeryor, Edward Lama, et al. *American Democracy in Africa in the Twenty-First Century?* Cherry Hill, NJ: Africana Homestead Legacy Publishers, 2000.

———., ed. *Globalization and Its Implications for Africa*. Cherry Hill, NJ: Africana Homestead Legacy Publishers, 2016.

World Bank. *Global Economic Prospects, June 2018: The Turning of the Tide?* Washington, DC: World Bank, 2018. doi: 10.1596/978-1-4648-1257-6. License: Creative Commons Attribution CC BY 3.0 IGO.

———. *Sub-Saharan Africa—Review of Selected Railway Concessions (English)*. Washington, DC: World Bank, 2006.

———. "World Development Indicators: GNI per Capita, Atlas Method" [Data File]. Washington, DC: The World Bank. http://data.worldbank.org/indicator/NY.GNP.PCAP.CD.

World Health Organization. *Noncommunicable Diseases Country Profiles 2014*. Geneva, Switzerland: World Health Organization, 2014.

World Health Organization. *World Health Statistics 2012*. Geneva, Switzerland: World Health Organization, 2012.
Yansané, Aguibou Y., ed. *Prospects for Recovery and Sustainable Development in Africa*. Westport, CT: Greenwood Press, 1996.
Zeleza, Paul Tiyambe. *A Modern Economic History of Africa, Vol. 1: The Nineteenth Century*. Dakar: Codesria, 1993.

Index

Abacha, Sanni, 118, 119, 121, 122, 123
Abeokuta Women's Union (AWU), 152
Abeokuta, 115
Abiola, Kudirat, 120
Abiola, M.K.O., 116, 117, 118, 119, 120, 121, 122, 123
Aboyade, Ojetunji, 50
Achebe, Chinua, 5
Adedeji, Adebayo, 21, 31
Affordable Care Act (ACA), 183
Afikpo, 152
African Americans, 115, 116, 120, 121, 123
African Charter for Popular Participation in Development and Transformation, 58
African Charter on Human and Peoples Rights, 132, 141
African Development Bank, 21, 31, 185
African diaspora, xv, 117, 120, 121
African Freedom Charter, 140
African Peer Review Mechanism (APRM), 40
African Priority Program for Economic Recovery (APPER), 40
African-Caribbean and Pacific Economic Partnership Agreement (ACP-EPA), 41
Afwerki, Isaias, 10
Agence Francaise de Development (AFD), 185
Aikhomu, Augustus, 117
Ake, Claude, 13, 64
Akinyemi, Bolaji, 119, 120
Akufo-Addo, Nana, 9
Akunyili, Dora, 162
Albert Schweitzer Hospital, 186, 193
Algeria, 5, 84
Alhassan, Jumai Aisha, 157
All People's Congress (APC), 9
All Progressive Congress (APC), 107, 139, 157
All Progressive Grand Alliance (APGA), 110
Alliance for Democracy (AD), 108, 110
al-Shabaab, 45
Amin, Samir, 13
amnesty, 166, 170
Amnesty International, 176
Amnesty International Report, 171
Angola, 8, 78, 79, 81, 87
Ansar al-Sharia, 45
anticolonialism, 119
Arab Spring, 9
Association for a Better Nigeria (ABN), 118

austerity measure, 14, 45, 56
authoritarian, 4, 5, 8, 11, 16, 39, 40, 103, 155
authoritarianism, xi

Babangida, Ibrahim, xv, 116, 118, 121, 136
Beijing Declaration and Platform for Action (Beijing Declaration or Beijing Platform), 151, 154, 156, 173
Bio, Julius Maada, 9
Biya, Paul, 43
Boko Haram, xvii, 45, 166, 171, 175
Bongolo Evangelical Hospital, 186
Brundtland Commission, 167. *See also* UN World Commission on Environment and Development (WCED)
Brundtland Report, 12
Buhari, Muhammadu, xvii, 135, 137, 139, 174
Burundi, xv, 102, 105, 108, 109, 112, 133, 165

Caisse Nationale d'Assurance Maladie et de Garantie Sociale (CNMGS), 181
Caisse Nationale de Garantie Sociale (CNGS), 182
Campaign for Democracy (CD), 120
Caribbean, 12, 41
Carrington, Walter C., 121
Chama Cha Mapinduzi (CCM), 8
Chibok girls, 166, 171
China, 45, 72, 82
Citizens' Forum for Constitutional Reform, 155
Civil Liberties Organization (CLO), 120
civil liberties, 7, 36
colonial, xi, xii, xiv, 4, 13, 21, 24, 25, 39, 52, 67, 68, 73, 78, 79, 81, 82, 83, 85, 86, 90, 93, 130, 152, 153
colonialism, 13, 21, 63, 67, 68, 77, 128, 152
Congressional Black Caucus (CBC), 116, 117, 119, 121, 123
Constitution Review Committee, 106
Constitutional Rights Project (CRP), 120
corruption, vii, 5, 11, 17, 26, 36, 43, 44, 45, 57, 80, 86, 87, 115, 174
Côte d'Ivoire, 5, 14, 88, 92
coup d'état, 26, 118

Dasuki, Ibrahim, 117
Delany, Martin R., 115
dependency, xiv, 45, 52, 65, 66
Derby, Idris, 43
Djibouti, 14
dos Santos, José Eduardo, 8

Economic and Financial Crimes Commission (EFCC), 43
Economic Commission for Africa (ECA), 13, 21, 24
economic growth, vii, xi, xii, 4, 6, 12, 13, 14, 17, 22, 24, 25, 26, 30, 38, 52, 66, 78, 175
economic liberalization, xi
Egypt, 19, 85
Ekpo, Margret, 152
El-Sisi, Abdel Fattah, 9
Enahoro, Anthony, 119, 120
Epetedo Declaration, 119
Eritrea, 10, 39, 79, 88
Ethiopia, 10, 14, 39, 88
Etiaba, Ngozi Virginia, 151
Eurocentric, 64

Falola, Toyin, 56, 73
Fanon, Franz, 13
Frank, Andre Gunder, 13
French Development Agency, 185
Fulani, 118, 136, 138, 139, 152

Gambia, 8, 9, 39, 43
Garvey, Marcus, 115
Gender and Equal Opportunity Bill, 174
gender equality, 55, 155, 167, 168, 172, 173, 174, 176
Ghana, vii, 4, 5, 9, 14, 78, 79, 80, 84, 105

Global Funds, 185
Global Partnership, 55, 172
Globalization, xvi, 11, 21, 27, 63, 70, 73, 88, 128, 140
Gross Domestic Product (GDP), 28, 37, 184
Gross National Product (GNP), 12, 37

Hausa, 118, 130, 138, 152
Hausa/Fulani, 118, 136, 138
HIV/AIDS, xviii, 12, 55, 161, 170, 171, 188, 189, 190, 191, 192, 193
How Europe Underdeveloped Africa, 65. *See also* Walter Rodney
Human Development Index (HDI), 37, 50

Igbo, xv, 128, 135, 136, 137, 138, 139, 152
imperialism, 23, 68
import-substitution, xiv, 80
Indigenous People of Biafra (IPOB), 135
Interim National Government (ING), 118
International Convention on Civil and Political Rights (ICCPR), 132, 140
International Covenant on Civil and Political Rights (ICCPR), 132, 140
International Criminal Court (ICC), 43
International Diabetes Federation (IDF), 191
International Financial Institutions (IFIs), 87, 88, 90, 93
International Monetary Fund (IMF), vii, xiv, 13, 21, 39, 55, 72, 80, 86
Ishaku, Darius Dickson, 157
Ivory Coast, 5. *See also* Côte d'Ivoire

Jackson, Jesse, 121
Jammeh, Yahya, 8, 39
Joint Task Force (JTF), 170, 171
Jonathan, Goodluck, 137, 138, 158, 174
Jubril, Sarah, 157

Kagame, Paul, 10, 43, 109
Kamara, Samura, 9
Kanu, Nnamdi, 137, 138, 139
Kenya African National Union (KANU), 131
Kenya, xv, 4, 5, 9, 43, 78, 79, 80, 81, 82, 84, 88, 89, 91, 103, 104, 128, 130, 132, 133, 152, 140
Kenyatta, Jomo, 4
Kenyatta, Uhuru, 9, 43
Kikuyu, 152
Kingibe, Baba Gana, 116
Kudirat Abiola Corner, 122

Lagos Plan of Action for Economic Development, 13
Lagos, 89, 152
Latin America, 12, 78, 81, 185, 186, 187
Libreville, 182
Libya, 27, 45, 120

malaria, 55, 172, 188, 189, 190, 191, 193
Malawi, xv, 81, 88, 102, 105, 107, 108, 109, 111, 112
malnutrition, 189, 191
marginalization, xvi, 11, 129, 131, 133, 136, 137, 150
market integration, 27, 28
maternal health/care, 53, 55, 172, 181, 184, 187, 188, 192
maternal mortality, 4, 15, 184, 193
McNamara, Robert, 29
MDGs, 25, 54, 56, 60, 174, 175. *See also* Millennium Development Goals (MDGs)
militancy, 45, 133, 166, 174, 175
military, 155, regimes
Millennium Development Goals (MDGs), xiii, 24, 25, 41, 50, 55, 58, 167, 168, 172, 192. *See also* MDGs
Mnangagwa, Emmerson, 8
modernist, 65, 66

modernization school/theory/argument, xiii, xiv, 12
Morsi, Mohamed, 9
mortality, 4, 15, 38, 41, 46, 50, 55, 172, 179, 184, 186, 188, 191, 192, 193, 195
MOSOP, 135
Movement for the Actualization of the Sovereign State of Biafra (MASSOB), 136
Movement for the Survival of Ogoni People (MOSOP), 134. *See also* MOSOP
Mubarak, Hosni, 9
Mugabe, Robert, 8, 43
multiparty, xi, 3, 5, 6, 9, 10, 11, 16, 103
Museveni, Yoweri, 10, 11, 43
Muslim Brotherhood, 9

NADECO, 120, 121, 122
Namibia, 109
National Agency for Food and Drug Administration, 162
National Assembly, 103, 104, 106, 107, 109, 111
National Democratic Coalition (NADECO), 119. *See also* NADECO
National Electoral Commission (NEC), 116
National Gender Policy, 156, 174
National Policy on Women, 156
National Republican Convention (NRC), 116
neocolonialism, xiv, 13, 21, 25, 56, 65, 72, 93
neoliberalism, 88
neo-Marxist, 13, 23
New Economic Partnership for African Development (NEPAD), 40
New International Economic Order (NIEO), 13, 40
Ngũgĩ, wa Thiong'o, 69, 70
Niger Delta, xvii, 133, 134, 135, 166, 170, 171, 174, 175
Nigerian Civil War, 136
Nigerian Railway Corporation (NRC), 84, 85
Nkrumah, Kwame, 4
Nkurunziza, Pierre, 108, 109
Northern Element Progressive Union (NEPU), 152
Nujoma, Samuel, 109
Nupe, 152
Nwosu, Humphrey, 116
Nyerere, Julius, 43

Obama, Barack, 9, 183
Obamacare, 183
Obasanjo, Olusegun, 54, 89, 106, 107, 111, 117, 134, 136, 137, 174
Obi, Peter, 151
Odinga, Raila, 10
Ogiek, xv, 128, 130, 131, 132, 133, 140
Ogoni Bill of Rights (OBR), 134
Ohanaeze Ndigbo, 138, 139
Okonjo-Iweala, Ngozi, 162
Organization of African Unity (OAU), 40

Pan-Africanism, 121
Patient Protection and Affordable Care Act (PPACA), 183
patriarchy, 159
patronage, 5, 57, 84, 104, 106, 108, 109, 111, 112
Paul Igamba Hospital, 185
PDP, 107, 110. *See also* People's Democratic Party (PDP)
People's Democratic Party (PDP), 104, 112, 157. *See also* PDP
Plan National de Development Sanitaire (PNDS), 183
political ecology, 19, xii, 23
political economy, xii, 12, 13
political rights, xii, 3, 6, 7, 16, 36, 156
Popular Movement for the Liberation of Angola (MPLA), 8
population, xiii, xv, 14, 19, 20, 22, 23, 24, 25, 26, 27, 28, 29, 30, 31, 38, 40, 49, 127, 128, 134, 135, 136, 138,

149, 154, 155, 161, 162, 179, 180, 181, 182, 190, 191, 194, 195
postcolonial, xiv, 5, 39, 40, 52, 77, 78, 79, 80, 81, 82, 84, 85, 90, 91, 93, 118, 153
poverty, vii, xii, xiii, 3, 4, 11, 14, 17, 22, 23, 24, 25, 26, 27, 29, 31, 32, 38, 39, 41, 45, 46, 49, 55, 58, 65, 72, 117, 153, 155, 168, 172, 174, 180, 181, 184, 190
precolonial, xiv, 4, 54, 79, 152
privatization, xiv, 14, 80, 87, 88, 89, 90, 91, 93
public funds, 56, 57

Radio Kudirat, 120
Rodney, Walter, 13, 64, 65
Rwanda, xv, xvi, 10, 39, 43, 102, 105, 109, 110, 112, 113, 128, 165, 174

Sachs, Jeffrey, 3
SAP, 45
Saro-Wiwa, Ken, 134, 135
Second World War, xi, 78, 80
Senegal, 14, 17, 88, 91
separation of powers, xii, 17, 111
Shonekan, Ernest, 118
Sierra Leone People's Party (SLPP), 9
Sierra Leone, 9, 39, 79, 87, 165
Sirleaf-Johnson, Ellen, 9
Social Democratic Party (SDP), 116
Somalia, 45, 165
South Africa, vii, 28, 79, 82, 86, 88, 103–4, 174, 193
South Sudan, 165
Soyinka, Wole, 119, 121
Structural Adjustment Program (SAP), 14, 39, 54, 80, 87. *See also* SAP
sub-Saharan Africa, 26, 28, 29, 54, 79, 181, 189, 191
Sudan, 39, 79, 81, 84, 88, 165
Supreme Council for Islamic Affairs, 117

Tanzam, 82
Tanzania, 5, 9, 14, 39, 43, 78, 82, 84, 88, 89, 91, 141
The Black Man's Burden, 24
Tofa, Bashir Othman, 116
Tonga, xv, 128, 129, 140
Trans-Africa, 121
transparency, 5, 17, 42, 46, 50, 58, 59

Uganda, 10, 11, 43, 78, 78, 81, 82, 88, 89, 91, 104
Ugandan Railway Corporation, 84
UN International Children's Emergency Fund, 183
UN Plan of Action, 11
UN Population Fund (UNFPA), 184
UN World Commission Conference on Environment and Development, 167
UN World Commission on Environment and Development (WCED), 167, 168
underdevelopment, xiv, 13, 23, 44, 45, 46, 54, 63, 64, 66, 67, 71, 73, 194
Unilateral Declaration of Independence (UDI), 82
United Nations Convention on Human Rights, 140
United Nations Development Program (UNDP), 37
United Nations Environmental Program (UNEP), 135
Universal primary education, 16, 42, 55, 172

Wachuku, Jaja, 116
Weah, George Oppong, 9
Willink Minorities Commission, 133
Wiredu, Kwasi, 67
Women in Politics Forum (WPF), 158
World Bank, vii, xiv, 13, 14, 21, 26, 29, 31, 32, 39, 45, 51, 55, 57, 72, 80, 82, 84, 86
World Health Organization (WHO), 135, 183,184, 190

Yar'Adua, Musa, 166
Yar'Adua, Umaru, 89, 138

Zambia, 5, 79, 80, 82, 84, 85, 88, 89, 128
Zamfara, 152
Zaria, 152
Zenawi, Meles, 10
Zimbabwe African National Union Patriotic Front (ZANU-PF), 8
Zimbabwe, xv, 8, 43, 82, 88, 128

About the Contributors

Funmi Adewumi (deceased) was a professor of Industrial Relations at Elizade University, Ilara-Mokin, Nigeria, until July 2017. He earned his PhD in Industrial Relations and Industrial Sociology from the University of Ibadan, Nigeria. He was formerly professor of Industrial Relations and dean of the College of Business and Social Sciences, Osun State University, Nigeria. He had also previously taught at the University of Ibadan. He has published widely in the field of Industrial Relations. Professor Adewumi was a consultant to a number of national and international NGOs and agencies.

Phillip E. Agbebaku, PhD, is professor in the Department of Political Science, Ambrose Alli University, Ekpoma, Nigeria. He was the director of the University's Entrepreneurship/Career Centre. He has participated in several local and international conferences, and has published extensively in the field of political science in monographs, edited books, and journals, which include *Journal of Social Sciences* (JSS), *International Review of Social Sciences and Humanities* (IRSSH), and the *Nigerian Forum.*

Rotimi Ajayi is professor in the Department of Political Science, Federal University of Lokoja, Lokoja, Kogi State, Nigeria. He was the former vice chancellor of Landmark University, Omu-Aran, Nigeria. He has many publications to his credit in the areas of comparative politics, political economy and public administration. His publications include three coedited books among which is *Understanding Government and Politics in Nigeria* (Omu-Aran: Landmark University, 2014).

Rufus T. Akinyele is professor in the Department of History and Strategic Studies, University of Lagos, where he obtained a PhD in history in 1990.

His research interests cuts across the related fields of African history, intergroup relations, and border studies. He is editor of *Ethnicity, Race and Nation Building in Africa* (Ibadan: Rex Charles, 2003); *African Integration: Images and Perspectives* (Lagos: University of Lagos Press, 2007); and *Borderlands and African Integration* (Lagos: Panaf Publishing Inc. 2008) and author of *Nigeria: Contesting for Space, Identity and Security* (Ibadan: Rex Charles, 2014). He has also published extensively in notable journals such as *Asian and African Studies*, *African Studies Review*, *Africa Development*, and *African Affairs*.

Tokunbo A. Ayoola, PhD, is the chair of the Department of History and International Relations, Elizade University, Ilara-Mokin, Ondo State, Nigeria, where he teaches African and African Diaspora History, Politics, and International Studies. His areas of specialization include transport history, railway studies, labor history, and economic and business history. His scholarly writings have appeared in academic journals including *Lagos Notes and Records* and *Lagos Historical Review*. He has also published chapters in edited volumes.

Gashawbeza W. Bekele is associate professor of geography at Tennessee State University. He obtained his PhD in geography from West Virginia University and his MPhil in development geography from the University of Oslo, Norway. His work and scholarship has focused on broadening our understanding of the relationship between international migration and development in Africa and industrial clustering and regional economic development in the United States. His recent publications include "Ethnic Identity Politics and the Sustenance of Africa's Predatory State," in Keneth Kalu, Olajumeke Yacob-Haliso, and Toyin Falola, eds., *Africa's 'Big Men': Predatory State-Society Relations in Africa* (New York, NY: Routledge, 2018), *The Long Struggle: Discourses on Human and Civil Rights in Africa and the African Diaspora* (Austin, TX: Pan African University Press, 2017, coedited with Adebayo Oyebade), and "Revisiting Africa's Brain Drain and the Diaspora Option," in Toyin Falola and Adebayo Oyebade (eds.), *The New African Diaspora in the United States: Identities and Homeland Connections* (New York: Routledge, 2016).

Ngozi U. Emeka-Nwobia holds a PhD in sociolinguistics and lectures in the Department of Linguistics and Literary Studies, Ebonyi State University, Nigeria. She is a Carnegie Scholar and Postdoctoral fellow of the American Council of Learned Societies (ACLS)'s African Humanities Program. She is a recipient of awards including the Social Science Research Council (SSRC)'s Next Generation Social Sciences Research in Africa; Doctoral Dissertation Research Fellowship Award; and Doctoral Dissertation Completion

Fellowship Award. She is currently undertaking collaborative research on literature, music, and prayer as sources of African values, spirituality, and Christian theology, funded by the Nagel Institute, Calvin College, Michigan.

Joseph Yinka Fashagba, PhD, is senior lecturer and head of Department of Political Science, Federal University Lokoja, Lokoja, Kogi State, Nigeria. He is a specialist in Legislative Studies, African Politics, and Democratic institutions. His papers have appeared in many scholarly journals. He has coedited three books including *Africa State Governance: Subnational Politics and National Power* (London: Palgrave Macmillan, 2015).

Mohammed Itakpe currently lectures in the Department of Political Science, Ambrose Alli University, Ekpoma, Nigeria. He holds a BSc and MSc in Political Science and has participated in several local and international conferences.

Tadesse Kidane-Mariam is a retired Emeritus Professor of geography from Edinboro University of Pennsylvania. He obtained his PhD in Geography from the University of Iowa, Iowa City, Iowa. He worked for the Ethiopian government as planner and minister of urban development and housing. His teaching and research interests focused on sustainable development, urban and regional planning, urbanization, urban development and housing, and environmental management. He has published many book chapters and articles in journals such as *Environmental Management*, *Journal of Tourism and Hospitality*, and *Arab World Geographer*. He was awarded the lifetime academic achievement award for distinguished teaching and public service at Tennessee State University's Annual Africa Conference on April 6, 2018.

William E. Odion, PhD, lectures in the Department of Political Science, Ambrose Alli University, Ekpoma, Nigeria. He has participated in several academic conferences. He has published extensively in scholarly journals including *Journal of Social Sciences* (JSS), *International Review of Social Sciences and Humanities* (IRSSH), *Nigerian Forum*, and *African Security Survey*. His research interests include African Politics and Development.

Sunday Layi Oladipupo is lecturer in the Department of Philosophy, Adekunle Ajasin University, Akungba-Akoko, Ondo State, Nigeria. He obtained his PhD in philosophy from Ambrose Alli University, Ekpoma, Edo State, Nigeria. He has written and published scholarly articles on African philosophy, moral, and sociopolitical philosophy. He is coeditor of *The Polemics of an African Philosopher: Essays in Honour of Professor Segun Ogungbemi* (Kano: Flash Printing & Publications, 2016).

Adaora Osondu-Oti is senior lecturer in the Department of International Relations and Diplomacy, Afe Babalola University, Ado-Ekiti, Nigeria. She obtained a PhD in international relations from Obafemi Awolowo University, Ile-Ife, Nigeria. Her research interests include human rights, women's rights and gender-related issues, Nigeria's foreign policy, security and conflict management, and China-Africa contemporary relations. She has published over twenty papers in both international and national journals and has contributed chapters in books. Dr. Osondu-Oti is a member of many professional bodies, including the Society for Peace Studies and Practice in Nigeria, Institute for French Research in Africa (IFRA) and Society for International Relations Awareness (SIRA).

Adebayo Oyebade is professor of history and chair of the Department of History, Political Science, Geography, and Africana Studies at Tennessee State University, Nashville. He obtained his PhD in history from Temple University, Philadelphia. His areas of specialization are African political and diplomatic history, history of the African Diaspora, the diplomatic history of the United States. He has written extensively on these areas in books, chapters in edited volumes, and scholarly journals. He is the author, editor, and coeditor of nine books, including *Culture and Customs of Angola* (Greenwood, 2007), *Hot Spot: Sub-Saharan Africa* (Greenwood, 2010, coauthored with Toyin Falola), *The United States' Foreign Policy in Africa in the 21st Century: Issues and Perspective* (Carolina Academic Press, 2014, edited), and *The New African Diaspora in the United States: Identities and Homeland Connections* (Routledge, 2017, coedited with Toyin Falola). His latest book is *The Long Struggle: Discourses on Human and Civil Rights in Africa and the African Diaspora* (Austin, TX: Pan African University Press, 2017), coedited with Gashawbeza W. Bekele. Oyebade is the recipient of a number of scholarly awards, including the Fulbright.

Udida A. Undiyaundeye, PhD, teaches in the Department of History and International Studies, University of Uyo, Uyo, Nigeria.

Biale Zua is a graduate assistant and a PhD candidate in the Department of Teaching and Learning, College of Education, Tennessee State University, Nashville. She obtained her master's degree in communication and language arts from the University Ibadan, Nigeria. Among her publications is *Written Communication* (Port Harcourt: Ecolaw Publications, 1988).

www.ingramcontent.com/pod-product-compliance
Ingram Content Group UK Ltd.
Pitfield, Milton Keynes, MK11 3LW, UK
UKHW020213290926
15470UKWH00001B/150

9 781498 564519